The Bad News
BIBLE

The Bad News
BIBLE
THE NEW TESTAMENT

DAVID VOAS

 **Prometheus Books**

59 John Glenn Drive
Amherst, NewYork 14228-2197

Published 1995 by Prometheus Books

99 98 97 96 95   5 4 3 2 1

Library of Congress Cataloging-in-Publication Data

Voas, David.
    The bad news Bible : the New Testament / David Voas.
        p.   cm.
    Includes index.
    Originally published London : Duckworth
    ISBN 0-87975-968-2
    1. Bible N.T.—Criticism, interpretation, etc. 2. Bible N.T.—
Controversial literature. I. Title.
BS2361.2.V63   1995
225.6—dc20   94-43298
                                                                      CIP

Printed in the United States of America on acid-free paper.

Introduction

Theology, once queen of the sciences, now seems merely queen of the cloisters, still gossiping about the same old stories long after the choir boys have grown up and moved on. It's a shame; those other disciplines may be more successful, but they aren't nearly as entertaining. Granted, theology – 'the study of God' – suffers from the suspicion that it has no subject, or at least none we can study. It is the only field with experts who don't know what they are talking about.

Their subject matter being inaccessible, theologians must resort to the odd couple of imagination and authority. There was great scope for creativity in the early days; the authors of the gospels and epistles were relatively unfettered by what had gone before. Once their writings were published and canonised, however, everything else became commentary; new doctrine had to be presented as explaining the old. Christian thinkers now have the job of showing that scripture makes sense, is consistent, and appears morally defensible. This can be difficult.

The scriptural Jesus does not live up to his Good Shepherd reputation. Moreover, the promise of a heavenly afterlife, so crucial to the appeal of Christianity, does not come from Jesus (or his ghost-writers). That might not matter, except that he specifically denies much of Sunday-school theology. Only the most selective quotation can give anyone confidence in salvation; the testimony attributed to Jesus weighs on the side of perdition.

As the biblical writers were themselves theologians, we have to decide how to regard their creation. The most conservative position is that every word is God's own truth. The relaxed view is that the authors were as prone to ignorance, credulity and prejudice as anyone else of that time or since. While most theologians hold that the scriptures were divinely inspired, this means to some only that they reflect an effort to understand what God was up to.

The problem of how to regard the Bible has been eclipsed in the headlines by the search for the historical Jesus. We are fascinated by personalities, and celebrities don't come any bigger than the son of God, even if disguised as an itinerant Palestinian exorcist. A claim that Jesus was an alien, or took drugs, will always grab attention. By contrast, people tend to regard the Bible as boring.

In fact, scripture could not be more amazing if it did assert that Jesus came from Mars. The problem is that people *think* they know what's in the Bible, or at least what kind of material it contains. Most of them are wrong: they are only familiar with a few church-approved extracts, and are astonished not just at how awful God is in the Old Testament, but also at how much less than perfect his son seems in the New. The message of Jesus isn't all good news (as the word 'gospel' literally means); paradise is an uncertain prospect at best. Taken as a whole, it could well be *The Bad News Bible*.

I am not referring to isolated passages; we know that the devil can cite scripture for his purpose. Whole books, not simply odd or out-of-context verses, are an embarrassment to modern Christians. Revelation is a bad joke. Mark, the earliest gospel and a likely source for Matthew and Luke, is a folk tale, short on teaching, long on demons and wonders, ending with a tacked-on scene in which the risen Jesus declares that immunity to snake bites and poison is the sign of salvation. As for Paul, the man could not keep his foot out of his mouth: weddings would be more interesting if the reading came not from I Corinthians 13 (on love) but from chapters 5, 6 and 7 (on fornication) or from chapter 11 (on the place of women). Most of the shorter letters are worse, and a couple should not be there at all (e.g. Philemon, with which Paul returned a runaway slave to his master, or the third letter of John, maligning an opponent).

We would like the Bible to say what we think it should say. In particular, we would like it to endorse the key elements of popular Christianity:

– Jesus was supremely good, even perfect
– love and forgiveness are the characteristic Christian virtues
– God takes an active interest in our individual well-being
– our sins will be forgiven
– belief plus a respectable life ensures passage to heaven

None of these doctrines receives strong support from the Bible – in fact all are contradicted in one place or another. What's remarkable, from such a partisan collection, is just how unhelpful the New Testament is. On the face of it Jesus was short-tempered, frequently wrong and sometimes intolerant. God is notable by his absence. Jews are blamed for as much as possible, and nobody seems to be in a hurry to forgive sinners. Only the all-too-fallible Paul encourages our expectations of heaven.

My intention is not to argue that all scripture is wrong-headed: much of it is admirable. I do think, though, that some corrective is needed to assumptions acquired at Sunday school and left unchallenged since, for want of a dispassionate look at the Bible. I try to be as fair as possible in quoting and summarising; indeed, the longest excerpts are the ethical favourites (from the Sermon on the Mount, for example).

To that extent *The Bad News Bible* does not set out to be a commentary, or a rival interpretation, but simply a brisk overview of the good, bad and indifferent. Of course it would be both naive and disingenuous to claim that the book is value-free. My aim is rather to strip off the old theological varnish in order to get a better look at the work underneath.

The Bible has been over-interpreted – Christian apologists have felt obliged to produce lengthy studies explaining away its contradictions, failed prophecies, uncongenial commandments and quaint world view. They have done such a good job of turning the documents into holy writ that now we have trouble reading them as anything else. I think we are the poorer for it.

The church insists on the humanity, as well as the divinity, of Jesus. The paradox is that to be human is to be less than perfect, and many people are unwilling to grant that Jesus had any imperfections. There is no difficulty in accepting that Jacob, Saul or Ezra could behave badly, but when scripture shows Jesus being rude or angry or mistaken, we are reluctant to believe it. Likewise any words of Jesus are assumed to contain the quintessence of wisdom, and hence to be immune from criticism. Here, reverence is the enemy of respect. Unless we are prepared to take Jesus seriously – and sometimes unseriously – the choice is between indifference and blind faith.

*

I am not trying to find the real Jesus, nor to return to primitive Christianity. My claim, indeed, is that theology and the church can properly assert authority over Christian belief and practice, because the Bible is unable to do the job.

The Bible is supposed to relate to doctrine much as a written constitution does to the law. Decisions and statutes are produced within a framework of fixed principles; rulings may be changed or superseded, but the final appeal is theoretically to the basic authority. There's a crucial difference, however: constitutions, unlike scripture, can be amended. Although biblical edicts are reinterpreted to meet changing conditions, the process can only go so far. With no provision for updates, a canon will eventually lose its authority; the gap between the immutable words and evolving sensibilities becomes too great.

Christianity, of course, is much more ambitious than the law. Whereas our legal system only pretends to be one imperfect attempt to regulate social behaviour, scripture claims to offer *the* prescription for human conduct. The Bible, moreover, includes history and prophecy as well as ethics. It states that certain events occurred, that other events will follow – with consequences for groups or individuals depending on their actions or beliefs – and that people ought to think and do specific things as a result.

Theologians are a flexible lot. Whenever a passage goes too far beyond what contemporary thinking will allow, an interpretation is imposed to make the problem disappear. All but the most conservative employ this approach freely in the case of science and history: where a biblical statement contradicts worldly fact, we describe it as symbolic, or incidental, or just blame the scribe. Many would admit that the Bible, however influential in the evolution of morality, is not now a source of ethical progress (at best passages may be used as a rubber stamp). I would suggest that even in the realm of doctrine – questions of faith, salvation, the Last Judgment and so on – theologians are now influenced more by recent philosophy and their immediate predecessors than by scripture. They develop ideas, and then look for scriptural warrant.

Following the progress made by nineteenth-century scholars in exploring the who, what, where, when and why of biblical authorship – the so-called higher criticism -- liberal theologians in the twentieth century embarked on the task of 'demythologising' Christianity. The irony is that historians of antiquity found this process less problematic than the modern laity they sought to accommodate. It is easy, that is to say, for a student of first-century eastern Mediterranean religious thought to see how the notion of a virgin birth emerged, but for many with less knowledge of that context, a laboured conception of Christianity without miracles is more difficult to accept than a neat parcel of supernatural beliefs.

The myth now most in need of exposure holds that the Bible is the ultimate source of authority for Christian doctrine. People look to scripture for inspiration, but to claim to consult it the way an American lawyer might use the US Constitution shows either innocence or cynicism. Even fundamentalists, who make the most obvious effort to treat the Bible as the authority in all things, will ignore (or reinterpret) any passages that sit uncomfortably with their other views. The primary authority is the one that tells them the nature of the world, Jesus and salvation; the Bible is a secondary source read through the lenses of that primary commitment.

*

In this book's predecessor on the Old Testament, *The Alternative Bible*, I suggested that the length, style and tone of the O.T. (in whatever translation) make it inaccessible to modern readers. The New Testament is not much better; though shorter, it is even more repetitive, with less action and fewer stories. Many of the teachings are over-familiar and so tend to be read in an unreflective way. I hope that editorial effort and good-humoured criticism has produced a more entertaining – not to say educational – version. (Readers can decide whose remarks are the most edifying.)

The Bad News Bible proceeds, as before, through a combination of narration and quotation from the Authorised Version (printed in bold italics). This is the version that was universal in the English-speaking world until the late nineteenth century and influenced so much of English literature. The book can therefore be used, like *The Alternative Bible*, as an anthology of famous biblical passages in their narrative context. God being the agent of events in the Old Testament, it was fitting that a member of his circle (the Archangel Michael) should tell the story. In the New Testament God has moved backstage, and two characters dominate the scene: Jesus (whose deeds and words are reported in the gospels) and Paul (who is the subject or author of much of the rest). A human being has therefore stepped in as observer and commentator.

This narrator is James, the brother of Jesus. It is apparent from the Bible that Jesus had siblings, though people embarrassed by the idea of Mary procreating further hold that they were actually cousins or step-brothers and sisters. The exact relationship is not crucial. We know that James (not to be confused with the disciples of the same name) belonged to Jesus' family, and that he was a leader of the early church in Jerusalem.

James reacts as a sympathetic yet critical insider. It seems from the gospels that Jesus was not always on close terms with his family. Indeed, it is generally thought that James only joined his brother's followers after the crucifixion. He led the Jewish tendency within early Christianity, viewing Jesus as a founder of a sect, not a new religion; as a result he disagreed with Paul a good deal. Of course it is not my intention that he should present the personality and world view of a first-century Palestinian; James is outside time, as in a sense is the Bible itself.

The Bad News Bible aims to make the least-read best-seller readable. If scripture turns out to contain less good news than is generally believed, a little reflection is no bad thing.

1

Matthew

Let me tell you about my ancestors. *Abraham begat Isaac; and Isaac begat Jacob; and ...* – but perhaps you know all that? Did you know that the harlot Rahab, the one who played a key role in the battle of Jericho, appears in our family tree? (She replaced the glum Naomi as Ruth's mother-in-law.)

Rahab wasn't the only black sheep, either. A few generations earlier Judah fornicated with his own daughter-in-law, whom he took for a prostitute. Their illegitimate son Perez provides our link to the patriarchs; I should probably have been named Jaime or José or something, like my brother. And our connection with the great king David, which is the whole point here, is through Bathsheba, whose previous husband was bumped off in order to avoid awkward questions about an unplanned pregnancy.

When they say that we come from the royal family, then, I don't start putting on airs. As far as I'm concerned, the only part that matters is that someone *begat Joseph the husband of Mary, of whom was born Jesus,* my brother. If our father had blue blood it didn't change the way we lived. Anyway, this business of counting 14 generations from Abraham to David, another 14 from David to the Babylonian captivity, and finally a further 14 generations (even if only 13 are listed) down to us, is strictly for the numerologists.

And besides, if we believe this fellow Matthew (whoever he is) the genealogy is irrelevant. What's the point of showing that by virtue of my father's ancestry Jesus belongs to the house of David, as the messiah should, if Joseph had nothing to do with his conception? Admittedly, no one I knew ever mentioned a virgin birth – not even Paul, and he probably wished that everybody could have had one.

Still, my job is just to let you know what stories people told, not to speculate about our parents. What Matthew says is that when *Mary was espoused to Joseph, before they came together, she was found with child of the Holy Ghost. Then Joseph her husband, being a just man, and not willing to make her a publick example, was minded to put her away privily.* While he was thinking about the best way to save her reputation, however, an angel appeared to him in a dream and revealed the culprit's identity.

Like a man whose wife becomes the king's mistress, my father apparently felt that he would have to make the best of the situation. I myself think it poor form that neither Mary nor the Holy Ghost told him what was happening before it became all too clear; acting furtive only makes the problem worse.

A speedy marriage seems the obvious solution, of course, but that might appear incompatible with a verse from Isaiah (which actually refers not to a virgin but to a 'young woman'): *Behold, a virgin shall be with child, and shall bring forth a son, and they shall call his name Emmanuel, which being interpreted is, God is with us.* Calling him Jesus must have been a mistake.

At any rate, Joseph was broad-minded about it all, *and took unto him his wife: And knew her not till she had brought forth her firstborn son.* Thereafter, we can presume, he enjoyed an ordinary conjugal life, undisturbed by further visits from on high.

2   Matthew seems to think that my good northern parents lived in the southern fleshpots of Judaea, perish the thought. *Now when Jesus was born in Bethlehem of Judaea in the days of Herod the king, behold, there came wise men from the east to Jerusalem, Saying, Where is he that is born King of the Jews? for we have seen his star in the east, and are come to worship him.* It's not clear to me why Magi, Persian astrologers, would go out of their way to adore a Jewish prince, but Herod didn't like what he heard. His experts told him that, judging from something the prophet Micah had said, Bethlehem would be a good place to look for the messiah.

Thinking that the wise men would save him the trouble of finding this new rival, Herod slyly told them to bring back word so that he too might pay his respects. Off they went, *and lo, the star, which they saw in the east, went before them, till it came and stood over where the young child was,* a mere five miles south. I've always wondered how the Magi did it. Apparently there was no doubt about which house (not stable) was their destination, though; by the sound of it, they didn't even bother to knock.

And when they were come into the house, they saw the young child with Mary his mother, and fell down, and worshipped him: and when they had opened their treasures, they presented unto him gifts; gold, and frankincense, and myrrh. And being warned of God in a dream that they should not return to Herod, they departed into their own country another way. There's no record of whether there were three or thirty of these fellows, incidentally.

Joseph, too, was warned in a dream (by an angel: did God feel awkward about dealing with him?) to escape with his family into Egypt. When the time was right they could leave; talking about the exodus, the prophet Hosea quoted God as saying *Out of Egypt have I called my son,* and it also seemed apt in these circumstances. Jesus was a latter-day Moses born to deliver his people, and Herod played the part of Pharaoh. Herod was exceedingly cross when the Persian magicians gave him the slip; he *sent forth, and slew all the children that were in Bethlehem, and in all the coasts thereof, from two years old and under.* He wasn't taking any chances.

I can't imagine that God would have wished my brother to be the cause, albeit indirect, of this 'massacre of the innocents'. Fortunately no one besides Matthew seems to have heard of it, though he finds it prefigured in Jeremiah's declaration *In Rama was there a voice heard, lamentation, and weeping, and great mourning, Rachel weeping for her children, and would not be comforted, because they are not.* It catches the mood, no doubt, but Bethlehem is quite some distance from Ramah, and its people trace their lineage through Leah, not Rachel. With Matthew, you can't take your eyes off the scriptures for a minute.

When Herod died Joseph had another instructional dream, and this time the angel told him that it was safe to go back. On the way, however, a further dream rerouted them from Judaea to the northern province of Galilee. They finally settled in the town of Nazareth, *that it might be fulfilled which was spoken by the prophets, He shall be called a Nazarene.* This seems to be a play on the word *nezer*, branch, which has messianic overtones, but I'd have to say it's rather strained.

BAPTISM AND TEMPTATION

As far as Matthew was concerned, nothing remarkable happened to Jesus during the next three decades. There was something in the air, though; everywhere you went, preachers were predicting the end, or the beginning, or both – it was often hard to be sure. One of these characters provided the catalyst for Jesus himself. He was known as John the Baptist ('the Dipper', to be literal) for his practice of immersing people in the river Jordan. Washing away sin, he proclaimed *Repent ye: for the kingdom of heaven is at hand.*

The prophet Isaiah referred to *The voice of one crying in the wilderness, Prepare ye the way of the Lord, make his paths straight.* John seemed to fit the bill. He certainly looked the part of the travelling man, wearing a camel-hair robe belted with leather, *and his meat was locusts and wild honey.* Charisma he didn't lack; something, at least, brought people from far and wide to confess their sins and be dunked in the river. It can't have been charm. When the religious elite came to be baptized *he said unto them, O generation of vipers, who hath warned you to flee from the wrath to come?*

While I applaud his emphasis on good works, I wish that he had promoted them for their own sake, or for the sake of others, rather than as a means of avoiding torment. John declared that

> *now also the axe is laid unto the root of the trees: therefore every tree which bringeth not forth good fruit is hewn down, and cast into the fire. I indeed baptize you with water unto repentance: but he that cometh after me is mightier than I, whose shoes I am not worthy to bear: he shall baptize you with the Holy Ghost, and with fire.*

Another reference to my brother, obviously. Having winnowed the wheat, *he will burn up the chaff with unquenchable fire.* That's bad news; I had hoped Jesus would be able to do something with the chaff.

To come back to the point, Jesus went along to be baptized by John. Now I know that my brother was supposed to be perfect, and there's no point in being washed clean of sin if you don't have any. Even John raised an objection. The usual answer is that Jesus felt it was the done thing, and that he should set an example. In my view he had a modest share of human failings, but perhaps that's just the way a sibling thinks.

The baptism itself seems to have made quite an impression on Jesus. As he emerged *the heavens were opened unto him, and he saw the Spirit of God descending like a dove, and lighting upon him: And lo a voice from heaven, saying, This is my beloved Son, in whom I am well pleased.* High praise, coming from God.

4   The first thing the divine spirit did, though, was to lead him *into the wilderness to be tempted of the devil. And when he had fasted forty days and forty nights, he was afterward an hungred.* I would have been hungry after the first day, myself. Anyway, the voice of temptation suggested that if he was the son of God, he could turn some stones into bread. Quoting scripture, Jesus reposted that *Man shall not live by bread alone*: very true, but he still has to eat. Next the devil urged that he throw himself off the roof of the temple, citing a psalm as assurance that angels would save him from so much as stubbing a toe. *Jesus said unto him, It is written again, Thou shalt not tempt the Lord thy God.* Especially by doing something so daft.

To make up for that last proposal, which to be honest was not very enticing, the devil took him to a mountaintop and offered possession of the kingdoms of the world below. All he wanted in exchange was a little respect – all right, a lot of respect, expressed prayerfully from a prone position – but Jesus just said *Get thee hence, Satan.* He apparently had no intention of becoming the messiah, at least in the expected political sense. We'd have to wait and see what he had in mind.

The devil having given up on Jesus, *angels came and ministered unto him.* The time had come to start preaching, especially now that John the Baptist had been thrown into prison. Jesus went back to Galilee, but moved from Nazareth to Capernaum, on the northern shores of the inland sea. As the prophet Isaiah said, *The people which sat in darkness saw great light.* To see the light meant seeing that the end was near, because his message (no surprises here) was *Repent: for the kingdom of heaven is at hand.*

But before the preaching, Jesus needed to assemble a gang. Walking by the shore he spotted two fishermen, *Simon called Peter, and Andrew his brother ... And he saith unto them, Follow me, and I will make you fishers of men. And they straightway left their nets, and followed him.* It was the same when he found another pair, *James the son of Zebedee, and John his brother ... they immediately left the ship and their father, and followed him.* I was reminded of the way Elisha walked away from his plough when Elijah told him to follow; either these fellows hated their jobs, or they were more impulsive than responsible adults should be. Some people just aren't prepared to work for a living.

Jesus wandered over Galilee with the lads, preaching in the synagogues. He became well known as a faith healer, *and they brought unto him all sick people that were taken with divers diseases and torments, and those which were possessed with devils, and those which were lunatick, and those that had the palsy; and he healed them.* He specialised in exorcism; if he mended any broken arms, I didn't hear about it.

THE SERMON ON THE MOUNT

My brother, of course, did more than cast out demons and preach the end of the world. He had a great deal to say about good and bad, right and wrong. Like Moses, he climbed a hill to offer a selection of his best sayings to the people. 5

The sermon begins with the 'Beatitudes':

Blessed are the poor in spirit: for theirs is the kingdom of heaven.
Blessed are they that mourn: for they shall be comforted.
Blessed are the meek: for they shall inherit the earth.
Blessed are they which do hunger and thirst after righteousness: for they shall be filled.
Blessed are the merciful: for they shall obtain mercy.
Blessed are the pure in heart: for they shall see God.
Blessed are the peacemakers: for they shall be called the children of God.
Blessed are they which are persecuted for righteousness' sake: for theirs is the kingdom of heaven.
Blessed are ye, when men shall revile you, and persecute you, and shall say all manner of evil against you falsely, for my sake.

It's high time that the gentle, the merciful, the pure and the peaceful were promised some reward. If the poor in spirit get the kingdom of heaven, though, what happens to the rich in spirit? And while the mournful must appreciate comfort, it would perhaps have been preferable to prevent the sorrow in the first place. (Likewise the persecuted might, given the choice, be a little less blessed.) Fairness is difficult to introduce after the fact.

Jesus told his listeners that *Ye are the salt of the earth: but if the salt have lost his savour, wherewith shall it be salted? it is thenceforth good for nothing.* So be salty – and spread yourself around.

Ye are the light of the world. A city that is set on an hill cannot be hid. Neither do men light a candle, and put it under a bushel, but on a candlestick; and it giveth light unto all that are in the house. Let your light so shine before men, that they may see your good works, and glorify your Father which is in heaven.

I wouldn't want you to be too ostentatious, but he was surely right to suggest that good deeds put everything else in the shade. If God is the ultimate Father (to use

Jesus' word), his reputation depends more on the behaviour than on the beliefs of his descendants.

We were raised to be good Jews, and Jesus denied that he would ever be anything else.

> *Think not that I am come to destroy the law, or the prophets: I am not come to destroy, but to fulfil. For verily I say unto you, Till heaven and earth pass, one jot or one tittle shall in no wise pass from the law, till all be fulfilled. Whosoever therefore shall break one of these least commandments, and shall teach men so, he shall be called the least in the kingdom of heaven.*

Surely not: Jesus himself was a chronic offender. But while he showed no great concern for every iota of scripture, it's true that he often argued for even higher standards. *For I say unto you, That except your righteousness shall exceed that righteousness of the scribes* (i.e. legal experts) *and Pharisees* (who as members of a special sect were widely respecte′ ıs devout, if over-serious), *ye shall in no case enter into the kingdom of heaven.*

Judging from his examples, in fact, I fear that heaven may be entirely empty of humankind. We already knew that a killer would face divine judgment, but Jesus added that *whosoever shall say, Thou fool, shall be in danger of hell fire.* That should take care of must of us; no wonder it's important to *Agree with thine adversary quickly, whiles thou art in the way with him.* If the fear of hell isn't enough, dread of the legal system should be, Jesus thought; once you're in its clutches, there'll be no escape *till thou hast paid the uttermost farthing.*

Not content with making rudeness a mortal sin, Jesus decided that thoughts could be as bad as words or deeds. Everybody knows the commandment *Thou shalt not commit adultery: But I say unto you, That whosoever looketh on a woman to lust after her hath committed adultery with her already in his heart.* I could have had a lot more fun at the same cost, it seems.

To avoid perdition, there's only one solution: *if thy right eye offend thee, pluck it out, and cast it from thee: for it is profitable for thee that one of thy members should perish, and not that thy whole body should be cast into hell. And if thy right hand offend thee, cut it off,* for the same reason; fortunately he didn't go any further. You could whittle yourself down to nothing before the week was out.

On the subject of divorce, I'm afraid that again Jesus made the Torah look like a model of liberality. He opposed it, full stop. According to Matthew he allowed an exception – a man might get rid of his wife *for the cause of fornication* (hers, not his, presumably) – but no one else recorded this concession. Apparently the sin is contagious: *whosoever shall marry her that is divorced committeth adultery.* That seems rather harsh, particularly if the new husband had nothing to do with breaking up the old marriage.

Jesus didn't like swearing – oaths, not curses. Instead of insisting that sworn statements be true, he declared *Swear not at all; neither by heaven; for it is God's throne, Nor by the earth; for it is his footstool ... But let your communication be, Yea, yea; Nay, nay: for whatsoever is more than these cometh of evil.* Or superstition, to be more exact; why should God feel obliged to strike down somebody's mother just because the person swore on her life?

Next Jesus produced one of his best-known sayings. In fact it comes from the prophets, but he popularised it – if you can really call it popular. Rather than follow the law of retaliation, he recommended *That ye resist not evil: but whosoever shall smite thee on thy right cheek, turn to him the other also.* If a man wants to sue the shirt off your back, give him your jacket as well; *And whosoever shall compel thee to go a mile, go with him twain.* No doubt some people can be shamed into righteousness, but most are only too glad to take advantage of any doormat that offers itself. Beyond its limited sphere of application, this precept is a thug's charter.

Letting yourself be exploited isn't enough, however. *Love your enemies, bless them that curse you, do good to them that hate you, and pray for them which despitefully use you, and persecute you.* In the first place, Jesus proposed, we're all God's children; *he maketh his sun to rise on the evil and on the good, and sendeth rain on the just and on the unjust.* If God wants to coddle the wicked, that's his business; I'm not eager to follow suit. But secondly, Jesus argued, there's no virtue in just loving your friends; *if ye love them which love you, what reward have ye? do not even the publicans the same?* Here I think he has a point. It's typical of the bad that they find bad everywhere, and characteristic of the good that they discover the best in all. Whether such generosity of spirit should be carried as far as love, I hesitate to say.

Jesus summed up with a literal counsel of perfection: *Be ye therefore perfect, even as your Father which is in heaven is perfect.* He probably has fewer temptations.

THE LORD'S PRAYER

Having begun by telling us not to hide our light under a bushel, Jesus continued the sermon by advising the reverse. God frowns on public displays of righteousness. Thus   6

> *when thou doest alms, let not thy left hand know what thy right hand doeth: That thine alms may be in secret: and thy Father which seeth in secret himself shall reward thee openly. And when thou prayest, thou shalt not be as the hypocrites are: for they love to pray standing in the synagogues and in the corners of the streets, that they may be seen of men. Verily I say unto you, They have their reward.*

After all, their prayers were merely intended to impress the neighbours; Jesus could be wonderfully sarcastic. For heaven's sake, pray in private behind closed doors, and *when ye pray, use not vain repetitions, as the heathen do: for they think that they shall be heard for their much speaking.*

God knows what you need without being told, so keep it short and to the point. (Some people carry the idea to its logical conclusion, and don't bother to pray at all.) Just to spell it out, Jesus even provided a sample prayer: the Lord's Prayer, as it came to be called.

> *Our Father which art in heaven, Hallowed be thy name.*
> *Thy kingdom come. Thy will be done in earth, as it is in heaven.*
> *Give us this day our daily bread.*
> *And forgive us our debts, as we forgive our debtors.*
> *And lead us not into temptation, but deliver us from evil:*
> *For thine is the kingdom, and the power, and the glory, for ever. Amen.*

Some of the transitions are a little abrupt, I must say. First we appeal for judgment day to arrive ('thy kingdom come'), and then we ask for something to eat while we wait. Since we can't pretend to be writing off debts, we're more comfortable with the variant 'forgive us our trespasses'. But here's the big question: why do we need fear that God might lead us into temptation, i.e. entice us to sin? I know he did a job on Job – killing his children and destroying his property in an effort to hear him curse – but most people don't need much encouragement. As we also have to be saved from the 'evil one' (to render the words more accurately), wrong-doers have plenty of help already.

Interestingly, Jesus went on to say that God would only forgive those who forgave others. A useful kind of reciprocity, though I wonder if it always works out fairly; it might seem unfortunate to fill hell with the victims of crimes too terrible to be forgiven. Does a mother have to forgive her child's killer before she can be excused an uncharitable thought?

As is well known, if generally disregarded, my brother had a low opinion of wealth and the pursuit of money. *Lay not up for yourselves treasure upon earth, where moth and rust doth corrupt, and where thieves break through and steal: But lay up for yourselves treasure in heaven ... For where your treasure is, there will your heart be also.* Nicely said, though I don't think it's in the nature of goodness to keep accounts.

Using an image that was less clear, Jesus declared that *The light of the body is the eye.* Apparently the idea was to contrast the evil eye, full of envy, with the good eye, trained on higher things. *If therefore the light that is in thee be darkness, how great is that darkness!* A choice must be made. *No man can serve two masters: for either he will hate the one, and love the other; or else he will hold to the one, and despise the other. Ye cannot serve God and mammon* (i.e. money). Given the importance most people attach to making and spending money, paradise won't be overcrowded.

If the poor thought that they were well set, Jesus disappointed them. He went on to say that it was a mistake to worry about food or drink or clothing. *Is not the life more than meat, and the body than raiment? Behold the fowls of the air: for they sow not, neither do they reap, nor gather into barns; yet your heavenly Father feedeth them.* (Lucky them, the hungry might reply.) Resign yourself to it, Jesus seemed to say; *Which of you by taking thought can add one cubit unto his stature?* Perhaps he was promoting perspective, but it sounded like fatalism.

Why bother about clothes? *Consider the lilies of the field, how they grow; they toil not, neither do they spin.* Despite such laziness, *even Solomon in all his glory was not arrayed like one of these* unemployed flowers. Imagine, then, how much more decorative we are in God's eyes than blooms that are here today and gone tomorrow.

To repeat: don't waste time asking how you are going to eat, drink, or be clothed, *For after all these things do the Gentiles seek,* if you'll excuse the ethnic slur. Instead, look forward to another world; *seek ye first the kingdom of God, and his righteousness; and all these things shall be added unto you. Take therefore no thought for the morrow: for the morrow shall take thought for the things of itself. Sufficient unto the day is the evil thereof.* As I recall, another Preacher used the same argument to recommend that one eat, drink and be merry. So seize the day – whether to pray or play is up to you.

THE GOLDEN RULE

Lest his followers become over-zealous in their puritanism, Jesus said *Judge not,*   7
that ye be not judged. What goes around comes around, *and with what measure ye mete, it shall be measured to you again.* Or as he would say to me in the midst of the planks and the sawdust when I was being critical, *why beholdest thou the mote* (the speck of wood) *that is in thy brother's eye, but considerest not the beam that is in thine own eye? ... Thou hypocrite, first cast out the beam out of thine own eye; and then shalt thou see clearly to cast out the mote out of thy brother's eye.* Being siblings, we naturally argued about whose failures were most beam-like.

Although he tried to be nonjudgmental, once in a while he would run out of patience. *Give not that which is holy unto the dogs, neither cast ye your pearls before swine,* was one particular sense of humour failure. People assume that he was referring to Gentiles, but in Mary's defence we weren't brought up to use those words for non-Jews. Pig-eater, maybe, but not pig.

He could be tremendously optimistic. *Ask, and it shall be given you; seek, and ye shall find; knock, and it shall be opened unto you: For every one that asketh receiveth; and he that seeketh findeth,* which hasn't been my experience, unfortunately. In support he argued that just as parents would not deny their children food – *Or what man is there of you, whom if his son ask bread, will he give him a stone?* – God will not refuse us what we ask. I wish we could be sure, on both counts.

Therefore all things whatsoever ye would that men should do to you, do ye even so to them: for this is the law and the prophets. Do as you would be done by, in other words. The great rabbi Hillel said that the whole law was founded on the principle that you should not do to others what you would not want done to yourself. By changing the emphasis from allowing to requiring what you would like Jesus made the rule stronger, though perhaps less clear. It makes sense to consult your own feelings when deciding what not to do; we tend to be hurt by the same things. Introspection is of little use, however, in discovering what someone else wants; beyond the necessities, desires are too diverse. Of course you can try to uncover them, but then the rule should be 'do as they would be done by', i.e. give people what they want.

Jesus confirmed my observation that not very many of us can expect salvation. He pictured two gates, one 'strait' (tight), one wide. *Enter ye in at the strait gate: for wide is the gate, and broad is the way, that leadeth to destruction, and many there be which go in thereat: Because strait is the gate, and narrow is the way, which leadeth unto life, and few there be that find it.* Do you not get any credit for looking?

Like salesmen, prophets feel a need to warn you about others of their kind. *Beware of false prophets, which come to you in sheep's clothing, but inwardly they are ravening wolves. Ye shall know them by their fruits. Do men gather grapes of thorns, or figs of thistles?* We're still left with the job of distinguishing between good and bad fruit. I don't believe that smooth and sweet is necessarily best; some of my brother's fruit seems thorny and hard to swallow. *Every tree that bringeth not forth good fruit is hewn down, and cast into the fire. Wherefore by their fruits ye shall know them.* A little severe, but I think he's right to judge people by what they do rather than what they profess.

Just to underline the point, Jesus said that belief was no passport to heaven. A lot of the faithful are going to be in for a shock.

> *Not every one that saith unto me, Lord, Lord, shall enter into the kingdom of heaven; but he that doeth the will of my Father which is in heaven. Many will say to me in that day, Lord, Lord, have we not prophesied in thy name? and in thy name have cast out devils? and in thy name done many wonderful works? And then will I profess unto them, I never knew you: depart from me, ye that work iniquity.*

That's a scene I'd be sorry to miss. (Mulling over nominations is such a pleasure; it's no wonder the idea of judgment day is so popular.)

The sermon was coming to a close. Taking it all to heart, Jesus said, makes you like the wise man who built his house on rock: the tempest came,

> *and beat upon that house; and it fell not: for it was founded upon a rock. And every one that heareth these sayings of mine, and doeth them not, shall*

be likened unto a foolish man, which built his house upon the sand: And the rain descended, and the floods came, and the winds blew, and beat upon that house; and it fell: and great was the fall of it.

And so, like Moses, he left us with a blessing and a curse.

The people who heard all this were, as you might imagine, *astonished at his doctrine,* but they were also impressed by his manner, *For he taught them as one having authority, and not as the scribes.* He did not bore them with the letter of the law: he spoke as if he knew what God had intended it to be.

HEALING

As Jesus came back down a leper accosted him and asked to be cured. Jesus obliged on the spot, but said *See thou tell no man.* No such luck, obviously.

8

Another supplicant, a centurion, found Jesus as he entered Capernaum. The person in need of healing was at home, which presented a problem: *Lord, I am not worthy that thou shouldest come under my roof.* Still, the officer had no doubt that a word from Jesus would suffice to drive away the illness, military fashion; *I am a man under authority, having soldiers under me: and I say to this man, Go, and he goeth; and to another, Come, and he cometh; and to my servant, Do this, and he doeth it.* He seemed to believe that Jesus was in charge of diseases (i.e. demons?).

Jesus was much impressed by the centurion's confidence, remarking that *I have not found so great faith, no, not in Israel.* Maybe he was wasting his time on his countrymen. People from beyond their borders would reach heaven, *But the children of the kingdom shall be cast out into outer darkness: there shall be weeping and gnashing of teeth.* I should think so too, after all their struggles over the centuries. At any rate, Jesus announced that the victim would be made well, sight unseen.

He did make a housecall in his next case, to cure his follower Peter's mother-in-law of the fever. There was no question of convalescence; *she arose, and ministered unto them.* I know a woman's work is never done, but that's ridiculous. The same evening *they brought unto him many that were possessed with devils: and he cast out the spirits with his word.*

Seeing the size of the crowds he was gathering, Jesus decided to decamp across the Sea of Galilee. When a scholar volunteered to join his crew, Jesus told him *The foxes have holes, and the birds of the air have nests; but the Son of man hath not where to lay his head.* Being an itinerant preacher wasn't a glamorous life. More shocking was his reply to a disciple who asked for leave to bury his father: *Follow me; and let the dead bury their dead.* Not very practical advice, and hardly in keeping with family values.

A storm blew up during their crossing, threatening to sink the ship. Like Jonah, Jesus was sleeping through the excitement. When his disciples awakened him he asked *Why are ye fearful, O ye of little faith? Then he arose, and rebuked the winds and the sea; and there was a great calm.* Judging from the exclamations that followed, his miracle cures on land hadn't prepared them for such a display.

They had no sooner landed than a regrettable incident cut short his sojourn across the water. Two deranged men, obviously possessed by demons, barred the way. Anticipating their expulsion, the demons asked to be sent into a herd of pigs feeding nearby. Jesus was gracious enough to oblige, *and, behold, the whole herd of swine ran violently down a steep place into the sea, and perished in the waters.* Needless to say this was a disaster for the farmers, not to mention the pigs. Thus *the whole city came out to meet Jesus: and when they saw him, they besought him that he would depart out of their coasts.* To be blunt, they ran him out of town.

9   Jesus didn't let this setback deter him. To his first patient back home, a paralytic, he said *Son, be of good cheer; thy sins be forgiven thee.* Given his condition there can't have been much to forgive. The man was in luck, though, because this adoption of the divine prerogative of forgiveness struck some people in attendance as blasphemous, and Jesus met the accusation by asking whether it was easier to say *Thy sins be forgiven thee; or to say, Arise, and walk?* His miraculous cures (the man did indeed get up and leave) showed his power to forgive, he claimed. No wonder doctors act so high and mighty.

And as Jesus passed forth from thence, he saw a man, named Matthew, sitting at the receipt of custom: and he saith unto him, Follow me. And he arose, and followed him. With that kind of effect on tax collectors, my brother should have been in business. For a time these writings were attributed to this man, which would make the story even odder: two words from a stranger made him walk away from his job, and he doesn't even say what was on his mind?

Naturally the Pharisees (being more strait-laced about their religion) disapproved of the way Jesus sat down to dinner with bailiffs, sharp operators and assorted riff-raff. He had a devastating reply: *They that be whole need not a physician, but they that are sick. ... I am not come to call the righteous, but sinners to repentance.* Besides, it's less boring.

Even the followers of John the Baptist questioned Jesus about the conspicuous failure of his disciples to observe the fasts. His excuse was that nothing so dreary should interfere with their appreciation of his company; *Can the children of the bridechamber mourn, as long as the bridegroom is with them?* There would be time enough for all that when he was gone. Moreover his thinking was radically different; he wasn't just patching up the old ways. *Neither do men put new wine into old bottles* (wineskins, to be more accurate), or both will suffer.

This speech was interrupted by an urgent – not to say overdue – summons: the daughter of an influential man had just died. Jesus was always on call. While *en route* a woman who for a dozen years had suffered from an issue of blood – some female problem, I imagine – crept up and touched his hem in the hope of being cured. Jesus turned and said *thy faith hath made thee whole*; it looked more like superstitious desperation than faith to me, but he was generous.

Arriving at the dead girl's house, Jesus shooed everyone away with the words *the maid is not dead, but sleepeth.* They all laughed, but *he went in, and took her by the hand, and the maid arose.* No sooner had he finished there than two blind men asked for his attention; his faith healing practice was threatening to get out of control. Perhaps that's why Jesus told his patients – obviously without success – *See that no man know it.* Some things you can't keep secret.

As they went out, behold, they brought to him a dumb man possessed with a devil. And when the devil was cast out, the dumb spake: and the multitude marvelled, saying, It was never so seen in Israel. But the Pharisees said, He casteth out devils through the prince of the devils. It was just sour grapes, of course.

And so he went from town to town, healing the afflicted and preaching the end of the world. It was clear to him that his listeners felt lost, and he told the disciples *The harvest truly is plenteous, but the labourers are few.* With so many people ripe for the plucking, the time had come to organise the work force.

THE KINGDOM OF HEAVEN

Jesus now had twelve disciples, and *he gave them power against unclean spirits,*   10
to cast them out, and to heal all manner of sickness and all manner of disease. Apart from Peter, Andrew, James, John and Matthew, already mentioned, the newly qualified exorcists and healers were Philip, Bartholomew, Thomas, another James, Lebbaeus, Simon the Zealot, and (last and definitely least) Judas Iscariot. *These twelve Jesus sent forth, and commanded them, saying, Go not into the way of the Gentiles, and into any city of the Samaritans enter ye not. But go rather to the lost sheep of the house of Israel.* This was strictly an operation for Jews only.

Spread the word, he told them: *The kingdom of heaven is at hand. Heal the sick, cleanse the lepers, raise the dead, cast out devils: freely ye have received, freely give.* They would take no money, or even shoes for that matter, relying on the hospitality extended along the way. On entering a town they were to *enquire who in it is worthy,* and stay with him (or her?) until moving on. *And whosoever shall not receive you, nor hear your words, when ye depart out of that house or city, shake off the dust of your feet. Verily I say unto you, It shall be more tolerable for the land of Sodom and Gomorrah in the day of judgment, than for that city.* That's called turning on the other's cheek.

Their paramedical skills notwithstanding, Jesus realised that the disciples faced a hostile world; *be ye therefore wise as serpents, and harmless as doves,* he said. When persecuted they could let their mouths do the talking, *For it is not ye that speak, but the Spirit of your Father which speaketh in you.* (God was everybody's father; usually Jesus didn't claim any special kinship.)

He moved into apocalyptic mode. Everyone would be turning against each other;

*the children shall rise up against their parents, and cause them to be put
to death. And ye shall be hated of all men for my name's sake: but he that
endureth to the end shall be saved. But when they persecute you in this city,
flee ye into another: for verily I say unto you, Ye shall not have gone over
the cities of Israel, till the Son of man be come.*

The messiah would usher in the divine kingdom, in other words, before they had
even finished their travels. The world is such a disappointment: it simply refuses
to end on schedule.

For some reason Jesus felt obliged to tell them that *The disciple is not above
his master, nor the servant above his lord.* If the master is called Beelzebub, his
followers will be labelled something worse. Nevertheless, he said, *preach ye upon
the housetops. And fear not them which kill the body, but are not able to kill the
soul: but rather fear him which is able to destroy both soul and body in hell.* My
brother, the fire and brimstone merchant.

God might not keep them from harm, but at least he'd take notice. *Are not two
sparrows sold for a farthing? and one of them shall not fall on the ground without
your Father.* (Without him allowing it, that should be – the sparrow doesn't knock
God off his perch.) *But the very hairs of your head are all numbered. Fear ye not
therefore, ye are of more value than many sparrows.* How very encouraging.

After mentioning that he would put in a good or bad word with God for his
supporters and opponents respectively, Jesus tried to clarify his mission. *Think not
that I am come to send peace on earth: I came not to send peace, but a sword.*
That's a shocker, I must say. *For I am come to set a man at variance against his
father,* he continued, *and the daughter against her mother, and the daughter in
law against her mother in law.* In short – and I'm sure I detected a glance in my
direction – *a man's foes shall be they of his own household.* He had us wrong,
though; we were just worried about him.

His insecurity with the family pained me; people who didn't love him more than
their own parents or children he rejected as unworthy. Jesus was so demanding, he
even insisted on martyrdom for his followers: *he that taketh not his cross, and
followeth after me is not worthy of me. He that findeth his life shall lose it: and
he that loseth his life for my sake shall find it.*

And so he sent his trainees out to gain practical experience. Relying as they did
on the hospitality of strangers, he sought to ensure a good reception: *whosoever
shall give to drink unto one of these little ones a cup of cold water only in the
name of a disciple, verily I say unto you, he shall in no wise lose his reward.* The
reward was unspecified (heaven? another glass of water?), which makes it more
tantalising.

THE RIVALS

Although imprisoned, John the (now inactive) Baptist was evidently in contact with his own disciples, because he sent a couple of them to ask Jesus what he claimed to be. *Art thou he that should come, or do we look for another?* My brother merely suggested that they take back news of his doings so that John could make up his own mind. Perhaps other people would decide that he was the messiah, but Jesus was very reluctant to say so himself. 11

While I was never quite sure how they viewed each other, there was obviously an element of rivalry between the two preachers. Jesus described John with a mixture of affection and condescension. He teased the people *What went ye out into the wilderness to see? A reed shaken with the wind? But what went ye out for to see? A man clothed in soft raiment?* Obviously not: the man looked like a beggar. *But what went ye out for to see? A prophet? yea, I say unto you, and more than a prophet.* His compliments had a sting in the tail, however. *Among them that are born of women there hath not risen a greater than John the Baptist: notwithstanding he that is least in the kingdom of heaven is greater than he.* Whatever that means, John's prospects in the next world sound limited.

Jesus remarked even more cryptically that *from the days of John the Baptist until now the kingdom of heaven suffereth violence, and the violent take it by force.* We're really in trouble if the mob is taking over heaven. The return of Elijah was supposed to herald the coming of the end, and John seemed to fit the bill as a latter-day Elijah: *He that hath ears to hear, let him hear.*

The fact that they were so different and yet alike didn't escape my brother, and he even made a joke about it. The public reminded him of children who refuse to play either of their games: *We have piped unto you, and ye have not danced; we have mourned unto you, and ye have not lamented.* On the one side they see John fasting and call him possessed, while on the other the *Son of man came eating and drinking, and they say, Behold a man gluttonous, and a winebibber, a friend of publicans and sinners. But wisdom is justified of her children.* The results would speak for themselves.

Unfortunately it seemed, on the contrary, that his good works hadn't made much of an impression. Not being one to tolerate disrespect, Jesus was obliged to curse his own town and two others with it. Capernaum *shalt be brought down to hell ... it shall be more tolerable for the land of Sodom in the day of judgment, than for thee.* That would make them prick up their ears.

Being obliged to make the best of a bad job, Jesus thanked God that his teaching was valued only by the simple, not by the wise. His reasoning escaped me, except that God apparently wanted it that way. He consoled himself with the thought that someone up above appreciated him: *All things are delivered unto me of my Father: and no man knoweth the Son, but the Father; neither knoweth any man the Father, save the Son, and he to whomsoever the Son will reveal him.* I can't decide whether this shows despair or hubris. It suggests that only God gave him recognition, which to all appearances is wrong, but also that he alone had worthwhile things to say about God, which would be unfortunate if true.

Jesus felt confident that he was a good master. *Come unto me, all ye that labour and are heavy laden, and I will give you rest. Take my yoke upon you, and learn of me; for I am meek and lowly in heart: and ye shall find rest unto your souls. For my yoke is easy, and my burden is light.*

12   Despite having said that not one iota of the old law should change, Jesus didn't feel constrained to recognise authority. One day while walking with him through a corn field, his disciples – weren't they supposed to be away preaching? – helped themselves to the crop. The Pharisees protested that it was the sabbath, when harvesting was forbidden. (I imagine that the farmer, had he been there, would have had a few objections of his own.) Citing a couple of less than convincing precedents, Jesus defended their action. He might have made more friends had he sounded less defensive, or perhaps more modest: *I say unto you, That in this place is one greater than the temple. … For the Son of man is Lord even of the sabbath day.*

The same issue arose when a man came to be healed on the sabbath. Jesus argued that one would rescue a sheep on the sabbath, and a man is worth more than an animal. In the circumstances – he wasn't dealing with anything life-threatening, just a case of a withered arm – the point didn't seem awfully relevant. Realising that the Pharisees would try to get rid of him, Jesus moved on. He healed everyone in the crowd that followed, but asked that they keep it quiet.

Then was brought unto him one possessed with a devil – the victim being blind and mute, it seemed a good diagnosis – and Jesus cured him. The Pharisees grumbled that he was only a good exorcist because Satan provided assistance. Jesus pointed out, very reasonably, that Satan wasn't in the business of driving out demons. And truthfully, I can scarcely imagine him making a pact with the devil. Jesus couldn't even tolerate neutrality: *He that is not with me is against me.* When you see things in black and white, tactical alliances don't come naturally.

Jesus didn't leave the matter there; to slander the work of God was blasphemy, and *blasphemy against the Holy Ghost shall not be forgiven unto men.* He spelt it out, showing once again how few have any assured future in the next life: *whosoever speaketh against the Holy Ghost, it shall not be forgiven him, neither in this world, neither in the world to come.* It's curious that divine spirits are so sensitive.

Returning to an earlier image, Jesus declared that *the tree is known by his fruit. O generation of vipers, how can ye, being evil, speak good things? for out of the abundance of the heart the mouth speaketh.* So a black heart necessarily produces bad deeds, while good deeds can only come from good character. I wouldn't have expected this from someone who worked amongst sinners; part of what makes humanity so complex is the fact that good people sometimes do bad things, and vice versa. *But I say unto you, That every idle word that men shall speak, they shall give account thereof in the day of judgment.* That's going to make it a long day, I'm afraid.

The group of scribes and Pharisees, having accepted this harangue with good grace, made a polite request: *Master, we would see a sign from thee.* Jesus exploded. *An evil and adulterous generation seeketh after a sign; and there shall no sign be given to it,* except that of Jonah. Just as he spent three days and three nights in the belly of the whale, *so shall the Son of man be three days and three nights in the heart of the earth.* I don't want to get ahead of myself, but the period he spent in the tomb (Friday evening to Sunday morning) doesn't add up to that. Anyway, this generation would be condemned: even Nineveh repented, with only Jonah there to preach. Similarly the Queen of Sheba went out of her way *to hear the wisdom of Solomon; and, behold, a greater than Solomon is here.*

The fate of the present generation was more than clear, but Jesus wanted to give this dead horse one more flogging. Drawing on his experience as an exorcist, he explained what a demon would do following its eviction.

When the unclean spirit is gone out of a man, he walketh through dry places, seeking rest, and findeth none. Then he saith, I will return into my house from whence I came out; and when he is come, he findeth it empty, swept, and garnished. Then goeth he, and taketh with himself seven other spirits more wicked than himself, and they enter in and dwell there: and the last state of that man is worse than the first. Even so shall it be also unto this wicked generation.

If they end up worse than before, is the victim to blame? I'd upbraid the exorcist for poor after-sales service. Perhaps it was intended to explain why patients didn't stay cured.

It seemed to me that Jesus needed a break; as the rest of the family felt the same, we decided to take him home. Someone let Jesus know that his mother and brothers were waiting outside. *But he answered and said unto him that told him, Who is my mother? and who are my brethren? And he stretched forth his hand toward his disciples, and said, Behold my mother and my brethren!* For my part, I wasn't offended, but our mother was hurt and anxious. Fringe religious activities have a way of scaring parents.

PARABLES

Later, in a calmer mood, Jesus went down to the seaside to tell stories. For some reason I couldn't quite fathom he sat in a boat, while everyone wanting to listen stood on the shore. His first parable concerned the different ways people might respond to his message: 13

Behold, a sower went forth to sow; And when he sowed, some seeds fell by the way side, and the fowls came and devoured them up: Some fell upon stony places, where they had not much earth: and forthwith they sprung up, because they had no deepness of earth: And when the sun was up, they were scorched; and because they had no root, they withered away. And some fell among thorns; and the thorns sprung up, and choked them: But other fell into good ground, and brought forth fruit, some an hundredfold, some sixtyfold, some thirtyfold.

Plain as such stories are, a surprising number of people are resolutely literal in their understanding. Recognising this, no doubt, his disciples bluntly asked *Why speakest thou unto them in parables?* I was perplexed by his answer. You already know the secrets of the kingdom of heaven, Jesus said, but the others don't. Apparently he intended to keep it that way. *For whosoever hath, to him shall be given, and he shall have more abundance: but whosoever hath not, from him shall be taken away even that he hath.* Parables, he suggested, allowed him to talk over the heads of common folk, and thus to follow in the footsteps of Isaiah, whose message was heard but not understood.

Just in case his disciples were not such an elite as he had suggested, he interpreted the story for them at some length. The birds eating the seed on the path are demons, I was interested to hear. And as a warning to the worldly, *He also that received seed among the thorns is he that heareth the word; and the care of this world, and the deceitfulness of riches, choke the word, and he becometh unfruit-ful.* Another reason not to work too hard, I'm happy to discover.

Jesus had another parable of the arable. A man sowed good seed, and in the dead of night *his enemy came and sowed tares* – i.e. weeds – *among the wheat.* When the weeds started to appear, the man realised that *An enemy hath done this.* He told his labourers not to pull them up, however, for fear of harming the wheat. At harvest time, he said, the first step would be to cut the weeds and burn them. This is meant to explain, I take it, why God produces Satan's crop as well as his own. Perhaps you were always destined to be hell-fodder, but at least your life in this world is no worse than anyone else's.

Unusually, Jesus portrayed the world to come as something that would develop and grow, rather than suddenly arrive. You'll have to excuse his botanical blind spots; I know that the mustard plant isn't a tree, let alone a large one, but we grew up in a town.

The kingdom of heaven is like to a grain of mustard seed, which a man took, and sowed in his field: Which indeed is the least of all seeds: but when it is grown, it is the greatest among herbs, and becometh a tree, so that the birds of the air come and lodge in the branches thereof.

I might have suspected that this was a utopian aberration in his apocalyptic vision, but the next parable seemed similar: the kingdom is like yeast gradually leavening a large quantity of flour. If the new age isn't going to come with a bang, what does that mean about judgment day?

Being rather slow, the disciples asked Jesus to explain his parable about the weeds in the wheat. He confirmed that at the end of the world angels would gather up the wrong-doers *And shall cast them into a furnace of fire: there shall be wailing and gnashing of teeth.* Like a visit to the dentist, only worse.

He tried out a few new ones on them. The kingdom of heaven is like buried treasure: its discoverer leaves it buried, selling his property to buy the field. (And then digs it up, I trust.) Similarly, *the kingdom of heaven is like unto a merchant man, seeking goodly pearls: Who, when he had found one pearl of great price, went and sold all that he had, and bought it.*

Because not everyone seems so ready to pay the price, though, Jesus pointed out what it would cost to decline. *Again, the kingdom of heaven is like unto a net, that was cast into the sea, and gathered of every kind.* When the catch was brought ashore the good fish were kept, and the bad discarded. The analogy didn't seem helpful (indeed, it's better to be bad if they were thrown back in), but the moral was the same: angels would toss the wicked on the fire, and there would be much sizzling and reflex jaw action.

Jesus asked if he had made himself clear, and they said *Yea, Lord,* you bet. Good, he replied, now you'll be able to produce both the old and the new (teachings, I suppose). At that he finally left to return home.

I'm afraid that our neighbours found this local boy back to teach in the synagogue not to their liking. They were quite sarcastic, in fact. *Whence hath this man this wisdom, and these mighty works? Is not this the carpenter's son? is not his mother called Mary? and his brethren, James, and Joses, and Simon, and Judas? And his sisters, are they not all with us? Whence then hath this man all these things?* In short, they thought he was a jumped-up apprentice.

I wanted him to take it gently, perhaps trying a little humility. *But Jesus said unto them, A prophet is not without honour, save in his own country, and in his own house. And he did not many mighty works there because of their unbelief.* Our loss, I'm sure, but miracles would be more impressive if they weren't confined to the credulous.

LOAVES AND FISHES

At that time Herod the tetrarch – not to be confused with Herod the Great – *heard* 14 *of the fame of Jesus, And said unto his servants, This is John the Baptist; he is risen from the dead.* Obviously his conscience was uneasy. It appears that he had kept John imprisoned at the urging of his wife Herodias, who resented the preacher's condemnation of their marriage (her previous husband, Herod's brother, was still alive). Although John's popular support had saved him from execution, on Herod's birthday his luck ran out.

I wasn't at the party, needless to say, but by all accounts it was a bawdy affair.

Salome *the daughter of Herodias danced before them, and pleased Herod. Whereupon he promised with an oath to give her whatsoever she would ask. And she, being before instructed of her mother, said, Give me here John Baptist's head in a charger. And the king was sorry,* but a promise is a promise, and besides he didn't want to disappoint his guests. I have no idea how they managed to bring the head to the palace – John was being held at a fortress nearly a hundred miles away – but it was duly given to Salome on a platter. I hope everyone had finished eating.

On hearing the news Jesus tried to slip away by himself for a while; John had, after all, been important to him, even if they had grown apart. He took a boat to a remote spot, but a crowd gathered where he landed, and he did some healing. As evening approached his disciples suggested that everyone should be sent off to eat. When Jesus told them to provide the food themselves, they replied that *We have here but five loaves, and two fishes.*

Telling everyone to sit down, Jesus performed a simple ritual: *looking up to heaven, he blessed, and brake, and gave the loaves to his disciples, and the disciples to the multitude. And they did all eat, and were filled: and they took up of the fragments that remained twelve baskets full.* The crowd was 5,000 strong, not counting women and children. (Why don't they count?)

If the prophet Elisha could feed a hundred men with twenty loaves, then I suppose Jesus could feed five thousand with five. It does seem odd, though, that no one acted surprised. I don't usually favour prosaic explanations of stories about my brother, but in this instance I'm not sure that anything supernatural was supposed to have occurred. No doubt some of the people were making an outing of it; all had travelled, and many must have come prepared. Jesus, by his example, moved them to share the picnic. To me, at least, that seems the best way to conjure a meal out of thin air.

I have no such explanation of the sequel. Jesus obliged the disciples to leave ahead of him in a boat while he sent the people on their way, and then said his prayers. Out at sea, the wind and water were giving the disciples a rough ride, but they had to wait until the early hours of the morning for assistance. *And in the fourth watch of the night Jesus went unto them, walking on the sea.* The sight made them even more terrified than they were already, but Jesus called out *Be of good cheer; it is I; be not afraid,* as if nothing could be more natural.

Peter, willing perhaps to try anything to get out of the boat, asked Jesus to call him over. *And when Peter was come down out of the ship, he walked on the water.* Like a beginner suddenly seized by fright, however, he saw the storm and began to sink. *And immediately Jesus stretched forth his hand, and caught him, and said unto him, O thou of little faith, wherefore didst thou doubt?* No need to be hard on the fellow; I think Peter did well, for a first attempt.

They clambered back into the boat and calm returned. *Then they that were in the ship came and worshipped him, saying, Of a truth thou art the Son of God.* Safely back on land, Jesus resumed his ordinary routine; the unwell came from miles around, *And besought him that they might only touch the hem of his garment: and as many as touched were made perfectly whole.*

In view of all these wonders, it does seem odd that the Pharisees had only the most mundane questions for him. *Why,* they asked, *do thy disciples transgress the tradition of the elders? for they wash not their hands when they eat bread.* Personally, I think Jesus should have admitted the mistake. Instead he became hostile, accusing them tit-for-tat of breaching the commandment about honouring thy father and mother. (Apparently they were allowing people to keep possessions that should have gone to the old folks, if the goods had been dedicated to God.) It was all rather undignified.

Jesus did make an astute observation, though: *Not that which goeth into the mouth defileth a man; but that which cometh out of the mouth, this defileth a man.* Worried, perhaps, by his lack of diplomacy, the disciples mentioned that he had offended the Pharisees. I gather from his response that it was intentional; he implied that they were weeds to be rooted up. To change metaphors, *they be blind leaders of the blind. And if the blind lead the blind, both shall fall into the ditch.*

Never afraid to make a fool of himself, Peter asked him to explain what he meant. Jesus rebuked him for being thick, but provided a gloss. Whatever goes into your mouth passes through your stomach and comes out the other end. By contrast, what comes out of your mouth is evidence of what lies in your heart, *For out of the heart proceed evil thoughts, murders, adulteries, fornications, thefts, false witness, blasphemies: These are the things which defile a man: but to eat with unwashen hands defileth not a man.* Well said: worse crimes have been committed. I don't think my mother would have been dissuaded, however, from teaching us to wash before meals.

Jesus left Galilee for the non-Jewish territories of Tyre and Sidon; whether things had become too hot for him, or he just wanted a break, I don't know. His reputation as an exorcist had spread even there, however, and a woman came to beg him to release her daughter from the devil. *But he answered her not a word.* As his disciples complained that they couldn't shake her off, he made it clear that he wasn't interested in treating Gentiles: *I am not sent but unto the lost sheep of the house of Israel.* When she still didn't give up, he tried racial abuse (the old pearls-before-swine argument): *It is not meet to take the children's bread, and to cast it to dogs. And she said, Truth, Lord: yet the dogs eat of the crumbs which fall from their masters' table.* I don't know whether it was her desperation or the impossibility of offending her that made him crack, but he pronounced the patient cured. He did it, as for his other Gentile client (the boy in the centurion's household), sight unseen: fear of contamination, perhaps?

Returning south towards Galilee, Jesus had the opportunity to repeat whatever it was he had done with the loaves and fishes. On this occasion, I must admit, it seems clear that the people in attendance had exhausted their supplies. That said, the disciples apparently had no idea that Jesus could make something out of nothing, because they asked where enough bread could be found to feed everyone. *And Jesus saith unto them, How many loaves have ye? And they said, Seven, and a few little fishes.* From there on the procedure was the same, though despite starting with more they ended up with less: there were just seven baskets of leftovers. It was a smaller crowd, too: *they that did eat were four thousand men, beside women and children.* They must have been hungrier than the first lot.

THE KEYS OF THE KINGDOM

16   When Jesus did such miraculous things, it's puzzling that he was seen as just another preacher/healer. The aristocratic Sadducees, following in the footsteps of the orthodox Pharisees, asked him for some sign that he might be more. He replied that it shouldn't be necessary. *When it is evening, ye say, It will be fair weather: for the sky is red.* In the morning, a red, gloomy sky means the reverse. So, then, *ye can discern the face of the sky; but can ye not discern the signs of the times?* There would be no sign except Jonah's (a three-day separation from the world), which seems to cast doubt on the reported miracles.

Even the disciples were confused. When Jesus told them to *beware the leaven of the Pharisees and of the Sadducees,* they thought it was a reproach for not bringing bread. He asked if it had not yet penetrated their skulls that bread wasn't a problem so long as he was around. He had been warning against the doctrine of his rivals, they realised, not their baking.

As they continued their travels, Jesus asked the disciples how people regarded him. They answered that he was variously identified as John the Baptist (probably not what he wanted to hear), Elijah (more flattering), Jeremiah (I suppose because the end was nigh, again), and various other prophets. He then enquired *But whom say ye that I am? And Simon Peter answered and said, Thou art the Christ, the Son of the living God.*

Jesus remarked that Peter's thought must have come from God, because it obviously hadn't come from anyone else. ('Christ' means the anointed one, i.e. the messiah, but no one expected the messiah to have divine parentage.) Peter was made dictator of the universe; anything he permitted or prohibited on earth would be the same in heaven. Making a pun on the name Peter ('Rock'), Jesus said:

> *thou art Peter, and upon this rock I will build my church; and the gates of hell shall not prevail against it. And I will give unto thee the keys of the kingdom of heaven: and whatsoever thou shalt bind on earth shall be bound in heaven: and whatsoever thou shalt loose on earth shall be loosed in heaven. Then charged he his disciples that they should tell no man that he was Jesus the Christ.*

Peter wouldn't have been my first choice to hold the keys of the kingdom; he was frankly a bit of a goon. Still, he was going to be running the show, by the sound of it. That didn't mean, however, that Jesus wanted people going around calling him the messiah.

Lest they have any unrealistic expectations, he told them that he was going to run into trouble with the authorities in Jerusalem, and would be (at least temporarily) killed. When Peter denied that such a thing could happen – he must still have been fallible at that stage – Jesus slapped him down: *Get thee behind me, Satan: thou art an offence unto me.*

Jesus repeated that they would win through losing. *For whosoever will save his life shall lose it: and whosoever will lose his life for my sake shall find it. For what is a man profited, if he shall gain the whole world, and lose his own soul?* On the day of judgment the heavenly powers *shall reward every man according to his works.* They wouldn't even have long to wait; it would happen in their own lifetimes. *Verily I say unto you, There be some standing here, which shall not taste of death, till they see the Son of man coming in his kingdom.* As he said, you win some, you lose some.

Six days later Jesus went up a mountain with Peter and two of the others. They saw him transfigured; he seemed to shine, as if he would glow in the dark. What should they see next but Moses and Elijah talking to him. Peter was so impressed that he offered to make three little huts, one for each of the dignitaries. Before Jesus had a chance to answer, however, a voice came out of a cloud saying *This is my beloved Son, in whom I am well pleased.* When the disciples picked themselves up off the ground, the visitors had disappeared. 17

As usual, Jesus told them to keep the episode to themselves. Realising God was preparing for a big event, they asked what had become of Elijah; he was supposed to come first. Jesus confirmed that he had come but, unhappily for him, hadn't been recognised. *Then the disciples understood that he spake unto them of John the Baptist.*

On their return a man fell to his knees before Jesus, hoping that he might succeed where the disciples had failed in curing his epileptic son. Jesus was in a foul temper (*O faithless and perverse generation, how long shall I be with you? how long shall I suffer you?*) but he did the business, ejecting the devil responsible. Why, the disciples asked, couldn't we do it?

> *And Jesus said unto them, Because of your unbelief: for verily I say unto you, If ye have faith as a grain of mustard seed, ye shall say unto this mountain, Remove hence to yonder place; and it shall remove; and nothing shall be impossible unto you.*

That's caused some disappointment and self-reproach, I imagine. Wait for the punchline, though: having said that their exorcism failed because they lacked faith, he casually remarked *Howbeit this kind* (of demon) *goeth not out but by prayer and fasting* – they had simply used the wrong technique. What a joker.

Jesus reminded his disciples that he was destined to be killed. *And they were exceeding sorry.*

Back in Capernaum a collector of the temple tax caught up with Peter, enquiring whether Jesus intended to pay. Answering 'yes' he went inside, only to have Jesus imply that he had spoken too hastily. I found it hard to grasp the rationale for avoidance, but fortunately Jesus found a way to stay out of trouble. Go down to the water, he told Peter, *and take up the fish that first cometh up; and when thou hast opened his mouth, thou shalt find a piece of money: that take, and give unto them for me and thee.* I wish he had paid mine while he was at it.

SIN AND FORGIVENESS

18   When the disciples expressed curiosity about the heavenly hierarchy, Jesus let them know that it wasn't what they were used to. *Except ye be converted, and become as little children, ye shall not enter into the kingdom of heaven.* I suppose he was trying to promote humility, but I've never noticed children being very humble. Child-lovers will be on top; disciplinarians are sunk, because

> *whoso shall receive one such little child in my name receiveth me. But whoso shall offend one of these little ones which believe in me, it were better for him that a millstone were hanged about his neck, and that he were drowned in the depth of the sea.*

I'll be more polite to children from now on. Jesus was a stern judge; *it must needs be that offences come; but woe to that man by whom the offence cometh!*

Jesus again recommended amputating any sinful members: a hand, a foot (the mind boggles), or of course an eye. *And if thine eye offend thee, pluck it out, and cast it from thee: it is better for thee to enter into life with one eye, rather than having two eyes to be cast into hell fire.* I wouldn't know which eye to blame.

Perhaps Jesus noticed that the violence was making his audience uneasy, because he told a reassuring parable about sheep. A shepherd will leave his whole flock on the hillside to look for a single stray. If he finds it, *he rejoiceth more of that sheep, than of the ninety and nine which went not astray.* This was an acute observation about human nature, I thought – and how good to know that God responds in just the same way.

What should be done with a sinner, then? Talk to him, Jesus said, and if he doesn't listen, bring a few more people in on it. Should that fail, tell everyone, and if there is still no correction, treat him as you would a Gentile or a tax-collector, i.e. with distaste.

That made good sense to the disciples, but his next couple of statements sounded most odd. First he extended what had been Peter's prerogative to all of them: anything they decided to prohibit, and anything they decided to permit, would likewise be allowed or forbidden in heaven. I can't understand why God should suddenly let people make the rules; they're prone to making bad ones, as he knows. Just as strangely, Jesus claimed that a request had only to be made by two of them for it to be granted by God. He reasoned that *where two or three are gathered together in my name, there am I in the midst of them.* That's all very well, but I've seen millions of petitioners go unanswered, never mind a pair.

Then came Peter to him, and said, Lord, how oft shall my brother sin against me, and I forgive him? till seven times? Jesus saith unto him, I say not unto thee, Until seven times: but, Until seventy times seven.

Clear enough, I thought, but then he told a parable. Once upon a time there was a king, and this king wanted to put his finances in order. There happened to be a man who owed him an absolutely staggering amount of money. As this man was without means, the king arranged for him to be sold, along with his wife and his children and all his possessions. When he begged for another chance, however, the king *was moved with compassion, and loosed him, and forgave him the debt.*

So far, so good, but then the lucky fellow went straight to someone who owed him a small sum and, grabbing him by the throat, demanded repayment. When this debtor asked that he be patient the man had him thrown into prison. The king was far from happy when he heard that his forgiveness hadn't proved contagious. In fact he revoked his pardon, ordering that the man be tortured until every last penny had been repaid. *So likewise shall my heavenly Father do also unto you, if ye from your hearts forgive not every one his brother their trespasses.*

There's nothing like divine encouragement. If you don't cultivate the right attitude, God will change his mind about forgiving all those sins you told him about. As I've said before, though, I don't see that unlimited forgiveness limited to those who forgive others is such a great idea. For the good-natured criminal – one who will assault and rob and not take it personally if someone else does the same to him – it's perfect. For the unhappy victim – one who persists in holding kidnapping and rape against the attacker – it's a peculiar path to hell.

THE FIRST SHALL BE LAST

Having given this sermon, Jesus left Galilee to travel south. He continued to work   19
as a healer. He was also consulted, however, on matters of doctrine and morality. When the question of divorce – a permanent favourite – came up again, Jesus insisted that matrimony originated by divine command; *What therefore God hath joined together, let not man put asunder.* He rejected the divorce code established by Moses as too permissive: remarriage was adultery, in his view.

This being so, his disciples suggested, it would be better not to marry. Jesus seemed to concede the point, though it wasn't a solution for everybody.

For there are some eunuchs, which were so born from their mother's womb: and there are some eunuchs, which were made eunuchs of men:

and there be eunuchs, which have made themselves eunuchs for the kingdom of heaven's sake. He that is able to receive it, let him receive it.

I think 'give it up' might be more accurate.

Then were there brought unto him little children, that he should put his hands on them, and pray. The disciples tried to shield him from nuisances, but Jesus wanted them to come. *And he laid his hands on them, and departed thence.*

When a man came to ask how he might achieve eternal life, Jesus told him to keep the commandments. I've done that, he replied; anything else? He should have quit while he was ahead. *If thou wilt be perfect, go and sell that thou hast, and give to the poor, and thou shalt have treasure in heaven,* Jesus said. That was enough for him; *he went away sorrowful: for he had great possessions.* No doubt he didn't like the idea of putting all his eggs in one basket.

Jesus declared that the wealthy would find it difficult to reach heaven. Not just difficult, but impossible: *It is easier for a camel to go through the eye of a needle, than for a rich man to enter into the kingdom of God.* Now maybe he said 'cable' rather than 'camel' – there's a dispute about exactly how funny he was trying to be – but the point stands. People who have more than they need can skip the harp lessons.

When his disciples heard it, they were exceedingly amazed, saying, Who then can be saved? No one we knew, by the sound of it. To forestall discouragement Jesus said *With men this is impossible; but with God all things are possible.* I've heard more reassuring statements.

Being the disciples' self-appointed shop steward, Peter bluntly put it to Jesus that they had given up everything to wander around the country with him: *what shall we have therefore?* Jesus made haste to promise them twelve thrones, from which they would lord it over the twelve tribes of Israel (curious – at least one among them would presumably be *persona non grata* in heaven). The good news was that everyone who had abandoned brothers, sisters, father, mother, children or property for his sake would live forever. The bad news – at least for his original disciples – was that *many that are first shall be last; and the last shall be first.* I'll stay near the end of the queue and hope for the best.

20   Jesus told another story to illustrate how heaven would work. The owner of a vineyard went out at dawn and hired labourers at an agreed wage for a day's work. At intervals throughout the day he went into the market and hired more workers, saying that he would pay them what was right. Even at the eleventh hour (counting from dawn until dusk) he was still recruiting, asking people *Why stand ye here all the day idle?*, to which they gave the answer that the employed find hard to grasp, *Because no man hath hired us.* He sent them off to join the others in the vineyard.

At sundown the workers received their wages; the paymaster gave everyone, from the last to appear through the first, the same amount. Not surprisingly the early arrivals felt disgruntled, and protested *These last have wrought but one hour, and thou hast made them equal unto us, which have borne the burden and heat of the day.* The lord of the manor pointed out that they had received the sum agreed, and the remuneration of the others was no concern of theirs; *I will give unto this last, even as unto thee. Is it not lawful for me to do what I will with mine own?*

He was quite right, in a way. It was his money, and paying the part-timers for a full day was an act of generosity. He seemed to be missing the point, though; the question was about fairness, not legal obligation. Bonuses shouldn't be distributed on the basis of last come, first served. Perhaps God is willing to give equal reward for unequal effort, but I wish he'd keep it quiet. It's not going to make this world any better if people know that *the last shall be first, and the first last: for many be called, but few chosen.* Motivation is all too low as it is.

Jesus was now heading in the direction of Jerusalem. He again told his disciples that he was going to be beaten and killed, before returning to life. Disturbing news, but the mother of James and John still had ambitions for them: *Grant that these my two sons may sit, the one on thy right hand, and the other on the left, in thy kingdom.* Some mothers just never give up.

I would have found it maddening: even while running a charity the staff persists in playing politics. Jesus told the brothers not to be hasty, asking *Are ye able to drink of the cup that I shall drink of ...?* Having affirmed that they were, lesser men might have felt conned by his response. *Ye shall drink indeed of my cup,* Jesus said, but the question of who sits where has already been decided by God. Besides, those who would be served must serve, *Even as the Son of man came not to be ministered unto, but to minister, and to give his life a ransom for many.*

As they were leaving Jericho two blind men called out to Jesus. He stopped and asked them what they wanted (he could be clairvoyant one moment and rather slow the next). They replied, patiently enough, *Lord, that our eyes may be opened. So Jesus had compassion on them, and touched their eyes: and immediately their eyes received sight.*

COMMOTION IN THE TEMPLE

Approaching Jerusalem, Jesus sent two disciples into a village, telling them to return with the donkey and its foal they would find there. I'm sure he must have made arrangements in advance; my brother wasn't one to go joy riding. No one else who tells this story mentions more than one donkey, but Matthew as usual had his eye on scripture, and Zechariah had mentioned that *thy King cometh unto thee, meek, and sitting upon an ass, and a colt the foal of an ass.* Misunderstanding the Hebrew parallelism – the prophet was echoing his own words, not describing a second ass – Matthew adjusted the picture accordingly.

Anyway, Jesus now had a donkey to ride. People cushioned the road with their coats, or with branches cut from trees. (They never did that when Jesus was walking, but you always get better service when you're not on foot.) The crowds shouted *Hosanna to the son of David,* which is a cry for help. The whole city was asking *Who is this? And the multitude said, This is Jesus the prophet of Nazareth of Galilee.*

Jesus went straight to the temple, but he wasn't in the mood for praying. The courtyard served as a small market, where pilgrims could change money and buy ritual offerings, though not yet souvenirs. Jesus caused a serious breach of the peace; he *overthrew the tables of the moneychangers, and the seats of them that sold doves, And said unto them, It is written, My house shall be called the house of prayer; but ye have made it a den of thieves.*

The lame and the blind gathered to be healed. The clergy were not pleased to have a stranger turn the temple into a health clinic, nor to have children shouting *Hosanna to the son of David,* as if he were the messiah. When they protested, Jesus – who could be terribly provoking – asked if they didn't know from the psalm that *Out of the mouth of babes and sucklings thou hast perfected praise?* (In fact that's only how it goes in the Greek translation, but never mind.) It must have been a relief when he went to spend the night at Bethany, a village just to the east of the city.

You didn't want to be around when Jesus was angry – not even if you happened to be a tree. When they left in the morning he was hungry, and stopped at a fig tree beside the road. Figs not being in season then I think he might more reasonably have looked elsewhere for his breakfast, but being forced to delay a meal can make you furious. Jesus cursed the tree, saying *Let no fruit grow on thee henceforth for ever. And presently the fig tree withered away.*

The disciples were much impressed by his fast-acting herbicidal powers. He told them, as he had before, that with faith and no doubts you could move mountains: *And all things, whatsoever ye shall ask in prayer, believing, ye shall receive.* Fortunately for fig trees and other objects of our temper, though regrettably for our general well-being, it seems that he was being overly optimistic.

When Jesus returned to the temple – and it speaks well for the tolerance of its guardians that he was allowed back – the priests asked him by what authority he was acting. Jesus countered with a question of his own: *The baptism of John, whence was it? from heaven, or of men?* They were caught in a cleft stick; it was too late to say that John was doing God's work, but he had too many supporters to deny it safely. *And they answered Jesus, and said, We cannot tell. And he said unto them, Neither tell I you by what authority I do these things.* So there.

He had a story for them, though. A man asked each of his two sons to work in the vineyard. One refused, but later thought better of it and went. The other said that he would, and then didn't. Which of the two obeyed? Obviously the repentant sinner, not the hypocrite. Likewise, Jesus said, *the publicans and the harlots go into the kingdom of God before you.* Priests tend not to find that amusing.

I give them full marks for patience: they sat still for another story. An absentee landlord sent a few servants to collect his share of the crop. The tenants beat or killed them, and did the same to the next group of envoys. The owner then decided to send his son – clearly a bad idea. He, too, was killed. What would the landlord do with these tenants, Jesus asked? Being good sports, they lobbed back the desired answer (no nonsense about forgiveness, you'll notice); *He will miserably destroy those wicked men, and will let out his vineyard unto other husbandmen, which shall render him the fruits in their seasons.* Jesus duly slammed home the moral: *The kingdom of God shall be taken from you.*

Needless to say *when the chief priests and Pharisees had heard his parables, they perceived that he spake of them;* subtlety wasn't his strong point. Fortunately Jesus still enjoyed the protection of the crowd, *because they took him for a prophet.* You can be as insulting as you like if the gang behind you is big enough.

JESUS AND THE PHARISEES

Jesus wasn't finished with them yet. The kingdom of heaven is like this, he said: 22 a ruler organised a wedding feast for his son, and none of the invited guests came. When reminders came around *They made light of it,* and some of the more sensitive even killed the royal messengers. The king didn't intend to let a few ungrateful people spoil the occasion, so *he sent forth his armies, and destroyed those murderers, and burned up their city.* Then he told his servants to go out into the streets and bring anyone they could find in to enjoy the feast. They did just that, summoning *both bad and good: and the wedding was furnished with guests.*

So far, clear enough: the priests and Pharisees hadn't acknowledged their invitations, and wouldn't be at the party. I'm at a loss to understand the conclusion, though. On his arrival, the king noticed someone who wasn't properly dressed for a wedding (but surely none of them were?). When he asked the man to explain himself, *he was speechless,* as you might expect. *Then said the king to the servants, Bind him hand and foot, and take him away, and cast him into outer darkness; there shall be weeping and gnashing of teeth. For many are called, but few are chosen.*

Now one possible moral is that great lords are dangerously unstable and should be avoided at all costs. While I presume Jesus had something else in mind, I wouldn't like to guess what. Not even the punchline made sense, unless the king went on to throw most of the other last-minute guests in the dungeon. Or perhaps it should be 'many are gulled, but few are chosen'.

Some of the Pharisees decided not to take all this lying down. They sent a few of their supporters, accompanied by agents of the state, to ask him whether it was right to pay taxes to Rome. Seeing that it was a trap, Jesus said *Why tempt ye me, ye hypocrites? Shew me the tribute money. And they brought unto him a penny. And he saith unto them, Whose is this image and superscription? They say unto him, Caesar's. Then saith he unto them, Render therefore unto Caesar the things which are Caesar's; and unto God the things that are God's.*

What you do when their claims conflict, Jesus didn't say, but the confrontation showed him at his muscular best. Later that day the Sadducees found him less magisterial. Mocking the idea of an afterlife, they told the story of a woman married to each of seven brothers in turn. *Therefore in the resurrection whose wife shall she be of the seven? for they all had her.* Jesus gave the dignified if slightly disappointing response that *in the resurrection they neither marry, nor are given in marriage, but are as the angels of God in heaven.* Some people would consider that paradise, I suppose.

He then offered a laughable argument for life after death. Did God not say *I am the God of Abraham, and the God of Isaac, and the God of Jacob? God is not the God of the dead, but of the living.* It follows that the patriarchs (and presumably others) are living. I'm hardly surprised that *when the multitude heard this, they were astonished at his doctrine.* I am the son of Joseph, and one must be conceived by the living, not the dead; is my father still alive?

If his sophistry needed work, at least Jesus was strong on doctrine. When one of the Pharisees asked him to name the greatest commandment, he gave a response that was both orthodox and original.

> *Thou shalt love the Lord thy God with all thy heart, and with all thy soul, and with all thy mind. This is the first and great commandment. And the second is like unto it, Thou shalt love thy neighbour as thyself. On these two commandments hang all the law and the prophets.*

All good Jews repeat the first phrase every day. The second part, also from the Torah, had received less emphasis, though it did remind me of the answer given by rabbi Hillel to a similar question. Still, I think Jesus deserves credit for placing love of humanity on a par with love of God.

He also had a fascinating comment on the ancestry of the messiah, who was conventionally expected to be a descendant of David. Jesus ridiculed this idea, citing the psalm of David that begins *The Lord said unto my Lord, Sit thou on my right hand, till I make thine enemies thy footstool.* Who would call his own offspring 'Lord'? Jesus obviously didn't believe that he had royal blood, which might also imply that he wouldn't have seen any reason to be born in Bethlehem.

23   Jesus continued to berate the Pharisees, those pious fellow Jews who paid so much attention to the law. He told his disciples to do as they said, but not as they did. I was surprised by that, because Jesus often disagreed with their rulings (about the sabbath, for example). Besides, it's unfair to accuse the Pharisees of hypocrisy; they might have been misguided, more concerned with the letter than the spirit of the law, but everyone acknowledged the rigour of their observance.

As far as Jesus was concerned, however, they did it all for show: *they make broad their phylacteries, and enlarge the borders of their garments, And love the uppermost rooms at feasts, and the chief seats in the synagogues,* and to be called 'rabbi'. Speaking of titles, he said *call no man your father upon the earth: for one is your Father, which is in heaven.* I don't see it, frankly; why should no one be addressed with respect, just because another is supremely deserving? Of course it's a different matter if the person insists on applying the title to himself; then we may well feel satisfaction that *whosoever shall exalt himself shall be abased; and he that shall humble himself shall be exalted.*

Jesus launched himself into a lengthy execration of the religious leadership. I was amazed by some of it; for example, he declared that they would go to the ends of the earth to make a convert, *and when he is made, ye make him two-fold more the child of hell than yourselves.* I confess, though, that I rather enjoyed the abuse he heaped on their care to tithe, i.e. to contribute a tenth of everything produced to God.

> *Woe unto you, scribes and Pharisees, hypocrites! for ye pay tithe of mint and anise and cummin, and have omitted the weightier matters of the law, judgment, mercy, and faith: these ought ye to have done, and not to leave the other undone. Ye blind guides, which strain at a gnat, and swallow a camel.*

That raised a chuckle, but my jaw dropped again when he compared them to whitewashed tombs.

> *Woe unto you, scribes and Pharisees, hypocrites! for ye are like unto whited sepulchres, which indeed appear beautiful outward, but are within full of dead men's bones, and of all uncleanness. Even so ye also outwardly appear righteous unto men, but within ye are full of hypocrisy and iniquity.*

My brother's reputation for being nonjudgmental never seemed very secure to me. He was often tolerant, but that isn't to say that he showed any particular reluctance to judge. He wasn't afraid to use strong language, either: *ye are the children of them which killed the prophets. ... Ye serpents, ye generation of vipers, how can ye escape the damnation of hell?* He could sound just like Jeremiah or Ezekiel. His words for the holy city, in fact, seem to come straight from the old-time tradition:

> *O Jerusalem, Jerusalem, thou that killest the prophets, and stonest them which are sent unto thee, how often would I have gathered thy children together, even as a hen gathereth her chickens under her wings, and ye would not! Behold, your house is left unto you desolate.*

THE END OF THE WORLD

Jesus made this reference to the temple more precise when he finally left it. He told   24
his disciples that *There shall not be left here one stone upon another, that shall not be thrown down.* They were in an apocalyptic mood, to judge by their discussion as they sat on the Mount of Olives. *Tell us*, his disciples said, *when*

shall these things be? and what shall be the sign of thy coming, and of the end of the world?

For a start, Jesus answered, many people would come along claiming to be the messiah.

> *And ye shall hear of wars and rumours of wars: see that ye be not troubled: for all these things must come to pass, but the end is not yet. For nation shall rise against nation, and kingdom against kingdom: and there shall be famines, and pestilences, and earthquakes, in divers places.*

All that would be just the beginning. They would be persecuted; there would be betrayal, and hatred, and wickedness, though anyone holding out would be saved. *And this gospel of the kingdom shall be preached in all the world for a witness unto all nations; and then shall the end come.* I don't know that gospel ('good news') is the term I'd use, to be honest.

When ye therefore shall see the abomination of desolation, spoken of by Daniel the prophet, stand in the holy place, (whoso readeth, let him understand:) then you'll know to take to the hills. Don't even go back to grab a coat: run. Pregnant women and nursing mothers will have a hard time of it, unfortunately. Just *pray ye that your flight be not in the winter, neither on the sabbath day: For then shall be great tribulation, such as was not since the beginning of the world to this time, no, nor ever shall be.* That would tend to spoil your sabbath.

It wouldn't take long, Jesus remarked, for humankind to be eradicated, *but for the elect's sake those days shall be shortened.* Again, don't pay any attention to people claiming to be the messiah, or alleging that he is in one place or another. *For as the lightning cometh out of the east, and shineth even unto the west; so shall also the coming of the Son of man be.* He would be all around; *For wheresoever the carcase is, there will the eagles be gathered together.* The 'eagles' here are actually vultures: highly appropriate, no doubt, if in rather poor taste.

Following this tribulation the sun, moon and stars would all go dark, and at the appearance of a sign everyone would weep and wail, *and they shall see the Son of man coming in the clouds of heaven with power and great glory. And he shall send his angels with a great sound of a trumpet,* to gather up the chosen ones. As for the rest, their fate was unclear.

What Jesus said next was the most exciting prediction of all. Just as new leaves on a fig tree tell you that summer is on its way, so *when ye shall see all these things, know that it is near, even at the doors. Verily I say unto you, This generation shall not pass, till all these things be fulfilled.* Luckily for us, it turned out to be not so verily the case.

At least he didn't risk naming a date, which is always a big mistake. *Heaven and earth shall pass away, but my words shall not pass away. But of that day and hour knoweth no man, no, not the angels of heaven, but my Father only* – and he wasn't telling. Some people thought Jesus knew everything, and were surprised at this confession of ignorance; I never had that problem.

The apocalypse would sneak up on people unawares, as it did in the time of Noah.

For as in the days that were before the flood they were eating and drinking, marrying and giving in marriage, until the day that Noe entered into the ark, And knew not until the flood came, and took them all away; so shall also the coming of the Son of man be. Then shall two be in the field; the one shall be taken, and the other left. Two women shall be grinding at the mill; the one shall be taken, and the other left. Watch therefore: for ye know not what hour your Lord doth come.

Like a burglar in the night, God's envoy will appear unexpectedly. To be more apt, he's like an absent householder. The servant whose master returns to find him working will be rewarded, but the one who is surprised while carousing with his friends will be chopped up into little pieces: *there shall be weeping and gnashing of teeth.*

For those looking forward to heaven, 'be prepared' is the best motto.　　25

Then shall the kingdom of heaven be likened unto ten virgins, which took their lamps, and went forth to meet the bridegroom. And five of them were wise, and five were foolish. They that were foolish took their lamps, and took no oil with them: But the wise took oil in their vessels with their lamps.

As it turned out, the moral had nothing to do with what can happen to a foolish virgin in the dark. The problem, rather, was that by the time the bridegroom turned up they were out of oil, and the others refused to share. As a result they were late for the wedding, and when they knocked on the door *he answered and said, Verily I say unto you, I know you not.* Apparently it's better to be ungenerous than unprepared.

The next parable was even more confusing. Before leaving on a long journey, a man distributed his wealth among his servants according to his assessment of their abilities. One received five talents (or sacks of money), another two talents, and a third just one. Through astute dealing the first two doubled their riches, while *he that had received one went and digged in the earth, and hid his lord's money.* If you don't have much to start with, you don't like to take chances.

When the man eventually returned he congratulated each of the successful investors, saying *Well done, thou good and faithful servant: thou hast been faithful over a few things, I will make thee ruler over many things: enter thou into the joy of thy lord.* The third servant returned the money he had been given, explaining *Lord, I knew thee that thou art an hard man, reaping where thou hast not sown, and gathering where thou hast not strawed: And I was afraid, and went and hid thy talent.* Personally I think he was right; if the big boss makes you responsible for part of the hoard, the last thing you want to do is risk losing it.

Regrettably the master didn't appreciate his caution.

Thou wicked and slothful servant … Thou oughtest therefore to have put my money to the exchanger, and then at my coming I should have received mine own with usury. Take therefore the talent from him, and give it unto him which hath ten talents. For unto every one that hath shall be given, and he shall have abundance: but from him that hath not shall be taken away even that which he hath. And cast ye the unprofitable servant into outer darkness: there shall be weeping and gnashing of teeth.

If you don't have the aptitude, you're out of luck. The rich get richer, and the poor go to the wall – if not to hell. He was a true blue champion of the enterprise culture, my brother.

Fortunately for his reputation, Jesus ended the sermon with a plug for altruism. On judgment day everyone would be herded before the throne, where *he shall separate them one from another, as a shepherd divideth his sheep from the goats: and he shall set the sheep on his right hand, but the goats on the left.* (Right-handed chauvinism, I fear.) Those on the right would be invited into the kingdom,

For I was an hungred, and ye gave me meat: I was thirsty, and ye gave me drink: I was a stranger, and ye took me in: Naked, and ye clothed me: I was sick, and ye visited me: I was in prison, and ye came unto me.

The chosen, not remembering any such occasion, are perplexed, but *the King shall answer and say unto them, Verily I say unto you, Inasmuch as ye have done it unto one of the least of these my brethren, ye have done it unto me.* That, to my mind, is the most affecting remark Jesus ever made. It ought, in fact, to be everyone's view: good done to one is good done to all.

Naturally the same principle applies to the bad, and thus *shall he say also unto them on the left hand, Depart from me, ye cursed, into everlasting fire, prepared for the devil and his angels.* Having not been charitable to the unfortunate, they were going to be even more unfortunate themselves.

THE LAST SUPPER

26   Passover was just two days away. Jesus knew that his time was almost up, though the priests were reluctant to arrest him. He started to act like a man about to die. At the house of Simon the leper in Bethany, *There came unto him a woman having an alabaster box of very precious ointment, and poured it on his head, as he sat at meat. But when his disciples saw it, they had indignation, saying, To what*

purpose is this waste? For this ointment might have been sold for much, and given to the poor. In earlier days I think Jesus might have agreed with them, but in the circumstances he was willing to be pampered: *she hath wrought a good work upon me. For ye have the poor always with you; but me ye have not always.*

It was after this that the disciple Judas Iscariot went to the chief priests and asked *What will ye give me, and I will deliver him unto you? And they covenanted with him for thirty pieces of silver.* (The amount had scriptural overtones.) I'm surprised they gave him anything; Jesus wasn't in hiding. The other mystery is why Judas was so aggrieved. I know that Jesus wasn't the easiest person to live with, but he usually upset only the conventionally religious.

Saying that *My time is at hand*, Jesus arranged to celebrate passover with his disciples. He must have spoilt their appetites by announcing in the middle of the meal, *Verily I say unto you, that one of you shall betray me. And they were exceeding sorrowful, and began every one of them to say unto him, Lord, is it I?* Jesus wasn't naming any names, but he said darkly that *it had been good for that man if he had not been born.* Judas was left to stew in his guilt.

And as they were eating, Jesus took bread, and blessed it, and brake it, and gave it to the disciples, and said, Take, eat; this is my body. And he took the cup, and gave thanks, and gave it to them, saying, Drink ye all of it; For this is my blood of the new testament, which is shed for many for the remission of sins. But I say unto you, I will not drink henceforth of this fruit of the vine, until that day when I drink it new with you in my Father's kingdom.

Even if my brother was inaugurating a new covenant (or testament) between God and the world, these were incredible things to say. He was a Jewish preacher, after all. Admittedly he wasn't rigorous about dietary restrictions, but the whole foundation of the law in this area is that you don't consume the life blood of any creature. The idea of drinking it would have been repellent to his disciples, and that's without even considering symbolic cannibalism. I wouldn't have expected them to show much appetite – and yet from their subsequent difficulties in staying awake, it appears that they ate all too well.

After dinner they went out to the Mount of Olives for a stroll. When Jesus predicted that they would all lose faith in him that night, Peter maintained that he would always be loyal, whatever happened to anyone else. Jesus replied *That this night, before the cock crow, thou shalt deny me thrice. Peter said unto him, Though I should die with thee, yet will I not deny thee.* His insistence that Jesus was wrong wasn't the best expression of faith, I have to say.

When they reached a place called Gethsemane, Jesus told them to wait while he prayed. He admitted to his closest disciples that *My soul is exceeding sorrowful, even unto death,* and asked them to keep him company. Walking a little further, he fell prostrate: *O my Father, if it be possible, let this cup pass from me: nevertheless not as I will, but as thou wilt.* On coming back he was aggrieved to find the others asleep. *What*, he asked Peter, *could ye not watch with me one hour?*

Watch and pray, that ye enter not into temptation: the spirit indeed is willing, but the flesh is weak.

So it seemed: returning from his prayers Jesus found them asleep again. He left a third time, and as before asked God to spare him, but in any case to do as he chose. While I don't know whose word we're taking for all this, his final remark when he came back to the disciples sounded very touching: *Sleep on now, and take your rest: behold, the hour is at hand, and the Son of man is betrayed into the hands of sinners.* Apparently he was being ironic, though, because he proceeded to rouse them.

Judas arrived with a large crowd of armed men, *And forthwith he came to Jesus, and said, Hail, master; and kissed him,* which was the sign to show the others whom they wanted. Jesus said *Friend, wherefore art thou come?* as he was seized. One of his followers drew a sword and cut off the ear of an arresting officer, but Jesus ordered *Put up again thy sword into his place: for all they that take the sword shall perish with the sword.* If he wanted to resist, he claimed defiantly, God would send twelve legions of angels to the rescue.

I rather had the impression that he had been hoping for just that, but I admire his bravado. Jesus went on to justify his acquiescence on the grounds that scripture would thereby be fulfilled, though without actually citing any passages. Evidently unconvinced, the disciples took to their heels and ran.

A court was assembled in the house of the high priest. Despite a quantity of false testimony – considering what he said in the temple, I'm surprised they needed it – they found it hard to convict him of anything. In frustration, the high priest insisted that Jesus state whether he was the messiah, *the Son of God*: an odd question, as no one imagined that the messiah would be divine. Jesus replied *Thou hast said: nevertheless I say unto you, Hereafter shall ye see the Son of man sitting on the right hand of power, and coming in the clouds of heaven.*

While not really an admission, it sounded blasphemous, and that was what they needed. After declaring that he should die, *they spit in his face, and buffeted him,* saying sarcastically that if he was indeed a prophet, perhaps he could name the assailants.

Peter, meanwhile, was sitting outside, having followed at a distance. A young woman came up and recognised him as someone who had been with Jesus. He denied it. A little later the same thing happened again. The people persisted, though, observing that his Galilean accent gave him away: *Surely thou also art one of them; for thy speech betrayeth thee. Then began he to curse and to swear, saying, I know not the man. And immediately the cock crew. And Peter remembered the word of Jesus, which said unto him, Before the cock crow, thou shalt deny me thrice. And he went out, and wept bitterly.*

THE CRUCIFIXION

In the morning the religious leadership handed Jesus over to the Roman governor, 27
Pontius Pilate. Judas, by now filled with remorse, returned the thirty pieces of
silver, admitting that he had betrayed an innocent man. When the priests said *What
is that to us?* he left and hanged himself. Being left with the blood money, they
decided, after some deliberation, to buy *the potter's field, to bury strangers in.*

Pontius Pilate adopted the approach pioneered by the chief priest, with the same
result. He asked *Art thou the King of the Jews? And Jesus said unto him, Thou
sayest.* Otherwise, he chose to remain silent. Not incriminating himself wasn't
enough to let him escape conviction, unfortunately.

It was the practice at passover that the governor would provide an amnesty to a
prisoner chosen by the people. The other candidate (only one? I hadn't realised we
were so law-abiding) was named Barabbas, and Pilate asked *Whom will ye that I
release unto you? Barabbas, or Jesus which is called Christ?* While this was
going on Pilate's wife sent a message saying *Have thou nothing to do with that
just man*; it seems that her dreams had been disturbed the previous night.

The priests had persuaded the crowd to ask for Barabbas. When Pilate demanded
to know what he should do with Jesus, everyone shouted *Let him be crucified,* and
only raised the volume when asked what he had done wrong. Seeing that argument
was pointless, Pilate *took water, and washed his hands before the multitude,
saying, I am innocent of the blood of this just person: see ye to it. Then answered
all the people, and said, His blood be on us, and on our children.*

I find it hard to believe that the people were so eager to see him die. Perhaps
their opinion of Jesus had changed, but it wouldn't say much for his charisma if
adoration turned to hatred in less than a week. Wanting to whitewash the Romans,
Matthew had Jews take the blame. It was a nasty trick – one that did more harm
than he could ever have imagined.

Jesus was turned over to the soldiers, who beat and abused him. Putting a crown
of thorns on his head, they mockingly called him 'King of the Jews'. When they
tired of maltreating the prisoner, they took him off to be crucified. A man from
north Africa who found himself in the wrong place at the wrong time was ordered
to carry the cross to *a place called Golgotha, that is to say, a place of a skull.*

The soldiers put Jesus on the cross, cast lots for his clothes, and then settled
down to watch him die. Crucifixion was a particularly vile form of execution used
for slaves, mutineers and criminal low life; death – usually by suffocation, when
the weight of the body prevented breathing – could take from a few hours to a few
days. The deterrence provided by the spectacle of public degradation was a bonus.
Anyone contemplating a career as messiah would doubtless have been discouraged
by the sign reading *THIS IS JESUS THE KING OF THE JEWS,* and by the
company he kept: thieves were crucified on either side of him.

Showing all the sensitivity one expects from voyeurs at an execution, people
jeered at him, suggesting that he come down from the cross. The priests jested that

He saved others; himself he cannot save. (They added that he had only to come down for them to believe his claims, and you do have to wonder why God takes such care to hide his light under a bushel.) The thieves on the neighbouring crosses joined in; you're never too busy to laugh.

At midday the sky turned dark, and about three hours later *Jesus cried with a loud voice, saying, Eli, Eli, lama sabachthani? that is to say, My God, my God, why hast thou forsaken me?* The despair was heart-wrenching. No one who heard it will ever forget it, or be able to pretend to forget it (even if a number of those watching seemed to think that Jesus was calling to Elijah!). It was painfully evident that my brother was subject to the same doubts and fears as the rest of humanity.

Using a rod, one person extended a sponge soaked in sour wine for him to drink. But Jesus, *when he had cried again with a loud voice, yielded up the ghost. And, behold, the veil of the temple was rent in twain from the top to the bottom; and the earth did quake, and the rocks rent; And the graves were opened; and many bodies of the saints which slept arose, And came out of the graves after his resurrection, and went into the holy city, and appeared unto many.* They must have kept it quiet, because no one else mentions the living dead walking the streets. A centurion on the scene was sufficiently impressed by the earthquake to remark that *Truly this was the Son of God.*

At sunset a wealthy follower of Jesus named Joseph, from Arimathaea, went to Pontius Pilate and asked to be given charge of the body. Pilate obliged, and Joseph placed the corpse, wrapped in cloth, in a tomb he had newly carved from the rock for his own future use. Blocking the entrance with a large stone he returned home, leaving Mary Magdalene (I'll come to her later) and another woman watching over the tomb.

The following morning a delegation from the temple came to warn Pontius Pilate that Jesus had announced *After three days I will rise again.* They advised vigilance, suggesting that his disciples might be tempted to remove the body and claim that he had been resurrected. Pilate concurred, and so the tomb was sealed, and a guard posted.

RESURRECTION

28   At dawn on Sunday two women paid a visit to the tomb: *Mary Magdalene and the other Mary* (not a disrespectful reference to my mother, I hope – but there were so many Marys it was hard to keep them all straight). There was another major earthquake, and *the angel of the Lord descended from heaven, and came and rolled back the stone from the door, and sat upon it.* (To catch his breath, perhaps?) *His countenance was like lightning, and his raiment white as snow;* the guards took one look at him and passed out.

The angel told the two Marys not to be afraid, that Jesus had been raised up, as promised, and that having seen the tomb they should go and tell the disciples that

Jesus was already on his way to Galilee, where he would meet them. (Moving the stone would appear to have been wasted effort.) As the women ran off to spread the news, whom should they bump into but Jesus himself. He didn't have much to say, just repeating the message the angel had already given them.

Meanwhile the guards went back to report to the religious authorities (not to the governor?). The priests gave them a generous bonus to spread the story that the disciples stole the body while they slept. People readily believed it, *and this saying is commonly reported among the Jews until this day.* Full marks to Matthew, then, for uncovering the bribery; I wonder how he did it.

The disciples, now down to eleven, went to a mountain in Galilee for their rendezvous with Jesus; the message from the Marys must have been more explicit than we knew. *And when they saw him, they worshipped him: but some doubted.* There's no satisfying some people. Jesus gave them their orders anyway:

All power is given unto me in heaven and in earth. Go ye therefore, and teach all nations, baptizing them in the name of the Father, and of the Son, and of the Holy Ghost: Teaching them to observe all things whatsoever I have commanded you: and, lo, I am with you alway, even unto the end of the world.

From what he had said, there shouldn't be long to wait.

2

Mark

1   Let me go back to beginning, and tell *the gospel of Jesus Christ, the Son of God,*
according to a certain Mark. He was probably the first to put the stories in writing,
after they had gone from mouth to mouth for a few decades. Mark did such a good
job that his successors – I'll mention no names, but we've just been hearing from
one of them – plagiarised his text for all it was worth, making a few changes here
and there, and adding in a lot of sayings.

Something else they added was the story of a virgin giving birth in Bethlehem;
that wasn't one that Mark had come across, it seems. He starts with John the Baptist
saying *There cometh one mightier than I after me, the latchet of whose shoes I
am not worthy to stoop down and unloose.* I suppose he meant my brother, though
he felt worthy enough to dunk Jesus in the river Jordan. When John landed himself
in prison, Jesus went back to Galilee to carry on the mission, preaching *The time
is fulfilled, and the kingdom of God is at hand: repent ye, and believe the gospel.*

While spreading the news and gathering disciples, he acquired a formidable
reputation as an exorcist. Demons recognised his true nature; in his first recorded
healing, the possessed person cried out *Let us alone; what have we to do with thee,
thou Jesus of Nazareth? art thou come to destroy us? I know thee who thou art,
the Holy One of God. And Jesus rebuked him, saying, Hold thy peace, and come
out of him.* The man had a fit, and the demon duly left.

After the sun had set that evening *they brought unto him all that were diseased,
and them that were possessed with devils.* The whole town was present, such is
people's taste in entertainment. *And he healed many* (not all?) *that were sick of
divers diseases, and cast out many devils; and suffered not the devils to speak,
because they knew him.*

So Jesus went from town to town; *he preached in their synagogues throughout
all Galilee, and cast out devils.* Though he tried to hush up gossip about his powers,
his efforts failed. Even when Jesus specifically instructed a cured leper to say
nothing to anyone, the man told the tale up and down the country; he was lucky
my brother was good natured. In the end Jesus had the utmost difficulty in avoiding
people.

2   Do you remember Jesus healing the paralysed man in Capernaum? What
Matthew didn't mention was that the crowd was so impenetrable that the man's
helpers broke in through the roof and lowered him on a stretcher. Queue jumping
at its worst, I thought, wondering what Jesus would tell the landlord about the roof,
but he liked to reward initiative. Asking whether it was easier to say to a paralytic

Thy sins be forgiven thee; or to say, Arise, and take up thy bed, and walk, Jesus did both. His reasoning was spurious, of course – being able to heal doesn't prove possession of the divine right to forgive – but everyone was much impressed.

You might recall that Jesus defended his disciples when they casually plucked corn on a sabbath. *The sabbath was made for man, and not man for the sabbath: Therefore the Son of man is Lord also of the sabbath.* I thought that the first sabbath was made for God, when he rested on the seventh day; still, I'm happy to give people priority. Jesus himself had no hesitation in healing on the sabbath. Since that was his principal occupation, I'd count him as an advocate of sabbath-day trading; certainly he was no friend of the sabbatarians.

With the religious authorities against him, it was the demons who gave Jesus the most credit. The *unclean spirits, when they saw him, fell down before him, and cried, saying, Thou art the Son of God. And he straitly charged them that they should not make him known.* The little devils could fall at his feet and make a spectacle of themselves, but he wasn't going to have them handling his publicity.

In need of help, Jesus designated twelve disciples to preach, and *to have power to heal sicknesses, and to cast out devils.* I've already mentioned their names, though it's worth adding that he gave the brothers James and John the tag *Boanerges, which is, The sons of thunder.* A rather war-like name for two ex-fishermen, I thought.

Such flights of fancy can't have helped his image; some of the people closest to him already feared that he was mad. Once, indeed, they *went out to lay hold on him: for they said, He is beside himself.* It's often said, I know, that those of us in the family had doubts about his sanity, but it's not true. He was no crazier than the rest of us.

When doctors of the law came from Jerusalem to declare that he was possessed by Beelzebub, they claimed that *by the prince of the devils casteth he out devils.* That's the problem with the exorcism business: it's only a matter of time before someone claims that you need exorcising yourself. Jesus showed how rational he could be, arguing

How can Satan cast out Satan? And if a kingdom be divided against itself, that kingdom cannot stand. And if a house be divided against itself, that house cannot stand.

Their suspicion was absurd, but he was in no mood to forgive and forget. Indeed, they had committed the one unforgivable sin: *he that shall blaspheme against the Holy Ghost hath never forgiveness, but is in danger of eternal damnation.*

Jesus sometimes concluded a parable by saying *He that hath ears to hear, let him hear.* It was never quite clear how much he wanted to be understood, or even whether he wanted to be understood. Taking what he said to the disciples at face value, he was positively elitist.

> *Unto you it is given to know the mystery of the kingdom of God: but unto them that are without, all these things are done in parables: That seeing they may see, and not perceive; and hearing they may hear, and not understand; lest at any time they should be converted, and their sins should be forgiven them.*

That was the whole idea, I thought, but maybe not. I was inclined to dismiss the statement as an aberration, or as someone's misunderstanding, but Jesus said something else along the same lines. (What happened to the notion that the meek shall inherit the earth?)

> *Take heed what ye hear: with what measure ye mete, it shall be measured to you: and unto you that hear shall more be given. For he that hath, to him shall be given: and he that hath not, from him shall be taken even that which he hath.*

In a sense this is quite an acute comment: you need some knowledge in order to learn, and the more you know the more you can master. Still, I had expected him to provide remedial education for the ignorant and sinful, not the news that they were doomed.

When the time came, God wouldn't hesitate to do what he had to do.

> *For the earth bringeth forth fruit of herself; first the blade, then the ear, after that the full corn in the ear. But when the fruit is brought forth, immediately he putteth in the sickle, because the harvest is come.*

I suppose we're still waiting for the fruit, whatever it might be. There were obviously advantages to being in Jesus' inner circle, because *when they were alone, he expounded all things to his disciples.*

WORKING MIRACLES

Having spent the whole day by the shore of the Sea of Galilee, Jesus said *Let us pass over unto the other side.* This led to the incident I've already mentioned; it was a bad night to spend in a boat, though being asleep on a cushion he didn't even notice the storm. That he managed to sleep while waves broke over the boat was miraculous in itself. Eventually the disciples woke him up, understandably sounding rather aggrieved: *Master, carest thou not that we perish?* When Jesus restored calm with a word they *said one to another, What manner of man is this, that even the wind and the sea obey him?*

5   *And they came over unto the other side of the sea, into the country of the Gadarenes.* They were greeted by a raving lunatic, whom not even chains and fetters had been able to control. One advantage of being demonically possessed,

however, was that he could see in an instant what everyone else was slow to discover: that Jesus was *Son of the most high God.* Using an old exorcist's trick to gain power over the evil spirit, Jesus asked *What is thy name? And he answered, saying, My name is Legion: for we are many.*

The demons, you'll recall, begged to be sent into the pigs grazing nearby, rather than being evicted from the country. Jesus consented, *And the unclean spirits went out, and entered into the swine: and the herd ran violently down a steep place into the sea, (they were about two thousand;) and were choked in the sea.*

On the positive side, of course, the newly exorcised man was *sitting, and clothed, and in his right mind,* but that didn't prevent the people from asking Jesus if he would mind taking his talents elsewhere. There was nothing for it but to turn the boat around and go back.

At least there was no shortage of work; he had no sooner arrived than the head of a synagogue came to him and said *My little daughter lieth at the point of death.* (I know that Matthew inserted a few episodes before this, but I can't help that.) On the way the unfortunate woman who had been bleeding for twelve years crept up through the crowd and touched his clothes, *And straightway the fountain of her blood was dried up; and she felt in her body that she was healed of that plague. And Jesus, immediately knowing in himself that virtue had gone out of him, turned him about in the press, and said, Who touched my clothes?*

The woman confessed, and Jesus told her to *go in peace.* Meanwhile a messenger came to tell the unhappy father that it was too late: the girl had died. Jesus went on to the house regardless, where he declared, to general derision, that *the damsel is not dead, but sleepeth.* Some people actually accept this as a diagnosis, so concerned are they to take every word he said literally. In any case Jesus woke her up, *And he charged them straitly that no man should know it; and commanded that something should be given her to eat.*

Our old acquaintances in Nazareth, as I've said, were not big fans of Jesus. *Is not this the carpenter, the son of Mary, the brother of James, and Joses, and of Juda, and Simon? and are not his sisters here with us? And they were offended at him.* They were rather offensive themselves; calling him the son of Mary (rather than of his father) carries a clear suggestion of illegitimacy. Remembering him from younger days, people evidently thought that he was too big for his sandals. I think it's fair to say that Jesus reciprocated their lack of regard. He didn't grace them with any miracles, *save that he laid his hands upon a few sick folk, and healed them.*

Jesus summoned his disciples and, sounding a bit like Noah, *began to send them forth by two and two; and gave them power over unclean spirits,* which always comes in handy. According to Mark they were to take nothing except a cloak, footwear and a staff (Matthew improved the story by excluding even sandals and staves.) Off they went, *and preached that men should repent. And they cast out many devils, and anointed with oil many that were sick, and healed them.*

All the commotion around Jesus was disconcerting to king Herod, who felt sure that *It is John, whom I beheaded: he is risen from the dead.* A bad conscience plays strange tricks.

When the disciples returned they tried to go off quietly by themselves, which led to the incident of the loaves and the five thousand. There Jesus sent them off on another ill-advised boat trip. Nine hours after darkness fell they were still struggling to row against the wind, when Jesus came *walking upon the sea, and would have passed by them.*

I'm surprised he would be so ungracious on his shortcut as to walk right past. The disciples were sufficiently alarmed, however, that he came over to reassure them, and when he stepped into the boat the wind eased. His walk could have been more pleasant if he had seen to it earlier.

7 Jesus was not at his best, as I've mentioned, when he was asked why his disciples didn't wash their hands before eating (he called the questioners hypocrites) or when the Gentile woman asked him to exorcise her daughter (he said that he wouldn't waste his talent on dogs). You had to see the healer in action to appreciate his way with people. For example, Jesus was presented with a man who was deaf and spoke badly; *he took him aside from the multitude, and put his fingers into his ears, and he spit, and touched his tongue; And looking up to heaven, he sighed, and saith unto him, Ephphatha, that is, Be opened.* You'd never have guessed that he lacked medical training.

8 After the feeding of the four thousand with seven loaves (not to be confused with the five thousand and the five loaves) Jesus told sceptics wanting evidence of his authority that *There shall no sign be given unto this generation.* Given that statement, I don't know what to make of all these reported wonders. Maybe we didn't hear about them at the time because Jesus tried to keep everything hushed up, but there's something odd about it.

Jesus had another opportunity to demonstrate his paramedical technique, this time with a blind man. Spittle, I should say, was highly regarded for medicinal purposes. My brother *took the blind man by the hand, and led him out of the town; and when he had spit on his eyes, and put his hands upon him, he asked him if he saw ought. And he looked up, and said, I see men as trees, walking.*

I might have been satisfied with that; even miracle cures can't always give perfect results. Jesus had another try, though, and this time the fellow *saw every man clearly.* As usual, Jesus asked his patient to keep quiet about what had happened. That wasn't so easy; how was the man supposed to explain the fact that he could see?

ON THE ROAD

Similarly, Jesus absolutely insisted that his disciples say nothing about him being the messiah. He made such a point of stopping that kind of talk that I began to suspect it was more than just caution or modesty holding him back. Maybe he didn't want us to be disappointed.

That said, he didn't hesitate to ask, where necessary, for the supreme sacrifice. *For what shall it profit a man, if he shall gain the whole world, and lose his own soul?* The time of reckoning was at hand, remember: *there be some of them that stand here, which shall not taste of death, till they have seen the kingdom of God come with power.* Either he was wrong, or some very old people are still waiting. 9

Jesus took his three friends Peter, James and John up the mountain to see his transfiguration – or to be more precise, the transfiguration of his clothes, which *became shining, exceeding white as snow; so as no fuller on earth can white them.* It takes a divine bleach to make clothes whiter-than-white.

Faced with a particularly severe case of epilepsy (or demonic possession, to use the accepted diagnosis), Jesus declared that *all things are possible to him that believeth. And straightway the father of the child cried out, and said with tears, Lord, I believe; help thou mine unbelief.* There's no better way to deal with doubt than by doing something wonderful, and so Jesus expelled the evil spirit from his son. I know my brother said that he wouldn't perform miracles, but his life would seem a lot less interesting if that had been the case.

Jesus told the disciples again that he was going to be killed, but as on every such occasion they seemed to be hearing it for the first time. Their conversation – *they had disputed among themselves, who should be the greatest* – made you wonder if they ever grasped it. Jesus had some bad news for people with ambition; *If any man desire to be first, the same shall be last of all, and servant of all.*

He went easy, though, on a fellow exorcist taking advantage of his reputation. When a disciple said *Master, we saw one casting out devils in thy name,* and put a stop to it because he wasn't one of us, *Jesus said, Forbid him not ... For he that is not against us is on our part.* Having previously heard Jesus say 'he that is not with me is against me', I was interested to hear the converse. There's no contradiction if everyone takes sides, but it does put people who want to stay neutral in a strange position.

The consequences of making the wrong choice might be uncomfortable. Like a person who passed up the opportunity to cut off a sinful hand, foot or eye, you might end up on the smouldering rubbish heap, *cast into hell fire: Where their worm dieth not, and the fire is not quenched.* On the other hand (if you still have both) perhaps it makes no difference, *For every one shall be salted with fire.* Raw flesh is too bland, I suppose.

Jesus set out his unequivocal opposition to divorce. While he was on the family 10 theme, *they brought young children to him, that he should touch them: and his disciples rebuked those that brought them. But when Jesus saw it, he was much displeased, and said unto them, Suffer the little children to come unto me, and forbid them not: for of such is the kingdom of God.* I had hoped that heaven would be rather more adult, to be honest.

When a man addressed him as *Good Master ... Jesus said unto him, Why callest thou me good? there is none good but one, that is, God.* This disclaimer of goodness, let alone perfect goodness, has embarrassed people who think that my brother was flawless. Of course the paradox of perfection is that if you admit it you're immodest, while if you don't you're a liar.

Having heard Jesus tell the man to dispose of all his possessions if he wanted to enter heaven, Peter nervously pointed out that they had given up everything to follow him. Jesus replied that those who had left family and property for his sake *shall receive an hundredfold now in this time, houses, and brethren, and sisters, and mothers, and children, and lands, with persecutions; and in the world to come eternal life.* That's what happened to Job; he lost everything, but received generous compensation in the end. I'd still find it a poor bargain. I'm happy with the mother I've got; I don't particularly want a hundred new ones, especially if persecution is part of the package.

The disciples, however, seemed all too interested in what was in it for them. They might at least have tried to show more sympathy for their leader's fate. When Jesus foretold what the Gentiles would do to the Son of man – *they shall mock him, and shall scourge him, and shall spit upon him, and shall kill him: and the third day he shall rise again* – James and John declared *Master, we would that thou shouldest do for us whatsoever we shall desire.* That request, you might recall (though Matthew put it in the mouth of their mother, presumably to avoid making them seem so disgracefully egotistical) was to sit in glory on either side of him. Showing the malicious side to his humour, Jesus agreed that they could share his fate, if not his position.

Mark often told his stories with only half Matthew's enthusiasm. Remember the two blind men who had their sight restored outside Jericho? Mark doesn't; he only
11   mentions one. Or how about the donkeys borrowed for the entrance into Jerusalem? I gather from Mark they made do with just one. According to him, in fact, they arrived too late to do anything at the temple; the ejection of the money-changers had to wait a day.

Jesus wasn't in a mood to be crossed, as the priests and the out-of-season fig tree discovered. Peter spotted it the next morning: *Master, behold, the fig tree which thou cursedst is withered away. And Jesus answering saith unto them, Have faith in God.* Discover the power of prayer.
12   I've already described how Jesus taunted the priests, scribes, Pharisees and Sadducees; I just wish God would clarify his religious preferences. Steps towards unity were resisted even by my brother. One scribe agreed that the commandments could be summed up in the instruction to love God and your neighbour – in fact, he suggested, this was more important than all the offerings and observances, and Jesus apparently concurred. Not content to leave matters there, however, Jesus ridiculed the tradition that the messiah would be descended from David, and then launched a personal attack on the teachers of law.

Beware of the scribes, which love to go in long clothing, and love salutations in the marketplaces, And the chief seats in the synagogues, and the

uppermost rooms at feasts: Which devour widows' houses, and for a
pretence make long prayers: these shall receive greater damnation.

He took a break to watch people in the temple making their contributions. While some were quite substantial, *there came a certain poor widow, and she threw in two mites, which make a farthing.* Jesus observed to his disciples that, relatively speaking, she had given more than anyone else, as the money was all that she had to live on. Sacrifice is always touching, but I hope the needy aren't expected to give their last farthings to the religious establishment.

THE COMING OF THE END

Jesus offered a lengthy description of the coming apocalypse. The wars, earth- 13 quakes and famines would be only the beginning; *Now the brother shall betray the brother to death, and the father the son; and the children shall rise up against their parents, and shall cause them to be put to death.* When the *abomination of desolation* arrives (whatever he, she or it might be), people should run for their lives, which most would lose in any case. Finally the skies would dim and the heavenly delegation would arrive. All these things would happen within the lifetime of his listeners, though he confessed that he didn't know when.

That being so, the best advice was

Watch ye therefore: for ye know not when the master of the house cometh,
at even, or at midnight, or at the cockcrowing, or in the morning: Lest
coming suddenly he find you sleeping. And what I say unto you I say unto
all, Watch.

To be honest, I think I'd rather be taken unawares.

For Jesus, at least, the end was now in sight. The woman took the perfume worth 14 a year's wages *and poured it on his head*; as he remarked, *she is come aforehand to anoint my body to the burying.* A benefactor known (as far as I could tell) to Jesus alone set aside a large room for the passover meal, which would be his last supper. Afterwards they went to the garden of Gethsemane, where Jesus battled with the terror of his coming execution while the disciples slept.

Arriving with the troops, Judas went and kissed his leader. This was no peck on the cheek, but a long kiss full of emotion. With that *they laid their hands on him, and took him.* A young man, scantily clad, had followed Jesus to the garden; they reached for his garb in an attempt to arrest him too, but *he left the linen cloth, and fled from them naked.* No one has ever been quite sure what that was all about.

The trial before the priests was a mess, with the witnesses contradicting each other while Jesus said nothing. In the end, though, he supposedly confessed to being the messiah, seated at God's right hand, which sounded blasphemous enough to let them reach a verdict. Meanwhile Peter was outside, fulfilling Jesus' prophecy that *Before the cock crow twice, thou shalt deny me thrice.* (Matthew removed the 'twice', which I think is a shame.)

15   The only person who could condemn Jesus to death, however, was Pontius Pilate. He was willing (and if truth be told, probably eager) to dispose of any Jewish troublemaker unfortunate enough to come before him. And so Jesus was taken off to Golgotha, apparently to general satisfaction; even the two thieves *that were crucified with him reviled him.* He died after some six hours on the cross, which as crucifixion went was a quick death. Indeed, when Joseph of Arimathaea asked for the body, *Pilate marvelled if he were already dead*, and called the supervising centurion to make sure.

16   The next day was the sabbath, but the following morning Mary Magdalene went with two other women (Matthew, I know, said it was only one) to put sweet-smelling oil on the body. They were surprised to see the stone rolled back, *And entering into the sepulchre, they saw a young man sitting on the right side, clothed in a long white garment; and they were affrighted.* The visitor told them not to be alarmed: *he is risen; he is not here.* Jesus had simply gone on ahead to Galilee. Not finding that reassuring they fled in terror, saying nothing to anyone.

Now when Jesus was risen early the first day of the week, he appeared first to Mary Magdalene, out of whom he had cast seven devils. With a history like that, it's no wonder that his followers didn't believe her story. But then, they didn't believe it when two of their own reported the same thing. Finally Jesus had to upbraid the disciples in person (or spirit) for their unbelief. His final orders were disturbing, to say the least.

Go ye into all the world, and preach the gospel to every creature. He that believeth and is baptized shall be saved; but he that believeth not shall be damned. And these signs shall follow them that believe; In my name shall they cast out devils; they shall speak with new tongues; They shall take up serpents; and if they drink any deadly thing, it shall not hurt them; they shall lay hands on the sick, and they shall recover.

If the signs of salvation are the ability to exorcise, to speak strange languages, to play with snakes, to drink poison, and to heal with a touch, failing which you go to hell, then I hope my brother enjoys his own company.

Having delivered those parting words, *he was received up into heaven, and sat on the right hand of God.*

3

Luke

People always want to tell the tale in their own way. A certain Luke admitted that *many have taken in hand to set forth* stories of my brother's life, but he wanted to produce a version for the benefit of a Roman official. *It seemed good to me also,* he declared, *having had perfect understanding of all things from the very first, to write unto thee in order, most excellent Theophilus, That thou mightest know the certainty of those things.*

To begin before the beginning, there was an old, childless couple named Elisabeth and Zacharias. He was a priest (Jewish, of course). One day while serving at the temple, Zacharias was selected to offer the incense in the sanctuary. *And there appeared unto him an angel of the Lord standing on the right side of the altar,* which came as something of a shock. *But the angel said unto him, Fear not ... thy wife Elisabeth shall bear thee a son, and thou shalt call his name John.*

The angel saw fit to mention that John *shall drink neither wine nor strong drink*; this handicap notwithstanding, he would *make ready a people prepared for the Lord.* Zacharias could clearly have used some preparation himself, because he reacted with the same incredulity Abraham and Sarah had shown two thousand years previously. His scepticism didn't go down well with the angel, whose huffy response was *I am Gabriel, that stand in the presence of God ... thou shalt be dumb, and not able to speak, until the day that these things shall be performed, because thou believest not my words.*

Personally, I wouldn't have much trouble keeping my doubts to myself in the divine presence. Zacharias was a good fellow, but honesty doesn't always pay.

Elisabeth did indeed become pregnant. When she was in her sixth month Gabriel came back for a repeat performance, this time to *a city of Galilee, named Nazareth,* where Joseph and Mary lived. Whereas Elisabeth had been a challenge because of her advanced years, Mary presented the opposite difficulty: she wasn't even married yet.

And the angel came in unto her, and said, Hail, thou that art highly favoured, the Lord is with thee: blessed art thou among women. Mary was afraid to guess where this might be leading. Sure enough, Gabriel continued by saying *thou shalt conceive in thy womb, and bring forth a son ...And he shall reign over the house of Jacob for ever; and of his kingdom there shall be no end.*

Mary replied by asking *How shall this be, seeing I know not a man?* – just the sort of question that had landed Zacharias in hot water. Gabriel was gentler with the young ones, though, and explained rather awkwardly that it was all something to do with the Holy Ghost: *therefore also that holy thing which shall be born of thee shall be called the Son of God.* I get rebuked when I refer to a child as 'it', and here an angel calls my brother that 'thing'.

As we say, *with God nothing shall be impossible* – at least when he sets his mind to it, which perhaps isn't as often as it should be – *And Mary said, Behold the handmaid of the Lord; be it unto me according to thy word.* To some people that sounds submissive, but to my mind it's distinctly assertive.

Gabriel had told her that Elisabeth, who apparently was a relative, was also undergoing an unplanned pregnancy. Mary wasted no time in travelling into the hills of Judah for a visit. *And it came to pass, that, when Elisabeth heard the salutation of Mary, the babe leaped in her womb; and Elisabeth was filled with the Holy Ghost: And she spake out with a loud voice, and said, Blessed art thou among women, and blessed is the fruit of thy womb.* Seeing the elderly lady possessed by a spirit did not disconcert my mother, who declaimed a proud, fierce hymn we came to know as the *Magnificat.*

> *My soul doth magnify the Lord,*
> *And my spirit hath rejoiced in God my Saviour.*
> *For he hath regarded the low estate of his handmaiden:*
> *for, behold, from henceforth all generations shall call me blessed.*
> *For he that is mighty hath done to me great things;*
> *and holy is his name.*
> *And his mercy is on them that fear him from generation to generation.*
> *He hath shewed strength with his arm;*
> *he hath scattered the proud in the imagination of their hearts.*
> *He hath put down the mighty from their seats,*
> *and exalted them of low degree.*
> *He hath filled the hungry with good things;*
> *and the rich he hath sent empty away.*

Mary was definitely not a woman you'd want to cross, despite her bloodless reputation.

Elisabeth had her son. Her family and friends wanted to name him after his father, but she insisted on calling him 'John'. This sounded an unlikely name, and they referred the matter to the mute Zacharias. *His name is John,* he scratched on the board to general astonishment. *And his mouth was opened immediately, and his tongue loosed, and he spake, and praised God.* He had learnt one lesson, anyway.

Once Zacharias started to speak, in fact, there was no stopping him.

> *Blessed be the Lord God of Israel;*
> *for he hath visited and redeemed his people.*
> *And hath raised up an horn of salvation for us*

in the house of his servant David.
As he spake by the mouth of his holy prophets,
which have been since the world began:
That we should be saved from our enemies,
and from the hand of all that hate us.

His son would be a prophet, preparing the way for the Lord, offering forgiveness

Through the tender mercy of our God;
whereby the dayspring from on high hath visited us,
To give light to them that sit in darkness and in the shadow of death,
to guide our feet into the way of peace.

John grew up holy, as suggested by the fact that he *was in the deserts till the day of his shewing unto Israel.*

FROM BABE TO TEEN

The story of my brother's birth is even better, of course. Luke, too, thinks that it   2
must have happened in Bethlehem. Recognising, unlike Matthew, that the family
lived in Nazareth, he asserts that they travelled south to join the other members of
their tribe during a general head count. He rather undermines his credibility,
unfortunately, by specifying that the census took place during the rule of a
particular governor – one who didn't take charge until a decade after Jesus
appeared.

Still, it all makes a good story. While in the ancestral town of Joseph (and
David), Mary *brought forth her firstborn son, and wrapped him in swaddling*
clothes, and laid him in a manger; because there was no room for them in the
inn. And there were in the same country shepherds abiding in the field, keeping
watch over their flock by night. And, lo, the angel of the Lord came upon them,
and the glory of the Lord shone round about them: and they were sore afraid.
And the angel said unto them, Fear not: for, behold, I bring you good tidings of
great joy, which shall be to all people. ... And suddenly there was with the angel
a multitude of the heavenly host praising God, and saying, Glory to God in the
highest, and on earth peace, good will toward men.

The shepherds were naturally curious to see what all the fuss was about, and
despite a lack of directions managed to find a babe fitting the description. Any
kings in the vicinity had less luck; there's no mention of Magi here. But if the family
missed out on the gold and frankincense, at least they didn't have to flee to Egypt.
Indeed, after a leisurely period in Bethlehem they positively dawdled in Jerusalem.

There, in the temple, they bumped into a certain Simeon, to whom the Holy
Ghost had revealed that *he should not see death, before he had seen the Lord's*
Christ. With Jesus in his arms, Simeon said

Lord, now lettest thou thy servant depart in peace,
according to thy word:
For mine eyes have seen thy salvation,
Which thou hast prepared before the face of all people;
A light to lighten the Gentiles,
and the glory of thy people Israel.

I don't know how long he had to wait; he didn't die on the spot, fortunately. An old prophetess named Anna was likewise impressed by the child, *and spake of him to all them that looked for redemption in Jerusalem.*

With all their secular and religious duties performed, *they returned into Galilee, to their own city Nazareth.* Every year, though, the family went back to Jerusalem for passover. The trip we made when Jesus was twelve was more eventful than usual; he stayed behind when the rest of us started out for home. The parents thought he was running around with his friends and relations, and so *went a day's journey; and they sought him among their kinsfolk and acquaintance. And when they found him not, they turned back again to Jerusalem, seeking him.* Three days later we found him showing off in the temple.

If it had been me, I would undoubtedly have ended up with a very sore bottom. Not only had he been selfish and naughty, he was rude to our parents. Mary said *Son, why hast thou thus dealt with us? behold, thy father and I have sought thee sorrowing. And he said unto them, How is it that ye sought me? wist ye not that I must be about my Father's business? And they understood not the saying which he spake unto them.* I don't know why they didn't understand; hadn't Gabriel's prenatal message been sufficiently clear?

My brother was probably no worse than any other bright child with a perturbed family background. Fortunately *Jesus increased in wisdom and stature, and in favour with God and man.*

3   John began preaching first, saying *to the multitude that came forth to be baptized of him, O generation of vipers, who hath warned you to flee from the wrath to come?* I was always perplexed at the way these fellows showed such fury themselves while urging kindness on everyone else; when *the people asked him, saying, What shall we do then? He answereth and saith unto them, He that hath two coats, let him impart to him that hath none; and he that hath meat, let him do likewise.* Tax collectors and soldiers seemed to get off more lightly; he simply told them to avoid extortion: *be content with your wages.*

By his own account, John was merely offering a foretaste of the real medicine. Someone would come to *gather the wheat into his garner; but the chaff he will burn with fire unquenchable.* Just who this might be became apparent when Jesus was baptized, *the heaven was opened, and the Holy Ghost descended in a bodily shape like a dove upon him.*

Luke also felt compelled to provide Jesus – or rather me, if Joseph wasn't his real father – with a genealogy. Unfortunately he didn't get together with Matthew on this, and so they ended up with irreconcilable lists. Not even the name of Joseph's father is the same. Luke traces the line all the way back through *Seth, which was the son of Adam, which was the son of God*. From son of God to son of God in 75 generations.

EARLY DAYS IN GALILEE

As far as the adult career of Jesus goes, though, Luke has only the occasional novelty to add. We already know how *the devil, taking him up into an high mountain, shewed unto him all the kingdoms of the world in a moment of time*. The next temptation (the order was reversed) was to jump off the top of the temple, *For it is written, He shall give his angels charge over thee, to keep thee: And in their hands they shall bear thee up, lest at any time thou dash thy foot against a stone*. Jesus resisted these megalomaniacal and suicidal impulses, and so the devil *departed from him for a season*.

Jesus made a reputation for himself in Galilee, but never won over his home town. Teaching at the synagogue in Nazareth, he quoted Isaiah: *The Spirit of the Lord is upon me, because he hath anointed me ... This day this scripture is fulfilled in your ears*. There was a stir in the audience, *And they said, Is not this Joseph's son?*

No doubt, Jesus said, you will confront me with the proverb *Physician, heal thyself*, insisting on seeing some good works locally. That isn't the way it works, he claimed. Even Elijah helped the widow in Sidon, and the Syrian general, when plenty of compatriots needed him just as much. I'm afraid our neighbours took this rather badly; they *rose up, and thrust him out of the city, and led him unto the brow of the hill whereon their city was built, that they might cast him down headlong*. He was lucky to escape.

The town of Capernaum gave Jesus a warmer welcome. People there brought their sick to him, *and he laid his hands on every one of them, and healed them. And devils also came out of many, crying out, and saying, Thou art Christ the Son of God*. He had to speak sternly to them; it's embarrassing when only devils recognise you.

The recruitment of the fishermen was not exactly as I had remembered it. Jesus told Simon Peter to go out on the lake; he replied *Master, we have toiled all the night, and have taken nothing: nevertheless at thy word I will let down the net*. As it happened their haul nearly swamped the boats. Sadly for the fish the catch was merely a demonstration of power: everything was abandoned on the shore as Peter, James and John went off with my brother.

There's a coda I should mention to the instruction that *new wine must be put into new bottles*. Lest that sound too radical, Jesus added that *No man also having drunk old wine straightway desireth new: for he saith, The old is better*. He knew his wine, and human nature, too.

After a night of prayer, Jesus *called unto him his disciples: and of them he chose twelve, whom also he named apostles.* There seems to be some dispute about who was included, because instead of Thaddaeus (alias Lebbaeus) is listed *Judas the brother of James* – not to be confused, of course, with *Judas Iscariot, which also was the traitor.*

According to Luke, Jesus *came down with them, and stood in the plain,* to deliver what we think of as the sermon on the mount. Most confusing. The eight beatitudes, moreover, are reduced to four, the gap being filled by four woes:

> *But woe unto you that are rich!*
> *for ye have received your consolation.*
> *Woe unto you that are full!*
> *for ye shall hunger.*
> *Woe unto you that laugh now!*
> *for ye shall mourn and weep.*
> *Woe unto you, when all men shall speak well of you!*
> *for so did their fathers to the false prophets.*

If you haven't already been disqualified, *Love your enemies, do good to them which hate you.* I have my doubts, but God might make it worth your trouble.

> *Judge not, and ye shall not be judged; condemn not, and ye shall not be condemned: forgive, and ye shall be forgiven: Give, and it shall be given unto you; good measure, pressed down, and shaken together, and running over, shall men give into your bosom.*

Hallelujah: give me that old-time religion.

7   Healing and exorcism are all very well, but after a time it takes something more to generate excitement. One day when the holy band was approaching a city, *behold, there was a dead man carried out, the only son of his mother, and she was a widow;* you can't be more deserving than that. Jesus approached, ordering *Young man, I say unto thee, Arise. And he that was dead sat up, and began to speak. And he delivered him to his mother.*

JESUS AND HIS FOLLOWERS

I have no objection to family entertainment, but the adult dramas were more to my taste. One evening Jesus was a guest at dinner, when a woman not known for her virtue *began to wash his feet with tears, and did wipe them with the hairs of her head, and kissed his feet, and anointed them with the ointment.* Etiquette manuals are unhelpful in this situation (should the others present excuse themselves, or pretend that nothing is happening, or join in?), and the host reflected that *This man, if he were a prophet, would have known who and what manner of woman this is that toucheth him.*

Jesus knew very well, and pointed out that the more there is to forgive, the greater the love of the forgiven for the forgiver. He also suggested that he rather enjoyed the experience:

I entered into thine house, thou gavest me no water for my feet: but she hath washed my feet with tears, and wiped them with the hairs of her head. Thou gavest me no kiss: but this woman since the time I came in hath not ceased to kiss my feet. My head with oil thou didst not anoint: but this woman hath anointed my feet with ointment. Wherefore I say unto thee, Her sins, which are many, are forgiven; for she loved much.

The other guests were shocked to hear him forgive her, that being regarded as God's business. But Jesus *said to the woman, Thy faith hath saved thee; go in peace.*

Jesus travelled not only with his twelve disciples, but also with *certain women,* 8 *which had been healed of evil spirits and infirmities, Mary called Magdalene, out of whom went seven devils, And Joanna the wife of Chuza Herod's servant, and Susanna, and many others, which ministered unto him of their substance* – that's to say they bankrolled the operation. It was enough to give me a bad case of fraternal envy. No doubt my brother would find me out, *For nothing is secret, that shall not be made manifest.*

After various miracles we already know about (the loaves, the transfiguration, 9 an exorcism) – though it seems that no one can agree on what he did when, or even in what order – Jesus *steadfastly set his face to go to Jerusalem.* When a village *en route* was inhospitable, the disciples James and John brightly asked *Lord, wilt thou that we command fire to come down from heaven, and consume them, even as Elias did?* Reading scripture can certainly put ideas in your head. Jesus was obliged to point out that *the Son of man is not come to destroy men's lives, but to save them. And they went on to another village.*

He often seemed to be harder on the faithful than on others. You'll recall that the supporter who wanted to bury his father was told to *Let the dead bury their dead.* Someone else said *Lord, I will follow thee; but let me first go bid them farewell, which are at home at my house. And Jesus said unto him, No man, having put his hand to the plough, and looking back, is fit for the kingdom of God.* Anyway, goodbyes are so upsetting.

Business was booming, and Jesus appointed another seventy disciples to act as 10 advance men. He sent them out in pairs to every town he intended to visit, saying

Go your ways: behold, I send you forth as lambs among wolves. Carry neither purse, nor scrip, nor shoes: and salute no man by the way. And into whatsoever house ye enter, first say, Peace be to this house.

If they received a welcome, they should stay, eating and drinking whatever their hosts provided, *for the labourer is worthy of his hire. Go not from house to house.* Jesus was not altogether clear on the concept of out-staying your welcome.

In any event, *the seventy returned again with joy, saying, Lord, even the devils are subject unto us through thy name. And he said unto them, I beheld Satan as lightning fall from heaven. Behold, I give unto you power to tread on serpents and scorpions, and over all the power of the enemy: and nothing shall by any means hurt you.*

Being generally pleased with the way work was going, Jesus offered credit where it was due: *I thank thee, O Father, Lord of heaven and earth, that thou hast hid these things from the wise and prudent, and hast revealed them unto babes.* I suppose they don't ask such awkward questions. To the disciples, he said

> *Blessed are the eyes which see the things that ye see: For I tell you, that many prophets and kings have desired to see those things which ye see, and have not seen them; and to hear those things which ye hear, and have not heard them.*

It's too bad God preferred a childlike congregation, because Jesus was often at his best precisely when confronted with a probing audience. Reflecting on the commandment to love your neighbour as yourself, a lawyer asked Jesus to define 'neighbour'. He offered a parable in reply.

> *A certain man went down from Jerusalem to Jericho, and fell among thieves, which stripped him of his raiment, and wounded him, and departed, leaving him half dead. And by chance there came down a certain priest that way: and when he saw him, he passed by on the other side. And likewise a Levite, when he was at the place, came and looked on him, and passed by on the other side. But a certain Samaritan, as he journeyed, came where he was: and when he saw him, he had compassion on him, And went to him, and bound up his wounds, pouring in oil and wine, and set him on his own beast, and brought him to an inn, and took care of him. And on the morrow when he departed, he took out two pence, and gave them to the host, and said unto him, Take care of him; and whatsoever thou spendest more, when I come again, I will repay thee. Which now of these three, thinkest thou, was neighbour unto him that fell among the thieves?*

Obviously the infidel Samaritan had a better claim than the respected leaders of his own faith. So, Jesus concluded, *Go, and do thou likewise.*

Help around the house, though, was a different matter. Once he was visiting a woman named Martha, whose sister Mary sat at his feet to listen to him talk. *But Martha was cumbered about much serving, and came to him, and said, Lord, dost thou not care that my sister hath left me to serve alone? bid her therefore that she help me. And Jesus answered and said unto her, Martha, Martha, thou art careful and troubled about many things: But one thing is needful: and Mary hath chosen that good part, which shall not be taken away from her.* Jesus seemed to hold the non-cook's belief that the meal would take care of itself.

THE WAY OF DAMNATION

In the middle of a homily on demonic possession, Jesus warned against the dangers of self-reliance. 11

> *When a strong man armed keepeth his palace, his goods are in peace: But when a stronger than he shall come upon him, and overcome him, he taketh from him all his armour wherein he trusted, and divideth his spoils.*

If that seemed incongruous in the context, it was even odder when at the end of the sermon *a certain woman of the company lifted up her voice, and said unto him, Blessed is the womb that bare thee, and the paps which thou hast sucked.* I wouldn't know what to say.

Jesus had no time for adult scepticism; childlike credulity was what he felt God preferred. *This is an evil generation: they seek a sign.* To my mind, people were just following his own advice. *No man, when he hath lighted a candle, putteth it in a secret place, neither under a bushel, but on a candlestick, that they which come in may see the light.* There's no point in being bright if you're going to put blinkers on.

I'm afraid, though, that he tended to blame everything on people with education – particularly legal education. *From the blood of Abel unto the blood of Zacharias, which perished between the altar and the temple: verily I say unto you, It shall be required of this generation. Woe unto you, lawyers! for ye have taken away the key of knowledge.* Making the present generation pay for the misdeeds of the fathers was something we were meant to change, I thought.

If they were all going to pay, he wanted to give them fair warning. Don't be afraid of violent people; they can only kill you. *Fear him, which after he hath killed hath power to cast into hell; yea, I say unto you, Fear him.* Having said that, bear in mind that God concerns himself with everyone. *Are not five sparrows sold for two farthings, and not one of them is forgotten before God?* (Matthew said they were two for a farthing; apparently there were discounts for volume.) 12

When someone asked for help in settling a disputed inheritance, Jesus told the parable of the rich fool. To my mind it should be called the parable of the rich sensible person, because after one particularly good harvest the man said to himself, *Soul, thou hast much goods laid up for many years; take thine ease, eat, drink, and be merry. But God said unto him, Thou fool, this night thy soul shall be required of thee: then whose shall those things be, which thou hast provided?* As far as I can see, his only mistake was in not retiring sooner.

What Jesus commanded, however, was *Sell that ye have, and give alms.* Since one never knows from one moment to the next when the end might come, it pays to be ready. *Let your loins be girded about, and your lights burning*. I should warn you that if you're not going to follow orders, you're better off not knowing them. God will be like a master returning to his house;

> *that servant, which knew his lord's will, and prepared not himself, neither did according to his will, shall be beaten with many stripes. But he that knew not, and did commit things worthy of stripes, shall be beaten with few stripes. For unto whomsoever much is given, of him shall be much required: and to whom men have committed much, of him they will ask the more.*

Although the end of the world was supposed to happen any day, my brother was starting to sound impatient.

> *I am come to send fire on the earth; and what will I, if it be already kindled? … Suppose ye that I am come to give peace on earth? I tell you, Nay; but rather division: For from henceforth there shall be five in one house divided, three against two, and two against three. The father shall be divided against the son, and the son against the father; the mother against the daughter, and the daughter against the mother; the mother in law against her daughter in law, and the daughter in law against her mother in law.*

He was a pain to have around the house, but I was secretly delighted by his distaste for family values.

13   A number of Galileans were killed by Pontius Pilate, and eighteen other people had died when a tower fell on them. Jesus denied that the victims had been more sinful than anyone else, without attempting to explain why, then, they had suffered as they did. At the same time, though, he warned everyone that *except ye repent, ye shall all likewise perish*. I'm still unclear on the connection between unholy living and early death.

Indeed, Jesus suggested that many people are not going to find themselves where they expect to end up. They will be left knocking on the door, saying *We have eaten and drunk in thy presence, and thou hast taught in our streets. But he shall say, I tell you, I know you not.*

THE ROAD TO SALVATION

14   Modesty is the best policy, Jesus advised, and it lends itself so well to gamesmanship. Take for example banquets where the guests are seated according to precedence:

> *When thou art bidden of any man to a wedding, sit not down in the highest*

room; lest a more honourable man than thou be bidden of him; And he that bade thee and him come and say to thee, Give this man place; and thou begin with shame to take the lowest room.

Far better to seat yourself at the bottom of the table, so that when your host comes and says *Friend, go up higher,* everyone will see how honoured you are. *For whosoever exalteth himself shall be abased; and he that humbleth himself shall be exalted.*

Extending hospitality to friends and family is a waste of time, Jesus said; they'll just return the invitation. What you need to do is to wine and dine the poor and disabled, *for they cannot recompense thee: for thou shalt be recompensed at the resurrection of the just.* You can score points in a big way.

Jesus told the story of a man who was giving a feast. His invited guests *all with one consent began to make excuse.* One had recently bought property, and another oxen, and each said *I pray thee have me excused. And another said, I have married a wife, and therefore I cannot come.* The host was none too pleased, and told his servant *Go out quickly into the streets and lanes of the city, and bring in hither the poor, and the maimed, and the halt, and the blind.* Even so he wasn't satisfied with the turnout, ordering the servant to *Go out into the highways and hedges, and compel them to come in, that my house may be filled. For I say unto you, That none of those men which were bidden shall taste of my supper.* The moral, I take it, is that people who take a place on the divine guest list for granted can look forward to almighty petulance.

God had said that he was a jealous god, and Jesus didn't tolerate any competition either.

If any man come to me, and hate not his father, and mother, and wife, and children, and brethren, and sisters, yea, and his own life also, he cannot be my disciple.

With demands like that, it was important to weigh things up before committing yourself. *For which of you, intending to build a tower, sitteth not down first, and counteth the cost, whether he have sufficient to finish it?* You might be embarrassed otherwise by starting something you can't finish. The price was quite clear: *whosoever he be of you that forsaketh not all that he hath, he cannot be my disciple.*

Just as the self-appointed elect are likely to be in for an unpleasant surprise, those who have gone their own way may get a better reception than they had expected. Jesus overheard the grumbles that *This man receiveth sinners, and eateth with them,* and responded with a few parables. If there are a hundred sheep and one of them strays, the shepherd will *leave the ninety and nine in the wilderness, and go after that which is lost;* having found it, he will tell everyone to *Rejoice with me; for I have found my sheep which was lost.* Jesus asserted that *joy shall*

15

be in heaven over one sinner that repenteth, more than over ninety and nine just persons, which need no repentance.

After a similar story of a lost coin, Jesus launched into the tale of the prodigal son. The younger of two sons asked his father for his share of the estate, *And not many days after the younger son gathered all together, and took his journey into a far country, and there wasted his substance with riotous living.* When a famine struck he was obliged to go to work feeding pigs.

> *And he would fain have filled his belly with the husks that the swine did eat: and no man gave unto him. And when he came to himself, he said, How many hired servants of my father's have bread enough and to spare, and I perish with hunger! I will arise and go to my father, and will say unto him, Father, I have sinned against heaven, and before thee, And am no more worthy to be called thy son: make me as one of thy hired servants. And he arose, and came to his father. But when he was yet a great way off, his father saw him, and had compassion, and ran, and fell on his neck, and kissed him.*

The father brushed aside his son's self-reproaches, pressing new clothes on him, and ordering the servants to *bring hither the fatted calf, and kill it; and let us eat, and be merry: For this my son was dead, and is alive again; he was lost, and is found.* The elder brother returned to find a feast in progress. He complained to his father that he had worked for years without putting a foot wrong, and had never received so much as a kid goat in return. *But as soon as this thy son was come, which hath devoured thy living with harlots, thou hast killed for him the fatted calf.* The father replied *Son, thou art ever with me, and all that I have is thine.* It was only right, though, to celebrate the reappearance of his brother.

MONEY MANAGEMENT

16 Jesus was prepared to go even further with sin. The owner of an estate dismissed its manager for incompetence. The soon-to-be-unemployed man realised that his future wasn't bright; *What shall I do? ... I cannot dig; to beg I am ashamed.* He decided to ensure that as many people as possible owed him favours. *So he called every one of his lord's debtors unto him, and said unto the first, How much owest thou unto my lord? And he said, An hundred measures of oil. And he said unto him, Take thy bill, and sit down quickly, and write fifty.*

Far from charging him with malfeasance, *the lord commended the unjust steward, because he had done wisely: for the children of this world are in their generation wiser than the children of light. And I say unto you,* Jesus concluded, *Make to yourselves friends of the mammon of unrighteousness; that, when ye fail, they may receive you into everlasting habitations.*

I'm all for hedging my bets. I was surprised to hear such a cynical defence of illicit behaviour, but then my brother was a good deal more worldly than most people suppose. Note his question: *He that is faithful in that which is least is faithful also in much: and he that is unjust in the least is unjust also in much. If therefore ye have not been faithful in the unrighteous mammon, who will commit to your trust the true riches?* If you can't handle yourself in the real world, how can you expect to win God's confidence?

Jesus was also quick to assert the opposite, however.

> *There was a certain rich man, which was clothed in purple and fine linen, and fared sumptuously every day: And there was a certain beggar named Lazarus, which was laid at his gate full of sores, And desiring to be fed with the crumbs which fell from the rich man's table: moreover the dogs came and licked his sores. And it came to pass, that the beggar died, and was carried by the angels into Abraham's bosom.*

The rich man died and went to hell. In the distance he could see Lazarus cozy in the patriarch's lap, and cried out for relief.

> *But Abraham said, Son, remember that thou in thy lifetime receivedst thy good things, and likewise Lazarus evil things: but now he is comforted, and thou are tormented. And beside all this, between us and you there is a great gulf fixed.*

Factors beyond our control and all that, old boy. Play the game; fair's fair, what?

The man being roasted asked that at least Lazarus be sent to tell his five brothers to repent. When Abraham objected that Moses and the prophets had already delivered their warnings, he stressed the effectiveness of a message from beyond the grave. Abraham was still being unsporting, though, and insisted – quite wrongly, I think – that *If they hear not Moses and the prophets, neither will they be persuaded, though one rose from the dead.* Presumably, then, my brother was just wasting his time.

While recognising the inevitability of wrong doing, Jesus was sometimes severe with wrong doers. *It were better for him that a millstone were hanged about his neck, and he cast into the sea, than that he should offend one of these little ones.* Having said that, Jesus encouraged forgiveness. Whereas earlier I quoted him as saying that someone should be forgiven 77 times, with no mention of repentance, here he makes the more sensible statement that *If thy brother trespass against thee, rebuke him; and if he repent, forgive him,* even if he sins and repents seven times in a day.

Though Jesus became known as a model of kindness and consideration, you wouldn't necessarily have guessed it. In his view, people deserved no credit for doing their duty: *which of you,* he asked, *having a servant plowing or feeding cattle, will say unto him by and by, when he is come from the field, Go and sit down to meat?* No one, of course: a man will tell his servant to make dinner and wait on him first. *Doth he thank that servant because he did the things that were commanded him?* Obviously not: he was only doing his duty. Neither, apparently, should we obedient servants expect any pats on the back from God.

To the question of *when the kingdom of God should come*, Jesus had an interesting answer: you can't tell. You won't be able to say *Lo here! or, lo there! for, behold, the kingdom of God is within you* – or perhaps 'among you', though it's not clear what he meant in either case. Something spectacular was yet to come; life might seem normal, *But the same day that Lot went out of Sodom it rained fire and brimstone from heaven, and destroyed them all. Even thus shall it be in the day when the Son of man is revealed.* Don't stop to pack your bags: *Remember Lot's wife.*

18   Don't let yourself be discouraged: *men ought always to pray, and not to faint.* A judge who didn't care tuppence for a widow's demand for justice finally granted it, he said, *lest by her continual coming she weary me.* Likewise, Jesus observed, *shall not God avenge his own elect, which cry day and night unto him, though he bear long with them?* Well, perhaps, though I presume God is more thick-skinned than the judge.

It's certainly unwise to take too much for granted.

Two men went up into the temple to pray; the one a Pharisee, and the other a publican. The Pharisee stood and prayed thus with himself, God, I thank thee, that I am not as other men are, extortioners, unjust, adulterers, or even as this publican. I fast twice in the week, I give tithes of all that I possess. And the publican, standing afar off, would not lift up so much as his eyes unto heaven, but smote upon his breast, saying, God be merciful to me a sinner. I tell you, this man went down to his house justified rather than the other.

You get no marks for effort; what God appreciates is breast-beating.

In any case, Jesus wasn't satisfied with perfect obedience to all the commandments; he would tell people *Yet lackest thou one thing: sell all that thou hast, and distribute unto the poor.* It clearly made things easier if you were poor from the outset, for *How hardly shall they that have riches enter into the kingdom of God!*

19   In practice Jesus was willing to compromise. When he arrived in Jericho he invited himself to stay with the chief tax collector (finding him sitting in a tree to get a better view). It makes sense to spend time with your most prosperous acquaintances; you get a better class of hospitality. The people in the street grumbled about the choice, and the man himself showed his recognition of the honour by saying *Behold, Lord, the half of my goods I give to the poor.* Rather than insisting on all of it, Jesus announced that *This day is salvation come to this house.*

There's another version of his parable of the talents. *A certain nobleman went into a far country to receive for himself a kingdom, and to return* – more than likely a reference to Archelaus, one of the Herods. He gave his servants money, which some of them managed to increase in his absence. One, though, simply kept it hidden, telling him frankly that his mercenary reputation had made him afraid to do otherwise. The master replied *Out of thine own mouth will I judge thee, thou wicked servant. Thou knewest that I was an austere man,* a specialist in unearned income: the money should have been put at interest. At least the servant was only relieved of his money; the man ordered his followers to bring in the people who had not wanted him as king, *and slay them before me.* I wish Jesus had told us the moral of the story.

THE FINAL DAYS

As Jesus entered Jerusalem his disciples (not, it seems, the residents) shouted out *Blessed be the King that cometh in the name of the Lord.* When some Pharisees suggested that he bring them under control, he said *I tell you that, if these should hold their peace, the stones would immediately cry out.* The sight of the city brought to mind its fate; here, at least, he was clairvoyant. He lamented *If thou hadst known, even thou, at least in this thy day, the things which belong unto thy peace! but now they are hid from thine eyes.* The day would come when *thine enemies ... shall lay thee even with the ground, and thy children within thee.*

Jesus told his parable of the vineyard, in which the owner's son is killed by the tenants. *What therefore shall the lord of the vineyard do unto them? He shall come and destroy these husbandmen, and shall give the vineyard to others. And when they heard it, they said, God forbid.*   20

The disciples were naturally curious to know when the end would come, and how they would know it was due. Despite having stressed that it would take people by surprise, Jesus described a long prelude of wars, earthquakes, famines, plagues, and celestial portents. In the mean time they would be betrayed by all and sundry; some would be killed, but paradoxically *there shall not an hair of your head perish. In your patience possess ye your souls.*   21

Passover was coming. *Then entered Satan into Judas surnamed Iscariot, being of the number of the twelve;* while he was plotting, Jesus was making arrangements for their last supper. He told Peter and John to follow a man carrying water, *And he shall shew you a large upper room furnished: there make ready.* When the time came Jesus passed them the food and the wine, apparently lacking appetite himself. That's understandable, but still, eating the passover meal is virtually a duty. The whole chronology is doubtful, however; perhaps it was some other dinner.   22

He hadn't even left the table when the disciples started to squabble about who should be in charge. Jesus told them not to behave like Gentile nobility, lording it over their subjects: *he that is greatest among you, let him be as the younger; and he that is chief, as he that doth serve. ... I am among you as he that serveth.*

Satan wasn't going to confine his attention to Judas. *And the Lord said, Simon, Simon, behold, Satan hath desired to have you, that he may sift you as wheat.* Permission had been granted. Having the devil make you do it can be enjoyable, but this didn't sound like one of those times.

The days of being meek and weedy were over. Life had been easy, *But now, he that hath a purse, let him take it, and likewise his scrip: and he that hath no sword, let him sell his garment, and buy one.* As you mention it, *they said, Lord, behold, here are two swords. And he said unto them, It is enough.* More than enough, I'd say, but I've never been eager to play soldier.

After dinner they went to the Mount of Olives, where Jesus prayed *Father, if thou be willing, remove this cup from me: nevertheless not my will, but thine, be done.* God's will coincided with Satan's, and Judas entered with the arresting party. There was a fracas, but Jesus was in no mood to resist; he even healed the severed ear of the high priest's servant.

With Jesus in custody, Peter came and sat in the courtyard. He had trouble fending off the people who recognised him, and by cock's crow had three times denied knowing the accused. *And the Lord turned, and looked upon Peter. ... And Peter went out, and wept bitterly.*

23   The allies of the priests brought Jesus before Pontius Pilate, *saying, We found this fellow perverting the nation.* Discovering that the prisoner was from Galilee, and so *belonged unto Herod's jurisdiction, he sent him to Herod, who himself also was at Jerusalem at that time.* Luke managed to push the blame for the execution yet further from the Romans.

Herod was initially intrigued by Jesus, but in the end he *and his men of war set him at nought, and mocked him, and arrayed him in a gorgeous robe, and sent him again to Pilate* – even the Roman soldiers were whitewashed, by assigning their bad behaviour to others. *And the same day Pilate and Herod were made friends together: for before they were at enmity between themselves.* At least some good came out of it.

Pilate was most reluctant to condemn Jesus, but bowed to the wishes of the mob. Just who was in this mob is all the more mysterious, given that as Jesus was led out *there followed him a great company of people, and of women, which also bewailed and lamented him.* He told them to save their tears for themselves, implying that things would become worse as the seasons advanced to winter. *For if they do these things in a green tree, what shall be done in the dry?* An interesting thought, that barren months bring out violence – one not supported by the evidence, I suspect.

And when they were come to the place, which is called Calvary, two criminals were crucified with Jesus, one on either side. *Then said Jesus, Father, forgive them; for they know not what they do.* One of the criminals joined in the general mockery, but the other – at least on this account – said that while they could have no complaints, *this man hath done nothing amiss. And he said unto Jesus, Lord, remember me when thou comest into thy kingdom.* Jesus promised *To day shalt thou be with me in paradise.*

Supposedly there was an eclipse of the sun, but as passover comes at the full moon and a solar eclipse only when there is no moon, maybe it just seemed that way. Jesus cried *Father, into thy hands I commend my spirit: and having said thus, he gave up the ghost. Now when the centurion saw what was done, he glorified God, saying, Certainly this was a righteous man.* So he was, which was why praising God wasn't my first reaction.

THE RETURN

Jesus was buried in a private tomb, thanks to the Jew from Arimathaea, *a man named Joseph, a counsellor; and he was a good man, and a just.* The women who had followed Jesus from Galilee wanted to prepare his body with spices; the next day being the sabbath, however, it wasn't until very early the following morning that they went to the tomb. They found it unblocked and empty – though not altogether empty, for *it came to pass, as they were much perplexed thereabout, behold, two men stood by them in shining garments: And as they were afraid, and bowed down their faces to the earth, they said unto them, Why seek ye the living among the dead?*

Not only the number of angels, but of women too, increased from earlier accounts. *It was Mary Magdalene, and Joanna, and Mary the mother of James, and other women that were with them, which told these things unto the apostles. And their words seemed to them as idle tales, and they believed them not.*

That would change, however. Later that day two of his followers were walking to the village of Emmaus when *Jesus himself drew near, and went with them;* for some reason, however, they didn't recognise him. When he asked why they seemed glum, they mentioned the recent catastrophe: *we trusted that it had been he which should have redeemed Israel.* He protested that, contrary to what they seemed to believe, the messiah was bound to suffer before his triumph.

They invited the 'stranger' to stop with them at the village. When he said the blessing at dinner *their eyes were opened, and they knew him; and he vanished out of their sight. And they said one to another, Did not our heart burn within us, while he talked with us by the way, and while he opened to us the scriptures?*

Having gone straight back to Jerusalem, they were told that *The Lord is risen indeed;* apparently Simon Peter had also seen Jesus. They described to the apostles and others *how he was known of them in breaking of bread. And as they thus spake, Jesus himself stood in the midst of them.*

There was consternation, of course, at the sight of what they took to be a ghost. Jesus tried to reassure them: *Behold my hands and my feet, that it is I myself: handle me, and see; for a spirit hath not flesh and bones, as ye see me have.* I don't know why it should be less frightening to have him there in the flesh than in the spirit, but he was determined to prove it. He asked *Have ye here any meat?*

And they gave him a piece of a broiled fish, and of an honeycomb. And he took it, and did eat before them.

The demonstration must have had a settling effect, because he was able to give them all a lesson in what Moses and the prophets had intended. According to scripture, he claimed, *it behoved Christ to suffer, and to rise from the dead the third day.* I don't recall reading anything like that myself, but no one was going to argue. *And he led them out as far as to Bethany, and he lifted up his hands, and blessed them. And it came to pass, while he blessed them, he was parted from them, and carried up into heaven.* I had generally heard that his ascension was some time later – 40 days later, for example – but perhaps I've just been indulging in wishful thinking.

4

John

In the beginning was the Word, and the Word was with God, and the Word was 1
God. The same was in the beginning with God. All things were made by him; and
without him was not any thing made that was made. In him was life; and the life
was the light of men. And the light shineth in darkness; and the darkness
comprehended it not.

And to think I just knew him as a brother. Jesus had come a long way, all right.
Even John the Baptist, great preacher that he was, would be dwarfed. *There was a*
man sent from God, whose name was John. The same came for a witness, to bear
witness of the Light, that all men through him might believe. He was not that
Light, but was sent to bear witness of that Light. That was the true Light, which
lighteth every man that cometh into the world.

Not everyone, unfortunately, could see the light. *He was in the world, and the*
world was made by him, and the world knew him not. He came unto his own,
and his own received him not. But as many as received him, to them gave he
power to become the sons of God, even to them that believe on his name: Which
were born, not of blood, nor of the will of the flesh, nor of the will of man, but
of God. And the Word was made flesh, and dwelt among us, (and we beheld his
glory, the glory as of the only begotten of the Father,) full of grace and truth.

Can Jesus be the only son, if all believers might become God's children? I
suppose they'll just be adopted. It was also a surprise to hear that *No man hath*
seen God at any time; Moses, to name but one, had seemed so certain.

At least I wasn't the only one to be confused. John had told people that *I baptize*
with water: but there standeth one among you, whom ye know not; He it is, who
coming after me is preferred before me, whose shoe's latchet I am not worthy to
unloose. And when my brother appeared, he declared *Behold the Lamb of God,*
which taketh away the sin of the world. He went on to explain, though, that when
he baptized Jesus *I knew him not*, which seems odd since not only were they
cousins, according to Luke, but John had even recognised his young colleague in
the womb. The experience of the baptism apparently persuaded him that *this is the*
Son of God, which makes his later doubts about Jesus (as recorded by Matthew)
all the more curious.

I trust that he was not too aggrieved when my brother poached some of his
disciples. Being persuaded that Jesus was the messiah (*which is, being interpreted,*
the Christ), Andrew brought along his brother Simon. Another potential recruit
sounded doubtful; when told by Philip about *Jesus of Nazareth, the son of Joseph,*

Nathanael replied *Can there any good thing come out of Nazareth?* His conversation with my brother went as follows, starting with Jesus:

> — *Behold an Israelite indeed, in whom is no guile!*
> — *Whence knowest thou me?*
> — *Before that Philip called thee, when thou wast under the fig tree, I saw thee.*
> — *Rabbi, thou art the Son of God; thou art the King of Israel.*

I'm not sure whether Nathanael was wickedly sarcastic or hopelessly credulous. At first Jesus seemed to suspect that his leg was being pulled; *Because I said unto thee, I saw thee under the fig tree, believest thou?* But his enthusiasm overcame his wariness: *thou shalt see greater things than these. Verily, verily, I say unto you, Hereafter ye shall see heaven open, and the angels of God ascending and descending upon the Son of man.* A ladder seems more practical, but what did Jacob know?

2   *There was a marriage in Cana of Galilee; and the mother of Jesus was there,* and all the rest of us, too. With the wine running out and disaster looming, Mary told my brother *They have no wine. Jesus saith unto her, Woman, what have I to do with thee? mine hour is not yet come.* His manners weren't divine, even if he was. Being the indulgent mother of a quick-tempered prodigy, she told the servants, *Whatsoever he saith unto you, do it.*

It's been observed that Mary's concern with the wine supply only makes sense if the wedding feast was for one of her own children (unless she was just there for the drink). That's quite right; as I recall, the party was for one of my sisters – not for Jesus, which is sometimes suggested. As he said, his turn hadn't come yet.

At any rate, Jesus told the servant to fill the six large waterpots, and then to take a sample to the master of ceremonies. When he *tasted the water that was made wine* – it was a blind tasting, no one having told him where it came from – he said *Every man at the beginning doth set forth good wine; and when men have well drunk, then that which is worse: but thou hast kept the good wine until now.* It does seem a shame that the miraculous vintage was squandered on the die-hards and tail-enders. Still, *This beginning of miracles did Jesus in Cana of Galilee, and manifested forth his glory; and his disciples believed on him.*

JESUS IN JERUSALEM

After this he went down to Capernaum, he, and his mother, and his brethren, and his disciples: but we didn't stay there long. Passover was coming, which meant a trip to Jerusalem. Travelling with Jesus could be a trial: if a particular custom offended him, he wasn't one to let people get on with it. Seeing money change hands in the courtyard of the temple – even for religious purposes – made him see red. *And when he had made a scourge of small cords, he drove them all out of the temple, and the sheep, and the oxen; and poured out the changers' money, and overthrew the tables; And said unto them that sold doves, Take these things hence; make not my Father's house an house of merchandise.* The temple was for killing animals, not buying them.

Everybody else reports this incident as happening towards the end, not the beginning, of his career, but for all I know it was a regular feature of his visits to Jerusalem. When asked for a sign of his authority, Jesus said *Destroy this temple, and in three days I will raise it up.* They didn't take him up on the offer, which was just as well, for *he spake of the temple of his body.* That could have been an unfortunate misunderstanding.

There was a man of the Pharisees, named Nicodemus, who came calling one **3** evening. Jesus told him that *Except a man be born again, he cannot see the kingdom of God.* Nicodemus wondered just how one went about being born again. Jesus explained that it was a spiritual rebirth; *That which is born of the flesh is flesh; and that which is born of the Spirit is spirit.* Using a Greek (?!) pun on spirit and wind, he commented that *The wind bloweth where it listeth, and thou hearest the sound thereof, but canst not tell whence it cometh, and whither it goeth: so is every one that is born of the Spirit.*

Nicodemus was still none the wiser, and asked *How can these things be?* Jesus was losing his patience; he said *Art thou a master of Israel, and knowest not these things?* It's a waste of time talking to people who can't understand anything. For some reason Jesus went on to claim that *no man hath ascended up to heaven, but he that came down from heaven, even the Son of man;* I wonder in that case where Elijah was going on his chariot of fire.

Evidently that was all going to change, *For God so loved the world, that he gave his only begotten Son, that whosoever believeth in him should not perish, but have everlasting life.* Belief is a prerequisite, of course. *He that believeth on him is not condemned: but he that believeth not is condemned already,* and that's before you even look at how they behave. Perhaps it's unnecessary, though, since *men loved darkness rather than light, because their deeds were evil.*

Jesus and his disciples went into Judaea to baptize, taking on John at his own game on his own turf. *And John also was baptizing in Aenon near to Salim, because there was much water there,* and that's all you need for a good baptism. His followers seemed unhappy at losing market share to the upstart, but John himself wasn't upset. *He must increase, but I must decrease;* it was only natural.

Bear in mind that the easiest way to please or offend a parent is to please or offend a child. *The Father loveth the Son, and hath given all things into his hand. He that believeth on the Son hath everlasting life: and he that believeth not the Son shall not see life; but the wrath of God abideth on him.* Not only was God on our side, he would chase the others well away from us.

Perhaps to avoid putting John the Baptist out of business altogether, Jesus **4** headed back towards Galilee via Samaria. He sat and rested by a well. *There cometh a woman of Samaria to draw water: Jesus saith unto her, Give me to drink.* She clearly wasn't swept off her feet by his manners, but asked out of curiosity *How is it that thou, being a Jew, askest drink of me ...? for the Jews have no dealings with the Samaritans.* Jesus replied that if she knew whom he was, she would have requested (and received) 'living water'. Being obliged to play the idiot, she enquired how he would get water without a bucket. He said that it would come from an inner source in each person, *springing up into everlasting life.*

When the woman expressed an interest, Jesus started a rather crass exchange.

— *Go, call thy husband, and come hither.*
— *I have no husband.*
— *Thou hast well said, I have no husband: For thou hast had five husbands; and he whom thou now hast is not thy husband: in that saidst thou truly.*
— *Sir, I perceive that thou art a prophet.*

Instead of telling him to go soak his head, she steered the conversation away from her private life and back to religion. He was happy to talk about the coming reformation (as well as to air his prejudices about Samaritans):

Ye worship ye know not what: we know what we worship: for salvation is of the Jews. But the hour cometh, and now is, when the true worshippers shall worship the Father in spirit and in truth: for the Father seeketh such to worship him. God is a Spirit: and they that worship him must worship him in spirit and in truth.

No doubt, the woman remarked, the messiah will make everything clear when he comes. *I that speak unto thee am he,* Jesus said. He had always gone to such trouble to stamp out those rumours, it was quite a surprise to hear this acknowledgement.

Many of his conversations followed the same pattern: cryptic statement, stooge-like question, lofty reply. So it went when the disciples told him *Master, eat:* he responded *I have meat to eat that ye know not of. Therefore said the disciples one to another, Hath any man brought him ought to eat? Jesus saith unto them, My meat is to do the will of him that sent me, and to finish his work.*

The signs seemed promising: *Lift up your eyes, and look on the fields; for they are white already to harvest. ... I sent you to reap that whereon ye bestowed no labour: other men laboured, and ye are entered into their labours.* His supporters were fortunate enough to be in the right place at the right time.

The Samaritan woman had done the rounds testifying *He told me all that ever I did,* and that helped to draw the crowds. Jesus himself did the rest; they went home saying *this is indeed the Christ, the Saviour of the world.*

Now after two days he departed thence, and went into Galilee. For Jesus himself testified, that a prophet hath no honour in his own country. In that case he should have stayed in Samaria, but why should I expect things to make sense? When a nobleman in Capernaum entreated Jesus to *heal his son: for he was at the point of death*, my brother sounded rather bitter: *Except ye see signs and wonders, ye will not believe.* The man repeated that he was just asking for his son to be cured. Jesus said *Go thy way; thy son liveth.*

This, after turning the water into wine at the wedding feast, was *the second miracle that Jesus did.* Performing miracles must have been hard work; it seemed to put him in a foul mood.

JEWS NOT FOR JESUS

Jesus went back to Jerusalem. *Now there is at Jerusalem by the sheep market a*   5 *pool, which is called in the Hebrew tongue Bethesda, having five porches. In these lay a great multitude of impotent folk, of blind, halt, withered,* including a man who had been disabled for 38 years. Jesus chose him to cure, saying *Rise, take up thy bed, and walk.* (Either that was his catch phrase, or this story has changed in the retelling.)

The poor fellow was hardly given a chance to celebrate. First the more orthodox Jews protested *It is the sabbath day: it is not lawful for thee to carry thy bed.* He answered that he was just doing as he was told; unfortunately Jesus wasn't around to stand up for him. *Afterward Jesus findeth him in the temple, and said unto him, Behold, thou art made whole: sin no more, lest a worse thing come unto thee.* Just what you want to hear from your doctor.

I should mention that whoever wrote this particular version of my brother's life was even more concerned than the others to show traditional Jews in a bad light. I have no objection to sectarian controversy, but exaggeration and abuse is dangerous. To provide a sample: *And therefore did the Jews persecute Jesus, and sought to slay him ... the Jews sought the more to kill him, because he not only had broken the sabbath, but said also that God was his Father, making himself equal with God.*

Jesus answered with a long harangue. *He that honoureth not the Son honoureth not the Father which hath sent him.* Authority has been delegated to the Son:

> *Marvel not at this: for the hour is coming, in the which all that are in the graves shall hear his voice, and shall come forth; they that have done good, unto the resurrection of life; and they that have done evil, unto the resurrection of damnation.*

Ouch. Much of this lost its force, I have to say, when he conceded that *If I bear witness of myself, my witness is not true.* A sound thought, but his independent evidence was not very strong. First there's John the Baptist: *He was a burning and a shining light: and ye were willing for a season to rejoice in his light.* Then, too, *the same works that I do, bear witness of me, that the Father hath sent me.* Finally,

Search the scriptures; for in them ye think ye have eternal life: and they are they which testify of me.

This appeal to scripture was the most important, and yet the weakest, plank in the argument. There's almost nothing in them to suggest life after death, and very little concerning a messiah, let alone any specific candidate. The law is even less helpful than the prophets. Jesus claimed that *had ye believed Moses, ye would have believed me: for he wrote of me.* I can't imagine which passages he had in mind.

6   *After these things Jesus went over the sea of Galilee*; he moved around more than a travelling salesman. The moment had come for the feeding of the five thousand. Peter mentioned that *There is a lad here, which hath five barley loaves, and two small fishes: but what are they among so many?* In the event, of course, there was plenty to go around, and Jesus told them to *Gather up the fragments that remain, that nothing be lost.*

The next day, Jesus told the crowd that *the bread of God is he which cometh down from heaven.* To spell it out,

> *I am the bread of life: he that cometh to me shall never hunger; and he that believeth on me shall never thirst. ... him that cometh to me I will in no wise cast out.*

Not everyone was happy; *The Jews then murmured at him ... And they said, Is not this Jesus, the son of Joseph, whose father and mother we know? how is it then that he saith, I came down from heaven?* That's not an easy question to answer, and Jesus replied that either you belonged to God's elect or you didn't. *Verily, verily, I say unto you, He that believeth on me hath everlasting life. I am that bread of life. ... and the bread that I will give is my flesh.*

This invitation to cannibalism caused even greater consternation. Jesus reiterated that *Whoso eateth my flesh, and drinketh my blood, hath eternal life; and I will raise him up at the last day.* I never knew whether salvation depended on faith or good works, and now he was introducing a different criterion: participation in the eucharist.

No one could be surprised that *Many therefore of his disciples, when they had heard this, said, This is an hard saying; who can hear it?* Jesus explained *It is the spirit that quickeneth; the flesh profiteth nothing.* Whatever he meant, it wasn't enough: *From that time many of his disciples went back, and walked no more with him. Then said Jesus unto the twelve, Will ye also go away?* Peter declared their loyalty. Jesus still sounded bitter, I'm afraid: *Have not I chosen you twelve, and one of you is a devil?* Good help is hard to find.

JESUS ON THE RUN

After these things Jesus walked in Galilee: for he would not walk in Jewry, 7
because the Jews sought to kill him. I don't think it was quite as bad as that – and anyway, what were those of us living in Galilee, if not Jews? We brothers got together and urged Jesus to travel south for the feast of tabernacles; he would never make his mark in the world while hiding out in the country. *If thou do these things, shew thyself to the world. For neither did his brethren believe in him.* Well, it's just that I hesitated to call myself a relative of God.

Jesus said that he wasn't going; *The world cannot hate you; but me it hateth, because I testify of it, that the works thereof are evil.* And so he stayed behind, apparently in a sulk, when we left for Jerusalem. *But when his brethren were gone up, then went he also up unto the feast, not openly, but as it were in secret.*

At the feast there was a certain amount of talk about Jesus; *some said, He is a good man: others said, Nay; but he deceiveth the people. Howbeit no man spake openly of him for fear of the Jews.* Unless they were afraid of themselves, it was presumably the religious authorities who discouraged the chatter. With the festivities half over, Jesus made a surprise appearance in the temple. His teaching met with some derision; *the Jews marvelled, saying, How knoweth this man letters, having never learned?*

When he wasn't annoying them, part of the audience found Jesus comical. He demanded *Why go ye about to kill me? The people answered and said, Thou hast a devil: who goeth about to kill thee?* It's true he was acting paranoid, but eventually someone really did get him. Jesus gave a rather desperate defence of healing on the sabbath, concluding with the plea *Judge not according to the appearance, but judge righteous judgment.*

His presence triggered a good deal of debate about whether or not he was the messiah. Against him was the tradition that the messiah would appear suddenly, as if from nowhere, and that was not the case with Jesus. That said, he had performed as many miracles as might have been expected. Then, too, he impressed people with his shout on the last day of the feast:

If any man thirst, let him come unto me, and drink. He that believeth in me, as the scripture hath said, out of his belly shall flow rivers of living water.

What's curious is that scripture says no such thing: not in the law, in the prophets, or in the other writings, has anyone found a verse to resemble it.

Still, with enough confidence you can carry anything off. *Many of the people therefore, when they heard this saying, said, Of a truth this is the Prophet. Others said, This is the Christ. But some said, Shall Christ come out of Galilee? Hath not the scripture said, That Christ cometh of the seed of David, and out of the town of Bethlehem, where David was?* They were quite right, of course, and in due time appropriate adjustments were made to the official biography.

When Nicodemus put in a word for Jesus with his fellow Pharisees, saying that it would be wrong to judge him without a hearing, they teased *Art thou also of Galilee? Search, and look: for out of Galilee ariseth no prophet.* That may not be strictly true, but we get the point: they thought we were hicks from the sticks.

8   One of my favourite anecdotes about Jesus is set at the Mount of Olives, when *the scribes and Pharisees brought unto him a woman taken in adultery.* They said that she was caught *in the very act. Now Moses in the law commanded us, that such should be stoned: but what sayest thou?* They thought they had him in a cleft stick: contradict the ancients or offend the civil authorities, who alone could impose the death penalty. *But Jesus stooped down, and with his finger wrote on the ground, as though he heard them not. So when they continued asking him, he lifted up himself, and said unto them, He that is without sin among you, let him first cast a stone at her.*

This made them stop and think, and as Jesus returned to writing on the ground, one by one they walked away. *When Jesus had lifted up himself, and saw none but the woman, he said unto her, Woman, where are those thine accusers? hath no man condemned thee? She said, No man, Lord. And Jesus said unto her, Neither do I condemn thee: go, and sin no more.*

Most of his debates with the Pharisees were less neatly resolved, unfortunately. One long controversy started with Jesus saying *I am the light of the world: he that followeth me shall not walk in darkness, but shall have the light of life.* Beautiful as this was, they declined to take his word for it. Jesus cited the rule that two witnesses were sufficient: *I am one that bear witness of myself, and the Father that sent me beareth witness of me.* His argument went from bad to worse when they asked *Where is thy Father? Jesus answered, Ye neither know me, nor my Father: if ye had known me, ye should have known my Father also.*

After that, I'm afraid, it degenerated into a mutual taunting session. Jesus said that he was going somewhere they couldn't follow. *Then said the Jews, Will he kill himself? because he saith, Whither I go, ye cannot come. And he said unto them, Ye are from beneath; I am from above ... ye shall die in your sins.*

Not everyone was hostile. *Then said Jesus to those Jews which believed on him, If ye continue in my word, then are ye my disciples indeed; And ye shall know the truth, and the truth shall make you free.* When, however, his supporters said that they already felt free, Jesus became abusive with them, too. *If ye were Abraham's children, ye would do the works of Abraham. But now ye seek to kill me, a man that hath told you the truth.* This got their backs up, and they replied *We be not born of fornication; we have one Father, even God.* Jesus retorted *Ye are of your father the devil, and the lusts of your father ye will do. He was a murderer from the beginning, and abode not in the truth, because there is no truth in him. When he speaketh a lie, he speaketh of his own: for he is a liar, and the father of it.*

Before he could start on their mothers, his audience suggested *Say we not well that thou art a Samaritan, and hast a devil?* When he denied being possessed, but declared that no one obedient to his teaching would die, they said *Now we know that thou hast a devil. Abraham is dead, and the prophets.* Jesus only repeated that he had a special relationship with God: *ye have not known him; but I know him: and if I should say, I know him not, I shall be a liar like unto you.* Furthermore, *Your father Abraham rejoiced to see my day … Then said the Jews unto him, Thou art not yet fifty years old, and hast thou seen Abraham? Jesus said unto them, Verily, verily, I say unto you, Before Abraham was, I am.*

Jesus had to make himself scarce to avoid being stoned for blasphemy. Unless he learned not to alienate his own supporters, his career was going to be rather short. Some people find me offensive, but next to my brother I'm a model of diplomacy.

PROMOTING GOD'S GLORY

A man who had been blind from birth started Jesus on his next adventure. As they 9 walked past the man, *his disciples asked him, saying, Master, who did sin, this man, or his parents, that he was born blind?* Jesus answered that neither was necessarily the case; he had been born that way so that God could show off.

At that Jesus got down to work, saying *I must work the works of him that sent me, while it is day: the night cometh, when no man can work. As long as I am in the world, I am the light of the world. When he had thus spoken, he spat on the ground, and made clay of the spittle, and he anointed the eyes of the blind man with the clay.* He told his patient to go and wash off the mud; the man returned able to see.

As usual Jesus had caused trouble for himself by going about his business on the sabbath. None the less, some of the Pharisees were favourably disposed towards him. *But the Jews did not believe … until they called the parents of him that had received his sight.* The parents confirmed that something had happened, but how or by whom they couldn't say: *he is of age; ask him: he shall speak for himself. These words spake his parents, because they feared the Jews: for the Jews had agreed already, that if any man did confess that he was Christ, he should be put out of the synagogue.* In fact a synagogue had no power to excommunicate at the time, though as it happens there was such authority later, when this story was written.

It would be a shame to let that distract us from the cured man's repartee. He had been told *Give God the praise: we know that this man is a sinner. He answered and said, Whether he be a sinner or no, I know not: one thing I know, that, whereas I was blind, now I see.* He eventually exasperated his interrogators, who kicked him out. Happily Jesus was there to reveal his credentials.

Verily, verily, as my brother liked to say, *He that entereth not by the door into* 10 *the sheepfold, but climbeth up some other way, the same is a thief and a robber.*

I never felt that way when I clambered over walls from one field to the next, but as Jesus said, the shepherd would use the main gate. The disciples didn't know what to make of this allegory, and he explained *I am the door of the sheep. All that ever came before me are thieves and robbers: but the sheep did not hear them.* Thank goodness for that – and how fortunate we ignored all those prophets and preachers.

He continued his homily:

I am the door: by me if any man enter in, he shall be saved, and shall go in and out, and find pasture. The thief cometh not, but for to steal, and to kill, and to destroy: I am come that they might have life, and that they might have it more abundantly. I am the good shepherd: the good shepherd giveth his life for the sheep. ... The hireling fleeth, because he is an hireling, and careth not for the sheep. ... And other sheep I have, which are not of this fold: them also I must bring, and they shall hear my voice; and there shall be one fold, and one shepherd.

Saying that he had been commissioned for this role by his Father fuelled the controversy. Many said *He hath a devil, and is mad*; others disagreed.

In Jerusalem for the feast of dedication that winter, Jesus continued the battle. People said *If thou be the Christ, tell us plainly.* He sidestepped that request, but made an even bolder claim: *I and my Father are one. Then the Jews took up stones again to stone him.* Displaying a bitter wit under pressure, Jesus asked which of his good deeds they intended to punish. Their response was that *For a good work we stone thee not; but for blasphemy; and because that thou, being a man, makest thyself God.*

Jesus declared that they had no cause to believe him if he did nothing godly. *But if I do, though ye believe not me, believe the works: that ye may know, and believe, that the Father is in me, and I in him.* That seemed a reasonable point to discuss, I thought, but he still had to make a run for it.

11   *Now a certain man was sick, named Lazarus,* not to be confused with the beggar who died and went to heaven. This man was the brother of Martha and Mary in Bethany, and a friend of Jesus. When Jesus heard of the illness *he said, This sickness is not unto death, but for the glory of God, that the Son of God might be glorified thereby.* Like blindness, in other words, it just gave the divine duo an opportunity to impress the masses. Not wanting to make things look too easy, *When he had heard therefore that he was sick, he abode two days still in the same place where he was.*

Having given Lazarus enough of a headstart to the grave, Jesus set out with his disciples for Judaea. He told them that his friend needed help in waking up; when they took him literally, as people often do, he *said unto them plainly, Lazarus is dead. And I am glad for your sakes that I was not there, to the intent ye may believe.* They would shortly see something to knock their sandals off.

Then when Jesus came, he found that he had lain in the grave four days already. The sisters of Lazarus were devastated; Martha told Jesus, *Lord, if thou hadst been here, my brother had not died.* He replied *Thy brother shall rise again.* When she acknowledged that he would *rise again in the resurrection at the last day,* Jesus tried to elaborate:

> *I am the resurrection, and the life: he that believeth in me, though he were dead, yet shall he live: And whosoever liveth and believeth in me shall never die. Believest thou this?*

The question sounded slightly doubtful, but she reassured him that he was the Son of God as far as she was concerned.

Next Mary came out and fell at his feet, and cried, and with *the Jews also weeping which came with her, he groaned in the spirit, and was troubled.* I should imagine so: my conscience would have roasted me. *Jesus wept. Then said the Jews, Behold how he loved him! And some of them said, Could not this man, which opened the eyes of the blind, have caused that even this man should not have died? Jesus therefore again groaning in himself cometh to the grave.*

Lazarus had been entombed in a cave. Jesus ordered that the stone blocking the entrance be removed. *Martha, the sister of him that was dead, saith unto him, Lord, by this time he stinketh: for he hath been dead four days.* Jesus was undaunted, and thanked his Father. In an aside to God, he justified his showmanship: *I knew that thou hearest me always: but because of the people which stand by I said it, that they may believe that thou hast sent me.*

The climax is spine-chilling; I wonder if any of the onlookers ever slept soundly again. Jesus *cried with a loud voice, Lazarus, come forth. And he that was dead came forth, bound hand and foot with graveclothes: and his face was bound about with a napkin. Jesus saith unto them, Loose him, and let him go.*

That's it, the end of the story. I would have liked to hear who was brave enough to unwrap him, and how he felt, and what he wanted to eat. The only epilogue, though, was a scene from the religious council, where the leadership wondered what to do with Jesus. *If we let him thus alone, all men will believe on him: and the Romans shall come and take away both our place and nation. And one of them, named Caiaphas, being the high priest that same year, said unto them, Ye know nothing at all, Nor consider that it is expedient for us, that one man should die for the people, and that the whole nation perish not.*

And so *from that day forth they took counsel together for to put him to death. Jesus therefore walked no more openly among the Jews,* though I knew he wouldn't be able to stay out of trouble for long. Passover was coming, and everyone was gathering in Jerusalem.

WASHING FEET

12 Six days before passover Jesus came back to Bethany, where the recently unbereaved household of Lazarus *made him a supper*. Mary poured expensive perfume on his feet, wiping them with her hair. *Then saith one of his disciples, Judas Iscariot, Simon's son, which should betray him, Why was not this ointment sold for three hundred pence, and given to the poor? This he said, not that he cared for the poor; but because he was a thief* – though if he was really picking the apostolic purse, it seems odd that he should have betrayed their chief fund raiser. Jesus reminded them that *the poor always ye have with you*, unlike himself.

A number of the curious gathered, not only, or even primarily, to see Jesus, *but that they might see Lazarus also, whom he had raised from the dead*. The chief priests decided that they would have to eliminate Lazarus, too, as he was the reason so many people were defecting to my brother's camp.

The next day Jesus, greeted by people bearing palm branches and shouting *Hosanna*, entered Jerusalem on a donkey. He declared that

> *The hour is come, that the Son of man should be glorified. Verily, verily, I say unto you, Except a corn of wheat fall into the ground and die, it abideth alone: but if it die, it bringeth forth much fruit. He that loveth his life shall lose it; and he that hateth his life in this world shall keep it unto life eternal.*

Though wavering for a moment in his resolve, Jesus concluded by saying *Father, glorify thy name. Then came there a voice from heaven, saying, I have both glorified it, and will glorify it again.* I wish he had come up with some other way of doing it; I don't find executions very glorious, myself.

The people were perplexed by his failure to meet messianic expectations. Jesus urged them to make the most of his presence.

> *Yet a little while is the light with you. Walk while ye have the light, lest darkness come upon you: for he that walketh in darkness knoweth not whither he goeth. While ye have light, believe in the light, that ye may be the children of light.*

These things spake Jesus, and departed, and did hide himself from them. That can't have helped.

But though he had done so many miracles before them, yet they believed not on him, because God wouldn't let them. Isaiah's prophecy of incredulity had to be fulfilled, which was accomplished with divine assistance: *He hath blinded their eyes, and hardened their heart*, to prevent them from having their misfortunes cured. And here I thought that free will was to blame for everything.

13 One evening before passover had started, Jesus rose from dinner, *laid aside his*

garments; and took a towel, and girded himself. After that he poureth water into a bason, and began to wash the disciples' feet, and to wipe them with the towel wherewith he was girded. Peter was initially alarmed, saying *Thou shalt never wash my feet. Jesus answered him, If I wash thee not, thou hast no part with me. Simon Peter saith unto him, Lord, not my feet only, but also my hands and my head.*

Jesus explained that he was setting an example to them; *The servant is not greater than his lord; neither he that is sent greater that he that sent him.* He seemed to have these the wrong way around, but you get the idea.

Jesus was very uneasy, and declared *that one of you shall betray me. Then the disciples looked one on another, doubting of whom he spake. Now there was leaning on Jesus' bosom one of his disciples, whom Jesus loved. Simon Peter therefore beckoned to him, that he should ask who it should be of whom he spake. He then lying on Jesus' breast saith unto him, Lord, who is it? Jesus answered, He it is, to whom I shall give a sop, when I have dipped it. And when he had dipped the sop, he gave it to Judas Iscariot, the son of Simon. And after the sop Satan entered into him. Then said Jesus unto him, That thou doest, do quickly.*

Judas didn't waste any time in leaving, and Jesus immediately seemed happier. Calling his disciples *Little children*, he said *A new commandment I give unto you, That ye love one another; as I have loved you, that ye also love one another.*

Very shortly there was going to be a lot of explaining to do. The disciples would need to persuade themselves, never mind anyone else, that the death of their leader was all for the best. Jesus had a good deal to say on the subject. 14

> *Let not your heart be troubled: ye believe in God, believe also in me. In my Father's house are many mansions: if it were not so, I would have told you. I go to prepare a place for you. And if I go and prepare a place for you, I will come again, and receive you unto myself; that where I am, there ye may be also.*

The disciple named Thomas wondered how they would be able to find this place. Jesus didn't exactly say, but he did make it clear that you'd need the right password to get in; *I am the way, the truth, and the life: no man cometh unto the Father, but by me.* My brother, the heavenly bouncer.

Give us a sight of God, Philip said, and we'll be satisfied. Jesus said *Have I been so long time with you, and yet hast thou not known me, Philip? he that hath seen me hath seen the Father.* It is odd, I must say, that they didn't recognise his divinity. You'd think they might have noticed something that unusual.

I can't help but think he was setting them up for disappointment, though. *He that believeth on me, the works that I do shall he do also ... And whatsoever ye shall ask in my name, that will I do.* Not even politicians make promises that sweeping.

THE HOLY GHOST

I will pray the Father, Jesus said, *and he shall give you another Comforter,* by way of consolation. This comforter, or advocate – Paraclete, in Greek – would be a kind of spirit, invisible to the rest of the world, *but ye know him; for he dwelleth with you, and shall be in you. I will not leave you comfortless: I will come to you.*

That sounded good to me, but *Judas saith unto him, not Iscariot, Lord, how is it that thou wilt manifest thyself unto us, and not unto the world?* These fellows never stopped with the questions. Jesus said that he was just passing on the word from higher up.

> *But the Comforter, which is the Holy Ghost, whom the Father will send in my name, he shall teach you all things, and bring all things to your remembrance, whatsoever I have said unto you. Peace I leave with you, my peace I give unto you: not as the world giveth, give I unto you. Let not your heart be troubled, neither let it be afraid. Ye have heard how I said unto you, I go away, and come again unto you. If ye loved me, ye would rejoice, because I said, I go unto the Father: for my Father is greater than I.*

15   That was a rare flash of modesty, it has to be said. Jesus was just as likely to say *I am the vine, ye are the branches ... without me ye can do nothing. If a man abide not in me, he is cast forth as a branch, and is withered; and men gather them, and cast them into the fire, and they are burned.* The instruction *continue ye in my love* begins to sound rather sinister.

Greater love hath no man than this, that a man lay down his life for his friends. Ye are my friends, if ye do whatsoever I command you. If you what? He seemed a bit unclear on how friendship works. The amusing part is that he went on *Henceforth I call you not servants,* but friends, on the grounds that friends are better informed – but that seemed to be the only difference. *Ye have not chosen me, but I have chosen you.*

Looking ahead, there would be not only the problem of explaining my brother's unfortunate demise, but also more than a few conflicts with traditionalists. Look at it this way, he said; *If the world hate you, ye know that it hated me before it hated you.* Having heard the word, people have no excuse. *He that hateth me hateth my Father also.* There's a bold claim for you; Jesus didn't hold with any wishy-washy ideas about everyone worshipping in his or her own way.

16   Jesus warned that *They shall put you out of the synagogues: yea, the time cometh, that whosoever killeth you will think that he doeth God service.* He admitted that *these things I said not unto you at the beginning, because I was with you.* Now that he was leaving, he just thought he'd mention that they were in the soup.

None of them, he noted, asked *Whither goest thou? – Quo vadis?* – though they felt heavy-hearted. *Nevertheless I tell you the truth; It is expedient for you that I go away: for if I go not away, the Comforter will not come unto you.* It still didn't sound like a good bargain to me. He rightly observed that *I have yet many things to say unto you, but ye cannot bear them now.*

Jesus carried on regardless. *A little while, and ye shall not see me: and again, a little while, and ye shall see me, because I go to the Father.* The disciples were, as usual, perplexed, and he offered an example.

A woman when she is in travail hath sorrow, because her hour is come: but as soon as she is delivered of the child, she remembereth no more the anguish, for joy that a man is born into the world.

They shouldn't be shy, he said; *ask, and ye shall receive, that your joy may be full.* Jesus conceded that he had never been very clear, *but the time cometh*, he promised, *when I shall no more speak unto you in proverbs, but I shall shew you plainly of the Father.* Fine, his disciples said, *now speakest thou plainly.* I doubt they were satisfied with his response:

Behold, the hour cometh, yea, is now come, that ye shall be scattered, every man to his own, and shall leave me alone: and yet I am not alone, because the Father is with me. These things I have spoken unto you, that in me ye might have peace. In the world ye shall have tribulation: but be of good cheer; I have overcome the world.

In a long prayer, Jesus asked God to protect his disciples. *While I was with them in the world, I kept them in thy name: those that thou gavest me I have kept, and none of them is lost, but the son of perdition; that the scripture might be fulfilled.* 17
I assume that Judas was the lost soul, though once again his reference to scripture had me stumped.

The sometimes messy fate of his disciples suggests that God wasn't paying full attention – a suspicion confirmed when I look back on the next part of the prayer, for unity amongst his future followers. If Jesus didn't get his point across, it certainly wasn't for want of trying; he asked

That they all may be one; as thou, Father, art in me, and I in thee, that they also may be one in us: that the world may believe that thou hast sent me. And the glory which thou gavest me I have given them; that they may be one, even as we are one: I in them, and thou in me, that they may be made perfect in one; and that the world may know that thou hast sent me, and hast loved them, as thou hast loved me.

The world will have to draw its own conclusions.

LAST WORDS

18   That turned out to be almost his last request. Jesus went with his disciples into a garden, whereupon Judas appeared with the arresting party carrying *lanterns and torches and weapons.* They asked for Jesus of Nazareth; *As soon then as he had said unto them, I am he, they went backward, and fell to the ground.* Why they were so clumsy is a mystery, but it's a wonder they didn't start a fire. *Then Simon Peter having a sword drew it, and smote the high priest's servant, and cut off his right ear. The servant's name was Malchus. Then said Jesus unto Peter, Put up thy sword into the sheath.*

There's no mention here of Jesus reaffixing the ear; I can't understand how Peter escaped scot-free, and even waited with the officials while Jesus was being held. Perhaps it does help to explain the denials, though; indeed, *One of the servants of the high priest, being his kinsman whose ear Peter cut off, saith, Did not I see thee in the garden with him?* That's not a conversation you'd want to continue.

The interrogation of Jesus by Pilate was all seriousness on one side and sarcasm on the other. Pilate walked in and asked *Art thou the King of the Jews?* Jesus enquired whether that was his idea, or someone else's. *Pilate answered, Am I a Jew?* He was curious to know how Jesus had managed to offend his own people. When the prisoner said that *My kingdom is not of this world,* Pilate asked *Art thou a king then?* Jesus would have done well to share a laugh at this point, but responded *for this cause came I into the world, that I should bear witness unto the truth.* Pilate, who could see that his humour was wasted, replied *What is truth? And when he had said this, he went out again unto the Jews, and saith unto them, I find in him no fault at all.*

His audience had no desire to see Jesus go free, however. When he was nominated for the holiday amnesty, *Then cried they all again, saying, Not this*
19   *man, but Barabbas. Now Barabbas was a robber.* Pilate had Jesus roughed up and, apparently hoping that the sight might generate some pity, presented to the crowd. *Then came Jesus forth, wearing the crown of thorns, and the purple robe. And Pilate saith unto them, Behold the man!* – *Ecce homo,* if you follow the Latin.

The priests were unrelenting, however. Pilate made one last attempt to find a way out, *but the Jews cried out, saying, If thou let this man go, thou art not Caesar's friend.* He sat in the seat of judgment; *it was the preparation of the passover, and about the sixth hour,* which is neither the day nor the time recorded elsewhere, but sounds about right to me. He demanded *Shall I crucify your King? The chief priests answered, We have no king but Caesar.* That was it: *they took Jesus, and led him away. And he bearing his cross went forth into a place called the place of a skull, which is called in the Hebrew Golgotha: Where they crucified him.*

Pilate wrote a sign to go on the cross, labelling him 'Jesus of Nazareth, King of the Jews'. The priests objected that this should read 'self-proclaimed king', but

Pilate answered, What I have written I have written. He was fed up with people who didn't laugh at his jokes.

Now there stood by the cross of Jesus his mother, and his mother's sister, Mary the wife of Cleophas, and Mary Magdalene. When Jesus therefore saw his mother, and the disciple standing by, whom he loved, he saith unto his mother, Woman, behold thy son! Then saith he to the disciple, Behold thy mother! And from that hour that disciple took her unto his own home. The identity of 'the disciple whom Jesus loved' – odd that it should be so clearly singular – has always been a great mystery. I have my suspicions, but it's not up to me to drag a person out of anonymity.

Having said *I thirst,* and been offered vinegar on a sponge, *he said, It is finished: and he bowed his head, and gave up the ghost.* Soldiers broke the legs of the men crucified on either side of him, *but when they came to Jesus, and saw that he was dead already, they brake not his legs: But one of the soldiers with a spear pierced his side, and forthwith came there out blood and water.*

Joseph of Arimathaea, assisted by Nicodemus, took *the body of Jesus, and wound it in linen clothes with the spices, as the manner of the Jews is to bury. Now in the place where he was crucified there was a garden; and in the garden a new sepulchre, wherein was never man yet laid.* That was where they left him.

JESUS RETURNS

The first day of the week cometh Mary Magdalene early, when it was yet dark, unto the sepulchre, and seeth the stone taken away from the sepulchre. She ran back, telling Peter and *the other disciple, whom Jesus loved,* that the body had disappeared. *So they ran both together: and the other disciple did outrun Peter, and came first to the sepulchre.* There they found only the linen winding cloth.

I'm not sure what they thought had happened, *For as yet they knew not the scripture, that he must rise again from the dead.* The men wandered off, leaving Mary weeping at the tomb. When she looked in, however, she saw two angels sitting where the body had been laid. They asked why she was crying. *Because they have taken away my Lord, and I know not where they have laid him. And when she had thus said, she turned herself back, and saw Jesus standing, and knew not that it was Jesus. Jesus saith unto her, Woman, why weepest thou? whom seekest thou?* She, supposing him to be the gardener, saith unto him, *Sir, if thou hath borne him hence, tell me where thou hast laid him, and I will take him away.*

Had it not been so serious, it would have been a farce: Jesus acting chivalrous and rather blank, Mary taking him for the custodian. When she did recognise him, he said *Touch me not – Noli me tangere – for I am not yet ascended to my Father.* I don't know what difference that made, or why he was being distant. Anyway, she carried a report back to the disciples.

Then the same day at evening, being the first day of the week, when the doors

20

were shut where the disciples were assembled for fear of the Jews, came Jesus and stood in the midst, and saith unto them, Peace be unto you. He showed them his wounds, and said that they would be his envoys, just as he had been God's. *And when he had said this, he breathed on them, and saith unto them, Receive ye the Holy Ghost: Whose soever sins ye remit, they are remitted unto them; and whose soever sins ye retain, they are retained.* With that sort of power, their organisation had quite a future.

The disciple Thomas wasn't there at the time, and when he heard that Jesus was walking around he said *Except I shall see in his hands the print of the nails, and put my finger into the print of the nails, and thrust my hand into his side, I will not believe* – a rash, if rational, statement. A week later, with doubting Thomas in attendance, Jesus once again passed through the locked door. He was solid enough when he wanted to be, though; *Then saith he to Thomas, Reach hither thy finger, and behold my hands; and reach hither thy hand, and thrust it into my side: and be not faithless, but believing. And Thomas answered and said unto him, My Lord and my God. Jesus saith unto him, Thomas, because thou hast seen me, thou hast believed: blessed are they that have not seen, and yet have believed.* I hope this is going to be an exception; there's no telling what people might start to believe.

Once you have things in black and white, of course, it's a different matter. These very words *are written, that ye might believe that Jesus is the Christ, the Son of God; and that believing ye might have life through his name.*

21   That might seem to be the end, but there's more. A number of the disciples had returned to their old trade in Galilee. *Simon Peter saith unto them, I go a fishing. They say unto him, We also go with thee.* They passed the whole night without a nibble. Now in the morning *Jesus stood on the shore: but the disciples knew not that it was Jesus.*

Hearing of their bad luck, *he said unto them, Cast the net on the right side of the ship, and ye shall find. They cast therefore, and now they were not able to draw it for the multitude of fishes. Therefore that disciple whom Jesus loved saith unto Peter, It is the Lord. Now when Simon Peter heard that it was the Lord, he girt his fisher's coat unto him, (for he was naked,) and did cast himself into the sea,* racing for the beach.

You could always rely on Peter for comic relief. Back on shore, Jesus was grilling fish and bread over a fire. Having hauled in the net, in which were 153 large fish, they accepted his invitation to breakfast. *And none of the disciples durst ask him, Who art thou? knowing that it was the Lord.* I'd have expected them to ask something, though.

After they had eaten, it was Jesus who did the asking. He quizzed Peter, *Simon, son of Jonas, lovest thou me more than these? He saith unto him, Yea, Lord; thou knowest that I love thee. He saith unto him, Feed my lambs.* Jesus repeated the question, Peter repeated the answer, and Jesus replied *Feed my sheep.* When Jesus went through the routine a third time, Peter felt aggrieved, *And he said unto him, Lord, thou knowest all things; thou knowest that I love thee. Jesus saith unto him, Feed my sheep.*

It's not wholly clear what that was all about. One assumes that Peter was being told to look after the flock, the thrice-repeated affirmation being intended to cancel out the previous denials. He was going to share the fate of Jesus, it seemed. *When thou wast young, thou girdedst thyself, and walkedst whither thou wouldest: but when thou shalt be old, thou shalt stretch forth thy hands, and another shall gird thee, and carry thee whither thou wouldest not. This spake he, signifying by what death he should glorify God.* Not a riddle one enjoyed solving, God's glory notwithstanding.

Jesus said *Follow me. Then Peter, turning about, seeth the disciple whom Jesus loved following; which also leaned on his breast at supper, and said, Lord, which is he that betrayeth thee? Peter seeing him saith to Jesus, Lord, and what shall this man do? Jesus saith unto him, If I will that he tarry till I come, what is that to thee?*

The point here, I should say, is not that they were habitually jealous and rude, but that the earlier records stood in need of correction. Contrary to Jesus' promise, the kingdom of God hadn't arrived in the lifetime of his companions. To sidestep the embarrassment, my friends suggested that there had been a misunderstanding; of his beloved disciple, *Jesus said not unto him, He shall not die; but, If I will that he tarry till I come, what is that to thee?* Hope that clears things up.

Incidentally, the mysterious loved one *is the disciple which testified of these things, and wrote these things: and we know that his testimony is true. And there are also many other things which Jesus did, the which, if they should be written every one, I suppose that even the world itself could not contain the books that should be written. Amen.*

5

The Acts of the Apostles

1   It would be a shame to leave the story there, especially since I've hardly made an appearance yet. Happily our friend Luke produced a sequel to his biography. He reminded its dedicatee where he had left off:

> *The former treatise have I made, O Theophilus, of all that Jesus began both to do and teach, Until the day in which he was taken up, after that he through the Holy Ghost had given commandments unto the apostles whom he had chosen: To whom also he shewed himself alive after his passion by many infallible proofs, being seen of them forty days.*

That's thirty-nine days longer than he previously told us; if he had written a third volume, Jesus might never have made it back to heaven at all.

What's more, Jesus wasn't about to let them go fishing in Galilee. He ordered the disciples to stay in Jerusalem; *ye shall be baptized with the Holy Ghost not many days hence.* Having given them their orders, *he was taken up; and a cloud received him out of their sight.* They were still staring up at the sky when *behold, two men stood by them in white apparel; Which also said, Ye men of Galilee, why stand ye gazing up into heaven?* Jesus would be coming back down the same way he went up, the angels said. (Regrettably they didn't specify when.)

The disciples returned to their upper room in the city. They *continued with one accord in prayer and supplication, with the women, and Mary the mother of Jesus, and with his brethren.* As a family we had had our differences with his followers, but these had been put aside.

One day when everyone was gathered – it was quite a crowd, about 120 people – Peter stood up and proposed naming a replacement for Judas. Matthew wrote that he had hanged himself, but Luke could do better than that: *Now this man purchased a field with the reward of iniquity; and falling headlong, he burst asunder in the midst, and all his bowels gushed out. And it was known unto all the dwellers at Jerusalem* – except Matthew, I suppose – and so the place is now called *The field of blood.*

Anyway, to qualify as twelfth man a nominee would need to have been with Jesus throughout, *Beginning from the baptism of John, unto that same day that he was taken up from us.* They found two candidates, *And they prayed, and said, Thou, Lord, which knowest the hearts of all men, shew whether of these two thou hast chosen.* A lottery was the approved method of soliciting divine guidance, *and the lot fell upon Matthias; and he was numbered with the eleven apostles.* Perhaps we should decide everything that way.

Seven weeks after passover comes the festival known as Shevuoth, or Pentecost. 2 *And when the day of Pentecost was fully come, they were all with one accord in one place. And suddenly there came a sound from heaven as of a rushing mighty wind, and it filled all the house where they were sitting. And there appeared unto them cloven tongues like as of fire, and it sat upon each of them. And they were all filled with the Holy Ghost, and began to speak with other tongues, as the Spirit gave them utterance.*

They didn't stay inside, however, because word of this phenomenon spread through Jerusalem: *every man heard them speak in his own language.* Needless to say, all were amazed. *Parthians, and Medes, and Elamites, and the dwellers in Mesopotamia, and in Judaea, and Cappadocia, in Pontus, and Asia, Phrygia, and Pamphylia, in Egypt, and in the parts of Libya about Cyrene, and strangers of Rome, Jews and proselytes, Cretes and Arabians, we do hear them speak in our tongues the wonderful works of God.*

I should qualify my statement; not everyone was impressed. *Others mocking said, These men are full of new wine.* Peter pointed out that it was too early: *these are not drunken, as ye suppose, seeing it is but the third hour of the day.* He argued that they were simply fulfilling a prophecy, though I fear he over-sold the event: the prophet Joel was describing judgment day in the relevant passage. Peter took even more extravagant liberties with a certain psalm, claiming that David foresaw *the resurrection of Christ, that his soul was not left in hell, neither his flesh did see corruption.*

Peter told them that *God hath made that same Jesus, whom ye have crucified, both Lord and Christ.* They were rather cut up by this, and asked *what shall we do? Then Peter said unto them, Repent.* They could still save themselves from the crimes of their generation. *Then they that gladly received his word were baptized: and the same day there were added unto them about three thousand souls.*

The movement seemed to be doing better without my brother than with him. Not even his special powers were missed; *many wonders and signs were done by the apostles. And all that believed were together, and had all things common; And sold their possessions and goods, and parted them to all men, as every man had need.* The leadership would come to need quite a lot, but at this stage everyone was trying to be a good communist.

One day as Peter and John went to afternoon prayers in the temple they passed 3 a beggar, a man crippled from birth. *Peter said, Silver and gold have I none; but such as I have give I thee: In the name of Jesus Christ of Nazareth rise up and walk. And he took him by the right hand, and lifted him up: and immediately his feet and ankle bones received strength. And he leaping up stood, and walked, and entered with them into the temple, walking, and leaping, and praising God.*

Peter disclaimed any special ability; all he did was invoke the name. (The general opinion was that a name carried with it some of the authority of the person, and that speaking the name called up that power.) It was time to repent, and to recognise Jesus, *For Moses truly said unto the fathers, A prophet shall the Lord your God raise up unto you ... And it shall come to pass, that every soul, which will not hear that prophet, shall be destroyed from among the people.*

PROBLEMS WITH AUTHORITY

4   The numbers of the faithful kept rising, but after this latest escapade Peter and John spent the night in a cell. The religious authorities demanded *By what power, or by what name, have ye done this?* Peter exercised his customary level of diplomacy by citing *the name of Jesus Christ of Nazareth, whom ye crucified,* and stressing that *Neither is there salvation in any other: for there is none other name under heaven given among men, whereby we must be saved.* It's Jesus or bust.

Now when they saw the boldness of Peter and John, and perceived that they were unlearned and ignorant men, they marvelled; the problem with being a priest is that there's always some provincial fisherman who thinks he knows better. They told Peter and John to give the preaching a rest, but the apostles declined to accept the order. They were released anyway; while people were so excited about the miracle cure, there was little else to be done.

Back home in the commune, they prayed until the building rocked; *the place was shaken where they were assembled together; and they were all filled with the Holy Ghost, and they spake the word of God with boldness. And the multitude of them that believed were of one heart and of one soul: neither said any of them that ought of the things which he possessed was his own; but they had all things in common. ... Neither was there any among them that lacked: for as many as were possessors of lands or houses sold them, and brought the prices of the things that were sold, And laid them down at the apostles' feet: and distribution was made unto every man according as he had need.*

5   When you're promoting communism, experience shows that purging a few helps to encourage the many. A man named Ananias and his wife Sapphira sold property, donating some – not all – of the proceeds to the movement. *But Peter said, Ananias, why hath Satan filled thine heart to lie to the Holy Ghost, and to keep back part of the price of the land? ... thou hast not lied unto men, but unto God. And Ananias hearing these words fell down,* and died on the spot.

And it was about the space of three hours after, when his wife, not knowing what was done, came in. And Peter answered unto her, Tell me whether ye sold the land for so much? And she said, Yea, for so much. Then Peter said unto her, How is it that ye have agreed together to tempt the Spirit of the Lord? behold, the feet of them which have buried thy husband are at the door, and shall carry thee out. Then fell she down straightway at his feet, and yielded up the ghost. A show trial, public confession and repentance are the usual preliminaries to execution, but death under interrogation is an accepted alternative.

And by the hands of the apostles were many signs and wonders wrought among the people, though it's hardly surprising that common folk tried to stay out of their way. Recruitment among the masses continued to bring good results, adding *multitudes both of men and women*. Although he had disclaimed any personal power, Peter was looking more regal by the day, *Insomuch that they brought forth the sick into the streets, and laid them on beds and couches, that at the least the shadow of Peter passing by might overshadow some of them. There came also a multitude out of the cities round about unto Jerusalem, bringing sick folks, and them which were vexed with unclean spirits: and they were healed every one.* Communists like to be pioneers in popular health care.

The authorities were less than happy to have this band of agitators on the loose. They *laid their hands on the apostles, and put them in the common prison. But the angel of the Lord by night opened the prison doors, and brought them forth*; their agents had infiltrated every department of the state. The apostles went straight back to their soap boxes before being rearrested and brought before the council.

There, the high priest demanded *Did not we straitly command you that ye should not teach in this name? and, behold, ye have filled Jerusalem with your doctrine.* The apostles didn't believe in conciliation (*The God of our fathers raised up Jesus, whom ye slew and hanged on a tree*) and were facing premature martyrdom when a Pharisee named Gamaliel intervened. Sending the prisoners outside, he gave the council some advice on dealing with revolutionaries.

He reminded them that *before these days rose up Theudas, boasting himself to be somebody;* when he was killed, however, his followers *were scattered, and brought to nought. After this man rose up Judas of Galilee in the days of the taxing, and drew away much people after him: he also perished; and all, even as many as obeyed him, were dispersed.* Rebels, rabble-rousers and saviours came and went with the seasons; his advice was to *let them alone: for if this counsel or this work be of men, it will come to nought: But if it be of God, ye cannot overthrow it.*

The apostles were let off with a beating, and renewed orders not to *speak in the name of Jesus.* They left *rejoicing that they were counted worthy to suffer shame for his name,* and promptly went back to preaching the good news about the messiah.

THE RISE AND FALL OF STEPHEN

Having encouraged each to give according to his ability, the apostles were then confronted with problems at the receiving end. As often happens there was an ethnic element in the dispute, which was between the foreign and native followers: *there arose a murmuring of the Grecians against the Hebrews, because their widows were neglected in the daily ministration.* The apostles didn't regard doling out charity as part of their job description; as they told everyone, *It is not reason that we should leave the word of God, and serve tables.*

A dose of tough-minded managerial discipline was just what the movement needed, I think. They were never going to get anywhere by following my brother's example and washing feet. Thus they proposed finding seven of the more capable Greek speakers, *whom we may appoint over this business.* The main apostolic board would set policy, stay in touch with God, and continue to expand the enterprise, while the new subsidiary would focus on the ethnic market in Jerusalem.

And the saying pleased the whole multitude: and they chose Stephen, a man full of faith and of the Holy Ghost, and Philip, and five others. The new appointees were a great success. *Stephen, full of faith and power, did great wonders and miracles among the people.*

Then there arose certain of the synagogue, which is called the synagogue of the Libertines – always one of my favourites – *disputing with Stephen. And they were not able to resist the wisdom and the spirit by which he spake.* Resisting was a problem for them, of course. Determined to see him tried by the council, they *set up false witnesses, which said, This man ceaseth not to speak blasphemous words against this holy place, and the law: For we have heard him say, that this Jesus of Nazareth shall destroy this place, and shall change the customs which Moses delivered us.* That doesn't sound so far from the truth to me, but he sat there looking as though butter wouldn't melt in his mouth, *And all that sat in the council, looking stedfastly on him, saw his face as it had been the face of an angel.*

7   *Then said the high priest, Are these things so?* If Stephen had been content to be quiet and look angelic he might have escaped with a slap on the wrist. Instead he expounded, at length, his view of the entire course of Jewish history from Abraham onwards. (New religious leaders feel compelled to do this.) There were minor departures from scripture, but nothing too shocking during the first thousand words or so, unless you count his belief that an angel rather than God himself had spoken to Moses at Mount Sinai. Suddenly, however, he saw fit to lecture them.

> *Ye stiffnecked and uncircumcised in heart and ears, ye do always resist the Holy Ghost: as your fathers did, so do ye. Which of the prophets have not your fathers persecuted? and they have slain them which shewed before of the coming of the Just One; of whom ye have been now the betrayers and murderers: Who have received the law by the disposition of angels, and have not kept it.*

This, clearly, was a man who wanted to be a prophet. His audience didn't respond too well; *they gnashed on him with their teeth.* Stephen, meanwhile, was entering into the higher stages of religious ecstasy, *And said, Behold, I see the heavens opened, and the Son of man standing on the right hand of God.*

I'm afraid that was the last straw. *Then they cried out with a loud voice, and stopped their ears, and ran upon him with one accord, And cast him out of the city, and stoned him.* It was a big day for the cause; not only did Stephen become its first post-crucifixion martyr, but we caught a glimpse of the man who would do more for the movement than anyone, bar none, except maybe Jesus. It was a highly charged moment, when *the witnesses laid down their clothes at a young man's feet, whose name was Saul* – better known later as Paul. I don't know quite what role he played – Stephen, incidentally, had cried out *Lord, lay not this sin to their charge* – but *Saul was consenting unto his death.*

8

THE ROAD TO DAMASCUS

And at that time there was a great persecution against the church which was at Jerusalem; and they were all scattered abroad throughout the regions of Judaea and Samaria, except the apostles. It was very kind of them to have left the ringleaders in place. *As for Saul, he made havock of the church, entering into every house, and haling men and women committed them to prison.*

Philip, one of the leaders of the foreigners, went to Samaria to preach. The people there were delighted, *hearing and seeing the miracles which he did. For unclean spirits, crying with loud voice, came out of many that were possessed with them: and many taken with palsies, and that were lame, were healed.* Even the resident magician, a fellow named Simon of whom everyone had said *This man is the great power of God*, became a believer.

Now when the apostles which were at Jerusalem heard that Samaria had received the word of God, they sent unto them Peter and John – to close the sale, you might say. The converts had been baptized, but no one had as yet been possessed by the Holy Ghost. A simple laying-on of hands by the distinguished visitors took care of that.

Thinking that this was a great trick, Simon the sorcerer *offered them money, Saying, Give me also this power, that on whomsoever I lay hands, he may receive the Holy Ghost.* Peter wasn't about to start franchising the operation:

Thy money perish with thee, because thou hast thought that the gift of God may be purchased with money. Thou hast neither part nor lot in this matter: for thy heart is not right in the sight of God. Repent therefore of this thy wickedness, and pray God, if perhaps the thought of thine heart may be forgiven thee. For I perceive that thou art in the gall of bitterness, and in the bond of iniquity.

Simon must have been rude, lazy, or – most likely, I imagine – superstitious, because he told Peter to do it himself: *Pray ye to the Lord for me, that none of these things which ye have spoken come upon me.*

The apostles went back to Jerusalem, while Philip was visited by *the angel of the Lord*, telling him to go south towards the Gaza road. On his way he came across *a man of Ethiopia, an eunuch of great authority under Candace queen of the Ethiopians*. The fellow was passing his time with the book of Isaiah. Philip took the opportunity to discuss both scripture and Jesus, and before long the man was volunteering for baptism. *And when they were come up out of the water, the Spirit of the Lord caught away Philip, that the eunuch saw him no more: and he went on his way rejoicing.* (Philip's departure could have that effect.) Philip, transported back to the north, continued his preaching.

9   *And Saul, yet breathing out threatenings and slaughter against the disciples of the Lord,* arranged to travel to Damascus to arrest anyone following 'the way', as we called it. A funny thing happened on the road to Damascus. The sky was lit up, *And he fell to the earth, and heard a voice saying unto him, Saul, Saul, why persecutest thou me? And he said, Who art thou, Lord? And the Lord said, I am Jesus whom thou persecutest: it is hard for thee to kick against the pricks.*

There are so many of them, for a start. What he meant was that Saul, like a mule kicking against the switch, was just making life hard for himself. Clearly the man's conscience was troubled. Jesus had little more to say, and Saul, who had been struck blind, was led by his companions into the city. Meanwhile a divine message was delivered to a disciple named Ananias (not the half-hearted benefactor, obviously), instructing him to *Arise, and go into the street which is called Straight, and enquire in the house of Judas for one called Saul, of Tarsus.* Given Saul's reputation this sounded like an especially bad idea, *But the Lord said unto him, Go thy way: for he is a chosen vessel unto me, to bear my name before the Gentiles, and kings, and the children of Israel.*

Ananias found Saul, laid hands on him, and said that he had been sent from Jesus, *that thou mightest receive thy sight, and be filled with the Holy Ghost. And immediately there fell from his eyes as it had been scales.* Before long his strength returned, *And straightway he preached Christ in the synagogues, that he is the Son of God.* Naturally this created quite a stir, coming from a known enemy of the sect. After a time *the Jews took counsel to kill him* – Saul had a knack for making himself unpopular – but he escaped to Jerusalem.

I'd have to admit that he met a cool reception; you hesitate to be too gullible in these matters. Barnabas, one of our benefactors, vouched for him, and before long Saul was offending people all over the city. When the Greek-speaking Jews decided to kill him, we sent him a few hundred miles up the coast to Tarsus for his own good.

Then had the churches rest throughout all Judaea and Galilee and Samaria, and were edified; and walking in the fear of the Lord, and in the comfort of the Holy Ghost, were multiplied. Those were the good old days, with Saul off our backs, but not yet organising the Gentile take-over.

Peter was getting better and better at imitating my brother. Sometimes, of course, he didn't hit exactly the right note. On one visit *to the saints which dwelt at Lydda,* he found a man who had been paralysed for eight years. *And Peter said unto him, Aeneas, Jesus Christ maketh thee whole: arise, and make thy bed.* Put them right to work, I'd tell him.

To give Peter credit, though, he was just as handy as Jesus had been when it came to miracle cures. He even achieved the ultimate on *a certain disciple named Tabitha, which by interpretation is called Dorcas* (i.e. Gazelle): *this woman was full of good works.* Unfortunately, she died. Peter was summoned to the bedside, where *all the widows stood by him weeping, and shewing the coats and garments which Dorcas made, while she was with them.* Clearly a hard woman to replace.

Peter sent them all out, prayed, *and turning him to the body said, Tabitha, arise. And she opened her eyes: and when she saw Peter, she sat up. And he gave her his hand, and lifted her up, and when he had called the saints and widows, presented her alive.* Only men were saints, but at least the widows had their seamstress back.

THE FIRST GENTILE

There was a certain man in Caesarea called Cornelius, a centurion, who was a   10
generous supporter of the Jewish people. One day he had a visit from an angel
telling him that word of his deeds had reached God, and that he should *send men
to Joppa, and call for one Simon, whose surname is Peter.* This he did.

Peter, meanwhile, was up on the roof praying. *And he became very hungry,
and would have eaten: but while they made ready, he fell into a trance, And saw
heaven opened, and a certain vessel descending unto him, as it had been a great
sheet knit at the four corners, and let down to the earth: Wherein were all manner
of four-footed beasts of the earth, and wild beasts, and creeping things, and fowls
of the air. And there came a voice to him, Rise, Peter; kill, and eat. But Peter
said, Not so, Lord; for I have never eaten any thing that is common or unclean.
And the voice spake unto him again the second time, What God hath cleansed,
that call not thou common.*

This invitation was repeated three times, before the giant tablecloth rose back
up into the clouds. *Now while Peter doubted in himself what this vision which he
had seen should mean* – it seemed so unlike God to insist that he eat exotic food
– the messengers arrived at the door. *While Peter thought on the vision, the Spirit
said unto him, Behold, three men seek thee. Arise therefore, and get thee down,
and go with them.*

When Peter arrived in Caesarea, *Cornelius met him, and fell down at his feet,
and worshipped him. But Peter took him up, saying, Stand up; I myself also am
a man.* Talking to his host's friends and relatives, he said *Ye know how that it is
an unlawful thing for a man that is a Jew to keep company, or come unto one of
another nation; but God hath shewed me that I should not call any man common
or unclean.* Not if he was edible, anyway.

When Cornelius related his story of the angelic summons, *Peter opened his
mouth, and said, Of a truth I perceive that God is no respecter of persons: But
in every nation he that feareth him, and worketh righteousness, is accepted with
him.* That's the inclusive part. They would have heard, though, *How God anointed
Jesus of Nazareth with the Holy Ghost and with power: who went about doing
good, and healing all that were oppressed of the devil;* how he was made to appear
after his execution, *Not to all the people, but unto witnesses chosen before of God.*

Jesus intends to be exclusive; *it is he which was ordained of God to be the Judge of quick and dead. To him give all the prophets witness, that through his name whosoever believeth in him shall receive remission of sins.*

As Peter was talking, *the Holy Ghost fell on all them which heard the word.* The circumcised Jewish followers were astonished to see this happen to Gentiles, *For they heard them speak with tongues, and magnify God.* Peter asked if anyone thought *that these should not be baptized, which have received the Holy Ghost as well as we?* Apparently no one objected, though with them being already possessed by the Holy Ghost, baptism seemed redundant to me.

11   *And the apostles and brethren that were in Judaea heard that the Gentiles had also received the word of God.* When Peter returned they protested to him that *Thou wentest in to men uncircumcised, and didst eat with them.* He told them the whole story, asking in his own defence *what was I, that I could withstand God?*

In fact, the writing was on the wall; we were losing control of the sect. My brother had wanted his followers to be better Jews, and now we were being joined by people who weren't Jews at all. Although most of the disciples who emigrated after Stephen's death preached only to other Jews, some of those settling in the large city of Antioch were less careful; they would turn just anyone into a believer. *Then tidings of these things came unto the ears of the church which was in Jerusalem: and they sent forth Barnabas,* to investigate. He was impressed by what he found, and brought Saul in from Tarsus to assist. *And it came to pass, that a whole year they assembled themselves with the church, and taught much people. And the disciples were called Christians first in Antioch.*

And in these days came prophets from Jerusalem unto Antioch. One of them, Agabus, predicted a great famine *throughout all the world: which came to pass in the days of Claudius Caesar,* at least if a moderate shortage in Judaea fulfils the prophecy. The faithful sent food relief to the mother country.

12   *Now about that time Herod the king stretched forth his hands to vex certain of the church. And he killed James the brother of John with the sword,* which did make us cross. *And because he saw it pleased the Jews, he proceeded further to take Peter also,* who was chained and kept under constant guard. Time was getting short when, *behold, the angel of the Lord came upon him, and a light shined in the prison: and he smote Peter on the side, and raised him up, saying, Arise up quickly. And his chains fell off from his hands.* The angel made Peter get dressed – the proprieties must be observed – and then they walked past one guardpost, and then another, and then *the iron gate that leadeth unto the city; which opened to them of his own accord.*

Only when he was safely out in the street did Peter realise that he hadn't been dreaming, *that the Lord hath sent his angel, and hath delivered me out of the hand of Herod, and from all the expectation of the people of the Jews.* He made his way to a supporter's house, *where many were gathered together praying. And as Peter knocked at the door of the gate, a damsel came to hearken, named Rhoda. And when she knew Peter's voice, she opened not the gate for gladness, but ran in, and told how Peter stood before the gate.* Clearly she wasn't going to win any prizes for common sense, but it seemed a bit hard when *they said unto her, Thou art mad. But she constantly affirmed that it was even so. Then said they, It is his angel.*

Peter, meanwhile, was still banging at the gate; a few minutes more and he would have been back in prison for disturbing the peace. They finally let him in, and he told them what had happened. *And he said, Go shew these things unto James, and to the brethren,* because by that time I was taking over from the old boys: a case of blood being stronger than water, you might say.

Now as soon as it was day, there was no small stir among the soldiers, what was become of Peter. And when Herod had sought for him, and found him not, he examined the keepers, and commanded that they should be put to death. I enjoy miraculous escapes as much as the next man, but I do fault God for not protecting the innocent from reprisals.

That said, God has always been an expert on retribution. A group of petitioners being present, *Herod, arrayed in royal apparel, sat upon his throne, and made an oration unto them. And the people gave a shout, saying, It is the voice of a god, and not of a man. And immediately the angel of the Lord smote him, because he gave not God the glory: and he was eaten of worms, and gave up the ghost. But the word of God grew and multiplied;* a little encouragement works wonders.

SPREADING THE WORD

Various prophets and teachers were now in Antioch. *As they ministered to the* 13 *Lord, and fasted, the Holy Ghost said, Separate me Barnabas and Saul for the work whereunto I have called them.* The Holy Ghost was not usually very talkative, so they didn't waste any time in travelling to Cyprus, where *they preached the word of God in the synagogues of the Jews.*

They had an opportunity to convert the governor, but a certain sorcerer was making things difficult for them. *Then Saul, (who also is called Paul,) filled with the Holy Ghost, set his eyes on him, And said, O full of all subtilty and all mischief, thou child of the devil, thou enemy of all righteousness, wilt thou not cease to pervert the right ways of the Lord?* As anyone can tell you, he was born to be a preacher. He told the man *thou shalt be blind* – something of a reverse healing – and the fellow *went about seeking some to lead him by the hand.* The governor, *when he saw what was done, believed, being astonished at the doctrine of the Lord.* He didn't become proconsul by taking unnecessary risks.

The missionaries continued their travels. The leaders of the synagogues were most hospitable, I thought; in one town they invited the visitors to preach, *saying, Ye men and brethren, if ye have any word of exhortation for the people, say on.* Paul didn't hesitate to abuse the welcome, proclaiming on behalf of Jesus that *by him all that believe are justified from all things, from which ye could not be justified by the law of Moses.*

Not surprisingly the local Jews lost patience with Paul and Barnabas, who declared in turn that they had forfeited their privileged access to the gospel; *seeing ye put it from you, and judge yourselves unworthy of everlasting life, lo, we turn to the Gentiles.* That will teach them. The Gentiles were grateful for the attention, *and glorified the word of the Lord: and as many as were ordained to eternal life believed.* For anyone else – those not marked for immortality – trying to be faithful is a waste of time: you can't fight predestination.

14   Paul and Barnabas moved on to another town. There as well, unfortunately, *the unbelieving Jews stirred up the Gentiles, and made their minds evil affected against the brethren.* They resumed their travels, and Paul was able to heal *a certain man at Lystra, impotent in his feet, being a cripple from his mother's womb, who never had walked.* Seeing the man erect and active, the people declared *The gods are come down to us in the likeness of men.*

They decided that Barnabas was Jupiter, and Paul Mercury, *because he was the chief speaker.* Their priest was on the point of sacrificing oxen for the god-like visitors when Barnabas and Paul *rent their clothes, and ran in among the people, crying out, And saying, Sirs, why do ye these things? We also are men of like passions with you, and preach unto you that ye should turn from these vanities unto the living God.*

It was most disappointing. *And there came thither certain Jews from Antioch and Iconium* – part of the international Jewish conspiracy, no doubt – *who persuaded the people, and, having stoned Paul, drew him out of the city, supposing he had been dead.* They supposed wrong, though; Paul got back on his feet and returned to town. I don't know whether he was brave, foolish or a glutton for punishment, but the man was certainly unusual.

He did leave with Barnabas the following day, thankfully. They moved from city to city preaching the good news, and also the bad, *that we must through much tribulation enter into the kingdom of God.* Ultimately they returned safely to Antioch, *And there they abode long time with the disciples.*

15   *And certain men which came down from Judaea taught the brethren, and said, Except ye be circumcised after the manner of Moses, ye cannot be saved.* So began the great penile fashion debate. When the arguments became fierce, Paul, Barnabas and various others travelled to Jerusalem for a meeting of all the apostles and elders.

The foreign missionaries arrived *declaring the conversion of the Gentiles*, which sounded like a good thing. A group of Christian Pharisees, however, said *That it was needful to circumcise them, and to command them to keep the law of Moses.* Here was the crux of the matter. Jesus, after all, had been a Jew preaching to Jews, taking for granted a belief in scripture and a willingness to conform to the Law, rightly interpreted. It didn't make sense to belong to a reformation movement if you had no intention of participating in what was being reformed. God had given Abraham instructions about the sort of penis he liked to see, and that was that.

As against this, Peter argued that God had decided to let the Gentiles join the party, *giving them the Holy Ghost, even as he did unto us.* Barnabas and Paul added their testimony. *And after they had held their peace,* it was left to me to find a solution; *James answered, saying, Men and brethren, hearken unto me: ... my sentence is, that we trouble not them, which from among the Gentiles are turned to God: But that we write unto them, that they abstain from pollutions of idols, and from fornication, and from things strangled, and from blood.* It was a reasonable compromise, if I say so myself. Cosmetic surgery in delicate places wouldn't be required, but some of the more overtly offensive practices would be discouraged.

This Council at Jerusalem concluded with the choice of two emissaries to accompany Paul and Barnabas back to Antioch, there to deliver the reassuring message to the faithful – *Which when they had read, they rejoiced for the consolation,* as you might well imagine. Any more onerous demands might have hindered our appeal considerably.

PAUL'S SECOND MISSION

And some days after Paul said unto Barnabas, Let us go again and visit our brethren in every city where we have preached the word of the Lord, and see how they do. Barnabas was agreeable, and proposed to take a certain John Mark along as travelling companion. Because of some personal history between them, Paul refused to have him along. *And the contention was so sharp between them, that they departed asunder one from the other: and so Barnabas took Mark, and sailed unto Cyprus; And Paul chose Silas, and departed.* It's always a shame to see established twosomes split up, particularly when it causes division in the church.

So began an unsettled time for Paul, acquiring new disciples, but constantly on the move. He found someone named Timothy, who had a Jewish mother and a Gentile father; wanting to take the fellow on his travels, Paul circumcised him. I don't know what was on his mind; Paul had always been among the leaders of the foreskin toleration tendency. Perhaps he was concerned about Jewish sensibilities, but that wouldn't have been characteristic. 16

As the troupe moved north and west, they *were forbidden of the Holy Ghost to preach the word in Asia.* There are foreigners and there are foreigners, after all. Thinking of heading east, the Spirit of Jesus (that's a new one) *suffered them not,* and so they ended up on the coast. *And a vision appeared to Paul in the night; There stood a man of Macedonia, and prayed him saying, Come over into Macedonia, and help us.*

They sailed to the northern end of the Aegean, ending up at Philippi. Things were looking good, until Paul lost his temper with a slave girl who possessed – or was possessed by – special powers. As Luke reports, she *brought her masters much gain by soothsaying: The same followed Paul and us, and cried, saying, These men are the servants of the most high God, which shew unto us the way of salvation. And this did she many days. But Paul, being grieved, turned and said to the spirit, I command thee in the name of Jesus Christ to come out of her. And he came out the same hour.*

When the girl's owners saw that she was ruined as a fortune-teller, they had Paul and Silas brought before magistrates, stripped, flogged, and chained in a cell. *And at midnight Paul and Silas prayed, and sang praises unto God*; that sort of treatment never seemed to dampen their spirits. *And suddenly there was a great earthquake, so that the foundations of the prison were shaken and immediately all the doors were opened, and every one's bands were loosed. And the keeper of the prison awaking out of his sleep, and seeing the prison doors open, he drew out his sword, and would have killed himself, supposing that the prisoners had been fled. But Paul cried with a loud voice, saying, Do thyself no harm: for we are all here.*

The superintendent was abject; he *fell down before Paul and Silas, And brought them out, and said, Sirs, what must I do to be saved? And they said, Believe on the Lord Jesus Christ, and thou shalt be saved.* He took them home, *and washed their stripes; and was baptized, he and all his, straightway.* Never mind circumcision, a bit of religious education before conversion wouldn't go amiss.

In the morning the magistrates sent word that they were free to leave the city, but that wasn't enough for Paul. He stood on his rights as a Roman citizen. The magistrates were alarmed to hear this, offering an apology for the public beating and subsequent bondage. One can only wonder why Paul didn't make his status known at the time.

17   The missionaries moved on to Thessalonica; after preaching in the synagogue for three weeks running, Paul was beginning to make converts. *But the Jews which believed not, moved with envy, took unto them certain lewd fellows of the baser sort, and gathered a company, and set all the city on an uproar.* Not finding the preachers at home, the mob took Jason, their host, *unto the rulers of the city, crying, These that have turned the world upside down are come hither also; Whom Jason hath received: and these all do contrary to the decrees of Caesar, saying that there is another king, one Jesus.*

Jason was released, but the faithful thought it best to pack the visitors off to their next stop. Unfortunately some outside agitators made life difficult for them there, too, and so Paul was shipped on to Athens. Although Silas and Timothy stayed behind, Paul sent for them the moment he arrived.

Now while Paul waited for them at Athens, his spirit was stirred in him, when he saw the city wholly given to idolatry. In fact it was a free market in ideas: the people were willing to consider, if not to believe, anything. He wasn't confined to the synagogue; *certain philosophers of the Epicureans, and of the Stoicks, encountered him. And some said, What will this babbler say?* Others explained that he was promoting the worship of foreign gods named 'Jesus' and 'Resurrection'.

Being intellectually curious, his audience invited him to address the council in a more formal setting. *(For all the Athenians and strangers which were there spent their time in nothing else, but either to tell, or to hear some new thing.) Then Paul stood in the midst of Mars' hill, and said,*

Ye men of Athens, I perceive that in all things ye are too superstitious. For as I passed by, and beheld your devotions, I found an altar with this inscription, TO THE UNKNOWN GOD. Whom therefore ye ignorantly worship, him declare I unto you. God that made the world and all things therein, seeing that he is Lord of heaven and earth, dwelleth not in temples made with hands; Neither is worshipped with men's hands, as though he needed any thing, seeing he giveth to all life, and breath, and all things; And hath made of one blood all nations of men for to dwell on all the face of the earth.

This God is not hard to find, *For in him we live, and move, and have our being; as certain also of your own poets have said, For we are also his offspring.* For a long time it didn't matter if you didn't look; *this ignorance God winked at.* Now, however, he orders people everywhere to repent, because he has scheduled a day of judgment. He has also chosen a judge, reinforcing that choice by raising him from the dead.

And when they heard of the resurrection of the dead, some mocked: and others said, We will hear thee again of this matter. So Paul departed from among them, never to return. I find that a shame, myself. Debating the free-thinkers in Athens was perhaps less heroic than braving persecution elsewhere, and the number of converts might have been disappointing, but doctrine can always benefit from rational inquiry.

Paul moved on to Corinth. There he moved in with a Jewish couple named   18
Aquila and Priscilla; as they were all tent-makers by trade, it was a convenient arrangement. He continued to visit the synagogue, apparently without causing an uproar. The arrival of Silas and Timothy seemed to light a fire in him, though; he *testified to the Jews that Jesus was Christ. And when they opposed themselves, and blasphemed, he shook his raiment, and said unto them, Your blood be upon your own heads; I am clean: from henceforth I will go unto the Gentiles.*

Converts still came forward. *Then spake the Lord to Paul in the night by a vision, Be not afraid ... I have much people in this city.* He carried on preaching there for a year and a half.

A remarkable incident occurred when a certain Galio was proconsul. The Jews brought Paul before his court, but the case was thrown out before it had properly begun. Galio declared that he was concerned with crimes, not theological disputes. *Then all the Greeks took Sosthenes, the chief ruler of the synagogue, and beat him before the judgment seat. And Galio cared for none of those things.* Now that we could beat up our enemies with impunity, I felt sure we were on the road to success.

Eventually Paul left for Syria, shaving his head as part of a vow before sailing across the sea. (I have no idea why he did it; one can only guess what impelled him to join a ship-load of sailors with a bald head.) After a stop-over in Ephesus he continued his journey as far as Antioch, where he remained for some time before setting out on another grand tour.

PAUL'S THIRD MISSION

And a certain Jew named Apollos, born at Alexandria, an eloquent man, and mighty in the scriptures, came to Ephesus. It wasn't clear that he had ever been properly baptized, let alone had the Holy Ghost descend on him, but we didn't turn away the likes of him. He was a great asset; *he mightily convinced the Jews, and that publickly, shewing by the scriptures that Jesus was Christ.*

19   Apollos ended up in Corinth, while Paul came back to Ephesus. There he found a number of believers, and asked them whether they had received the Holy Ghost. *And they said unto him, We have not so much as heard whether there be any Holy Ghost.* It didn't take Paul long to put things right; he rebaptized them – they had previously only had the inferior John-style baptism – and *the Holy Ghost came on them; and they spake with tongues, and prophesied.* If that's the sign of success, there's a lot of remedial work to be done.

After a few months Paul withdrew his followers from the synagogue, but he continued teaching in the area for two years. *And God wrought special miracles by the hands of Paul:* handkerchiefs or other bits of cloth that he had touched were taken to the sick, *and the diseases departed from them, and the evil spirits went out of them.*

Naturally he had imitators, but no one else really developed the knack. There were, notably, *certain of the vagabond Jews, exorcists,* who ordered out demons in the name of Jesus. One day seven of them were at work when *the evil spirit answered and said, Jesus I know, and Paul I know; but who are ye?* The possessed man leapt up and assaulted them with such ferocity that *they fled out of that house naked and wounded.* As a result of this incident *the name of the Lord Jesus was magnified;* whether you needed baptism or exorcism, our group did it best.

We were able to attack the competition less directly, too. Many people who had previously used old-fashioned magic *brought their books together, and burned them before all men: and they counted the price of them, and found it fifty thousand pieces of silver.* (It's cheating if you just burn the cheap editions.) *So mightily grew the word of God and prevailed;* too much reading just makes people confused.

Book-burning doesn't usually lead to trouble, but disparaging graven images is more delicate. A spokesman for the silversmiths was up in arms because Paul had been teaching that their images were not sacred, *So that not only this our craft is in danger to be set at nought; but also that the temple of the great goddess Diana should be despised.* The uproar was awe-inspiring; a couple of Paul's companions were taken to the theatre, where *all with one voice about the space of two hours cried out, Great is Diana of the Ephesians.*

Further trouble was averted thanks to the persuasive powers of the town clerk. Everyone knows, he said, that Ephesus is the city of Diana, the guardian of her heaven-sent image. *Seeing then that these things cannot be spoken against, ye ought to be quiet, and to do nothing rashly.* The arrested men had committed no offence, and in any case there were courts and rulers to handle complaints. *And when he had thus spoken, he dismissed the assembly.*

Paul didn't push his luck, leaving Ephesus with all due haste. He travelled into   20
Greece and Macedonia; it was around this time that he wrote his famous letters to the Corinthians and the Romans. It was also during this period that he revived someone he had bored to death. When a group of believers had gathered to hear Paul preach, he *continued his speech until midnight.* A certain young man had unwisely chosen to sit in a third-storey window, *and as Paul was long preaching, he sunk down with sleep, and fell down from the third loft, and was taken up dead.*

And Paul went down, and fell on him, and embracing him said, Trouble not yourselves; for his life is in him. Having provided his diagnosis, Paul went back upstairs and carried on talking and eating until dawn, when he finally left. *And they brought the young man alive, and were not a little comforted.*

Paul began his journey back to Palestine, hoping to reach Jerusalem in time for Pentecost. He avoided Ephesus, for which I don't blame him, though his excuse about being pressed for time sounded rather hollow when he summoned the church elders there to meet him in another town. He clearly felt sorry for himself, reminding them how he had been *Serving the Lord with all humility of mind, and with many tears, and temptations, which befell me by the lying in wait of the Jews.* Now, he said, *I go bound in the spirit unto Jerusalem, not knowing the things that shall befall me there,* although the Holy Ghost had been warning him at every opportunity that he would be persecuted. You couldn't describe Paul as a good listener, even to voices from above.

This was good-bye, he said; you *shall see my face no more.* He had sought no financial gain;

Yea, ye yourselves know, that these hands have ministered unto my necessities, and to them that were with me. I have shewed you all things, how that so labouring ye ought to support the weak, and to remember the words of the Lord Jesus, how he said, It is more blessed to give than to receive.

I can't recall my brother saying that, but I'm sure he'd be glad to accept the attribution. *And they all wept sore, and fell on Paul's neck, and kissed him.*

Paul continued his journey. At Tyre there were disciples *who said to Paul*   21
through the Spirit, that he should not go up to Jerusalem. He ignored them, moving on to the house of Philip in Caesarea; *And the same man had four*

daughters, virgins, which did prophesy. Apparently they were saving themselves, though, because the only prophecy Paul heard came from the man Agabus: *he took Paul's girdle, and bound his own hands and feet, and said, Thus saith the Holy Ghost, So shall the Jews at Jerusalem bind the man that owneth this girdle, and shall deliver him into the hands of the Gentiles.*

It's just as well they weren't planning to gag him, or we might never have heard the prophecy. Everyone tried to persuade Paul not to go, but he was adamant. And so the party moved on to Jerusalem where, as Luke reports, *the day following Paul went in with us unto James; and all the elders were present.*

Paul described his success among the Gentiles. I congratulated him, but felt obliged to confront him with the allegation that he was leading Jews astray, *saying that they ought not to circumcise their children, neither to walk after the customs.* We had to act quickly to improve his reputation. I suggested that he sponsor a few of our followers in a purification ritual, thereby demonstrating that he was righteous and obedient to the Law.

PAUL IN COURT

I fear that my efforts at public relations failed miserably. Paul was recognised in the temple, and dragged outside by some people with an inclination to violence; had it not been for the rapid response of Roman troops, that might have been the end of him. *Then the chief captain came near, and took him, and commanded him to be bound with two chains; and demanded who he was, and what he had done.* Unable to get a sensible response from the crowd, the commandant had Paul brought in to help with their enquiries. The mob, meanwhile, continued to shout *Away with him.*

The officer was surprised to hear Paul address him in Greek; he had taken him for a notorious Egyptian revolutionary. Rather put out, *Paul said, I am a man which am a Jew of Tarsus, a city in Cilicia, a citizen of no mean city: and, I beseech thee, suffer me to speak unto the people.* In fact he was a Roman citizen, which was even more impressive, but once again he chose not to advertise it. He was granted permission to address the crowd, which he did in their language.

22   Not only was he a Jew, Paul said in his own defence, but he had been *brought up in this city at the feet of Gamaliel,* the great rabbi. He had been zealous in persecuting heretics – the partisans of Jesus – until his revelation on the road to Damascus. Incidentally, he admitted that his companions on that occasion *heard not the voice of him that spake to me*; had they been contradicting the original story that they did hear a voice? Following his conversion he had another vision, this time at the temple in Jerusalem, in which Jesus ordered him to *Depart: for I will send thee far hence unto the Gentiles.*

The crowd, which found the speech veering too close to blasphemy for its liking, began to shout *Away with such a fellow from the earth: for it is not fit that he should live. And as they cried out, and cast off their clothes, and threw dust into the air, The chief captain commanded him to be brought into the castle.* I felt sorry for Paul, missing such a spectacle.

As the soldiers were tying him up for a good whipping, Paul casually asked *the centurion that stood by, Is it lawful for you to scourge a man that is a Roman, and uncondemned?* He must have enjoyed the consternation. The commandant came over *and said unto him, Tell me, art thou a Roman? He said, Yea. And the chief captain answered, With a great sum obtained I this freedom. And Paul said, But I was free born.* So there.

Given that they couldn't beat it out of him, the only way of discovering what all the fuss was about was to convene a hearing before the religious council. It got 23
off to a bad start. Paul said that his conscience was clear, the high priest ordered his henchmen to give him a smack, and Paul responded by saying *God shall smite thee, thou whited wall* – not the snappiest insult I'd ever heard. When the underlings exclaimed *Revilest thou God's high priest?*, Paul said that he hadn't recognised the man.

Noticing that the court contained both Pharisees and Sadducees, Paul decided to divide and conquer: *Men and brethren, I am a Pharisee, the son of a Pharisee: of the hope and resurrection of the dead I am called in question.* As the possibility of an afterlife was one of the main issues separating the two camps, they were soon arguing amongst themselves. Once again the commandant had to give up on framing charges.

The next day *certain of the Jews banded together, and bound themselves under a curse, saying that they would neither eat nor drink till they had killed Paul.* About 40 of them were involved. Paul's nephew heard of their plotting and warned his uncle, who sent him on to tell the commandant. This officer, in turn, organised a large escort to transport Paul to Caesarea. It was time to pass the parcel to Felix, the governor.

A few days later the high priest arrived in Caesarea with his assistants to make 24
the case for the prosecution. They declared that *we have found this man a pestilent fellow, and a mover of sedition among all the Jews throughout the world, and a ringleader of the sect of the Nazarenes.* Paul responded that he had been minding his own business in Jerusalem.

> *But this I confess unto thee, that after the way which they call heresy, so worship I the God of my fathers, believing all things which are written in the law and in the prophets: And have hope toward God, which they themselves also allow, that there shall be a resurrection of the dead, both of the just and unjust. And herein do I exercise myself, to have always a conscience void of offence toward God, and toward men.*

Felix deferred judgment, granting Paul a considerable degree of freedom while keeping him under arrest. Paul even had the opportunity to brief the governor and his Jewish wife on the new faith in Jesus. But *as he reasoned of righteousness, temperance, and judgment to come, Felix trembled, and answered, Go thy way for this time; when I have a convenient season, I will call for thee.* Say in about a century. In fact, though, he invited Paul in for a chat with some regularity, hoping that it might dawn on him to offer some financial incentive for a favourable verdict.

I've always wondered what became of those people who vowed to fast until they had assassinated Paul; we never heard any more about them. Paul was still in custody when, two years later, Porcius Festus replaced Felix as governor. (The Romans kept Judaea for people with silly names.)

THE APPEAL TO CAESAR

25   The Jewish leadership urged Festus to prosecute Paul, who continued to deny any wrongdoing. *But Festus, willing to do the Jews a pleasure, answered Paul, and said, Wilt thou go up to Jerusalem, and there be judged of these things before me?* His reply, in a word, was 'no'; Paul said *I appeal unto Caesar. Then Festus, when he had conferred with the council, answered, Hast thou appealed unto Caesar? unto Caesar shalt thou go.*

I suspect that here Paul made a tactical error, but it's easy to be wise after the event. A little while later Agrippa, one of the Herods and king of various northern parts, came to visit with his sister Bernice. Festus told them about the prisoner left over from the days of Felix, and of how his accusers had no conventional charges, but just *certain questions against him of their own superstition, and of one Jesus, which was dead, whom Paul affirmed to be alive.* The natives were always arguing over some damn thing or another.

Agrippa expressed an interest in seeing this character, and so a special hearing was arranged. Festus said that he would be grateful for any suggestions about what to write to the emperor when Paul was sent to Rome for judgment, *For it seemeth to me unreasonable to send a prisoner, and not withal to signify the crimes laid against him.*

26   Paul was given the floor, and he launched into his standard sermon. As a youth he had been devout, indeed, *that after the most straitest sect of our religion I lived as a Pharisee.* He became an enemy of the Jesus brigade, *and being exceedingly mad against them, I persecuted them even unto strange cities.* That changed after the vision on the road to Damascus. He still maintained, however, that everything was as Moses and the prophets had said it would be (or at least as he said they said it would be): *That Christ should suffer, and that he should be the first that should rise from the dead, and should shew light unto the people, and to the Gentiles.*

Festus lost his patience at this point, shouting *Paul, thou art beside thyself; much learning doth make thee mad. But he said, I am not mad, most noble Festus; but speak forth the words of truth and soberness. For the king knoweth of these things, before whom also I speak freely: for I am persuaded that none of these things are hidden from him; for this thing was not done in a corner. King Agrippa, believest thou the prophets? I know that thou believest. Then*

Agrippa said unto Paul, Almost thou persuadest me to be a Christian. And Paul said, I would to God, that not only thou, but also all that hear me this day, were both almost, and altogether such as I am, except these bonds.

If only everyone were more like us; life would be so much easier (and less interesting). Paul's listeners were at least persuaded that he had done nothing criminal. In fact, Agrippa remarked, *This man might have been set at liberty, if he had not appealed unto Caesar.* I hate it when that happens.

Paul did not have an easy voyage to Rome. The first leg passed off smoothly 27 enough, but on the second they ran into trouble. Being late in the season it was dangerous to sail the Mediterranean, and while on Crete *Paul admonished them, And said unto them, Sirs, I perceive that this voyage will be with hurt and much damage, not only of the lading and ship, but also of our lives.* Not surprisingly, since he was just a prisoner, the master and owner of the ship overruled him.

In the event they hit a tremendous storm, *And when neither sun nor stars in many days appeared,* Luke reported, *and no small tempest lay on us, all hope that we should be saved was then taken away.* Eventually Paul got up and, having said 'I told you so', revised his original prediction: *I exhort you to be of good cheer: for there shall be no loss of any man's life among you, but of the ship.* He explained that an angel had come to say that *thou must be brought before Caesar: and, lo, God hath given thee all them that sail with thee.*

They did in the end spy land, and after an uneasy night worrying about the rocks, made for the shore. The adventure wasn't over, though. The ship ran aground, and waves smashed the stern. *And the soldiers' counsel was to kill the prisoners, lest any of them should swim out, and escape. But the centurion, willing to save Paul, kept them from their purpose; and commanded that they which could swim should cast themselves first into the sea, and get to land: And the rest, some on boards, and some on broken pieces of the ship. And so it came to pass, that they escaped all safe to land.*

They were shipwrecked on Malta where, thankfully, *the barbarous people* 28 *shewed us no little kindness: for they kindled a fire, and received us every one.* Paul was out gathering wood when a viper bit him, *And when the barbarians saw the venomous beast hang on his hand, they said among themselves, No doubt this man is a murderer, whom, though he hath escaped the sea, yet vengeance suffereth not to live. ... Howbeit they looked when he should have swollen, or fallen down dead suddenly: but after they had looked a great while, and saw no harm come to him, they changed their minds, and said that he was a god.* Ah, the fickleness of popular opinion.

Paul confirmed his reputation by healing first the father of the chief magistrate, and then all and sundry, through prayer and laying-on of hands. Doubtless the regret was general when, after three months, the party took to the sea once more. This time it was smooth sailing; Paul reached Rome without further drama.

Paul had his own house in Rome, though he was obliged *to dwell by himself with a soldier that kept him*; I suspect he was happy with the arrangement. Soon after his arrival he summoned the local Jewish leadership, and told them how he came to be there, blaming their counterparts in Jerusalem. They responded graciously;

> *We neither received letters out of Judaea concerning thee, neither any of the brethren that came shewed or spake any harm of thee. But we desire to hear of thee what thou thinkest: for as concerning this sect, we know that every where it is spoken against.*

An entire day was set aside for him to talk, at the end of which *some believed the things which were spoken, and some believed not.* Not a bad result, I would have thought. Paul, though, was a hard man to please, and didn't accept even partial failure gracefully. He quoted the prophet Isaiah at them: *Hearing ye shall hear, and shall not understand; and seeing ye shall see, and not perceive.* As they didn't appreciate the good news, *Be it known therefore unto you, that the salvation of God is sent unto the Gentiles, and that they will hear it.*

Justice moved exceedingly slowly, but he didn't have a bad time in Rome. *Paul dwelt two whole years in his own hired house, and received all that came in unto him, Preaching the kingdom of God, and teaching those things which concern the Lord Jesus Christ, with all confidence, no man forbidding him.* Eventually his luck ran out, but he still had several good years ahead of him.

6

Romans

Paul, who always seemed to be on tour, conducted his missionary work by correspondence as well. He wrote his letters before Matthew, Mark, Luke and John put pen to paper. I know that some people say he was manic, domineering, and a (repressed) homosexual, but then so was Alexander. Paul took a struggling Jewish sect and turned it into a multi-national operation. I won't pretend to be happy about his policies (and he certainly changed the way people thought about my brother), but you can't deny his success.

The best statement of his doctrine comes from one of the later letters, apparently 1 addressed to the followers in Rome. He describes himself as *Paul, a servant of Jesus Christ, called to be an apostle,* which gives you a hint of his talent for self-promotion; as far as I know he never even met my brother. He could be ingratiating and offensive by turns.

> *First, I thank my God through Jesus Christ for you all, that your faith is spoken of throughout the whole world. For God is my witness, whom I serve with my spirit in the gospel of his Son, that without ceasing I make mention of you always in my prayers.*

He had always wanted to pay them a visit, though it hadn't yet been possible. He wasn't prejudiced;

> *I am debtor both to the Greeks, and to the Barbarians; both to the wise, and to the unwise. So, as much as in me is, I am ready to preach the gospel to you that are at Rome also.*

Very good of him, I'm sure. His message was that *The just shall live by faith*; what that meant would shortly emerge.

First, however, a few frighteners were in order, *For the wrath of God is revealed from heaven against all ungodliness and unrighteousness of men.* While the divine attributes are invisible, their effects are in plain view; it's inexcusable that people *glorified him not as God, neither were thankful.* In consequence God *gave them up to uncleanness through the lusts of their own hearts, to dishonour their own bodies between themselves* (always a popular punishment). They *worshipped and served the creature more than the Creator.*

Paul had something of an obsession with unnatural passion; he couldn't help but spell out what was on his mind.

> *God gave them up unto vile affections: for even their women did change the natural use into that which is against nature: And likewise also the men, leaving the natural use of the woman, burned in their lust one toward another; men with men working that which is unseemly, and receiving in themselves that recompence of their error which was meet.*

Sexual licence was only the beginning; once you've done it with another chap, it's all downhill from there.

> *God gave them over to a reprobate mind, to do those things which are not convenient; Being filled with all unrighteousness, fornication, wickedness, covetousness, maliciousness; full of envy, murder, debate, deceit, malignity; whisperers, Backbiters, haters of God, despiteful, proud, boasters, inventors of evil things, disobedient to parents, Without understanding, covenantbreakers, without natural affection, implacable, unmerciful.*

Is anyone feeling insecure? Not the fellows Paul had in mind, annoyingly enough, *Who knowing the judgment of God, that they which commit such things are worthy of death, not only do the same, but have pleasure in them that do them.*

2   Lest his readers congratulate themselves on not being so inclined, Paul held that everyone was guilty; *wherein thou judgest another, thou condemnest thyself.* Quite so. Speaking of judging, Paul knew the sentence as well as the verdict:

> *after thy hardness and impenitent heart treasurest up unto thyself wrath against the day of wrath and revelation of the righteous judgment of God; Who will render to every man according to his deeds: To them who by patient continuance in well doing seek for glory and honour and immortality, eternal life: But unto them that are contentious, and do not obey the truth, but obey unrighteousness, indignation and wrath, Tribulation and anguish.*

According to Paul, I thought, deeds are always damning, but I don't want to get ahead of myself. He did emphasise an important point: *there is no respect of persons with God,* who pays no attention to rank or race. If anything Jews would suffer, because having been given the Law they would be held to its standards. *For as many as have sinned without law shall also perish without law: and as many as have sinned in the law shall be judged by the law.* By contrast the Gentiles, *having not the law, are a law unto themselves,* tested simply by conscience.

Behold, thou art called a Jew, and restest in the law, and makest thy boast of God, And knowest his will, and approvest the things that are more excellent, being instructed out of the law; the result is just that your sins give God a bad name. There's no point in being circumcised unless you do him credit.

FAITH AND WORKS

Paul could foresee the objections (even if he had trouble answering them). *What* 3 *advantage then hath the Jew?* Considerable: God spoke to the children of Israel. But will their sins lead him to renege on his promises? *God forbid: yea, let God be true, but every man a liar.* Then God would be unjust if he exacted retribution? By no means. Since our infidelity puts his constancy in such a good light, though, why not say *Let us do evil, that good may come?* Paul lost patience with his own arguments, storming that anybody who talked that way deserved damnation.

Going back to his starting point, Paul asserted that everyone, Jew or non-Jew, is subject to sin. He cited multiple passages from scripture (*There is none righteous, no, not one,* etc.) in support. The law exists just so that *all the world may become guilty before God.* Sounding for all the world like a moral anarchist, he claimed that the law simply produces *knowledge of sin.*

Having laid the ground, Paul was ready to announce his conclusion. Whatever your background, if you had faith in Jesus, God would give you a free pardon. *For all have sinned, and come short of the glory of God; Being justified freely by his grace through the redemption that is in Christ Jesus.* One great wrong – the death of Jesus – was designed to put the rest of us right.

Keeping the commandments, therefore, won't get you into God's good books; only faith in Jesus will do that. This immediately raises a problem, of course: *Do we then make void the law through faith? God forbid.* Paul wouldn't find it easy, however, to define the place of morality.

Defending the doctrine of justification by faith (as opposed to works) calls for 4 a comprehensive reinterpretation of scripture. Paul considered the example of Abraham at some length. We normally think of Abraham's obedience, that is his deeds, as justifying the covenant God made with him – an agreement that itself required action, not least circumcision. Paul argued that faith came first, with obedience being essentially beside the point; law can only produce punishment, and *where no law is, there is no transgression.*

What mattered was the faith of Abraham before he was circumcised, *Who against hope believed in hope, that he might become the father of many nations.* Paul is naughty to claim that *being not weak in faith,* Abraham ignored his wife's infertility and their advanced years; *He staggered not at the promise of God.* On the contrary, he not only staggered, he fell about laughing. I don't think Abraham truly believed that Sarah would bear a son until it happened. The moral, anyway, is supposed to be that we too will be considered righteous, *if we believe on him that raised up Jesus our Lord from the dead.* (There will be more to it, I'm afraid.)

Such a reconciliation carries the promise of future reward, which should make 5 us happy.

And not only so, but we glory in tribulations also: knowing that tribulation worketh patience; And patience, experience; and experience, hope: And hope maketh not ashamed; because the love of God is shed abroad in our hearts by the Holy Ghost which is given unto us.

Whatever happens we can't lose.

Paul pointed out how impressive it is that *while we were yet sinners, Christ died for us.* All credit to my brother, but why did anyone have to die? And if Jesus was to bear our sins, wouldn't that involve some consequence beyond merely dying, however unpleasantly? He didn't save us from death, because we still die, and yet if he saved us from a worse fate, he succeeded without suffering it himself. Now eternal exile from heaven: that would have been a sacrifice.

Sin seems to be a hereditary, or at the very least a chronic, condition of humanity. It was *by one man* (Adam) *sin entered into the world, and death by sin,* and we haven't stopped sinning since. Jesus provided a remedy, however, *For as by one man's disobedience many were made sinners, so by the obedience of one shall many be made righteous.*

As if there wasn't enough trouble in the world already,

6

the law entered, that the offence might abound. But where sin abounded, grace did much more abound ... What shall we say then? Shall we continue in sin, that grace may abound? God forbid. How shall we, that are dead to sin, live any longer therein?

Baptism lets us share the death that Jesus died, and just as he was raised up, *even so we also should walk in newness of life.* We can say good-bye to our sinful selves,

Knowing that Christ being raised from the dead dieth no more; death hath no more dominion over him. For in that he died, he died unto sin once: but in that he liveth, he liveth unto God. Likewise reckon ye also yourselves to be dead indeed unto sin, but alive unto God through Jesus Christ our Lord.

We should keep our bodies from becoming slaves to sin, despite God's saving grace. Having first-hand experience of the subject, Paul said that

I speak after the manner of men because of the infirmity of your flesh: for as ye have yielded your members servants to uncleanness and to iniquity unto iniquity; even so now yield your members servants to righteousness unto holiness.

I think he believed that purity somehow follows automatically from faith. If not there's a problem, *For the wages of sin is death; but the gift of God is eternal life.* Perhaps we should be worried after all.

SIN AND THE SPIRIT

Paul noted that a woman is bound to her husband only during his lifetime; his death 7 releases her to go with another man. The expected parallel would have been that the law has now died, but he seemed to get lost in his metaphor. Rather, it is you who have died to the law, and *ye should be married to another, even to him who is raised from the dead, that we should bring forth fruit unto God.*

Whatever Paul had in mind, he clearly thought that coming out from under the law was a good thing. *What shall we say then? Is the law sin? God forbid.* Remarkably enough, however, he maintained that the law not only defined sin, but actually created it, forbidden fruit being sweeter.

> *I had not known sin, but by the law: for I had not known lust, except the law had said, Thou shalt not covet. But sin, taking occasion by the commandment, wrought in me all manner of concupiscence. For without the law sin was dead.*

Well, it's certainly a novel excuse ('the Bible made me do it'). Indeed, he was ready to shuffle off the responsibility altogether: *it is no more I that do it, but sin that dwelleth in me.*

To give him credit, Paul put his finger on a common frustration; *For the good that I would I do not: but the evil which I would not, that I do.* In his case, though, there seemed to be something more; he felt himself physically possessed by sin, powerless against his own body. His intellect knew what was right,

> *But I see another law in my members, warring against the law of my mind, and bringing me into captivity to the law of sin which is in my members. O wretched man that I am! who shall deliver me from the body of this death? I thank God through Jesus Christ our Lord. So then with the mind I myself serve the law of God; but with the flesh the law of sin.*

For someone who believed that God's grace had superseded the law, he had a raging case of guilt.

Fortunately, Paul said, we have been liberated; *God sending his own Son in the* 8 *likeness of sinful flesh, and for sin, condemned sin in the flesh.* His idea that sin was no longer deadly must have been a great comfort, but the companion thought – that Jesus died to free us from our baser natures – doesn't help a bad conscience.

> *For they that are after the flesh do mind the things of the flesh; but they*

that are after the Spirit the things of the Spirit. For to be carnally minded is death; but to be spiritually minded is life and peace.

Sin has made our bodies dead meat, but our spiritual selves can save us. We can become, in fact,

the sons of God. For ye have not received the spirit of bondage again to fear; but ye have received the Spirit of adoption, whereby we cry, Abba, Father. The Spirit itself beareth witness with our spirit, that we are the children of God: And if children, then heirs; heirs of God, and joint-heirs with Christ.

If God ever dies, we could inherit the world. The first time I was joint-heir with Jesus, I just ended up sawing lumber.

Our pain is a modest price to pay, according to Paul, *For I reckon that the sufferings of this present time are not worthy to be compared with the glory which shall be revealed to us.* I reckon he's right; that's why people join up, anyway. Of course, it's hard to be patient; *we know that the whole creation groaneth and travaileth in pain together until now.* Even Paul admitted that the labour seemed inordinately long.

We do, at least, have an ally in the Spirit (which one I'm not sure), who intercedes with God on our behalf. It's hard to see the point, though; God has a master plan for human resources:

we know that all things work together for good to them that love God, to them who are the called according to his purpose. For whom he did foreknow, he also did predestinate to be conformed to the image of his Son, that he might be the firstborn among many brethren. Moreover whom he did predestinate, them he also called: and whom he called, them he also justified: and whom he justified, them he also glorified.

As Paul remarked, *If God be for us, who can be against us?* Or as he only implied, if God is against us, why not give up?

Since God handed over his own son, Paul argued, he can hardly fail to give us everything. Our enemies can take a big leap off a short pier. *Who shall lay any thing to the charge of God's elect? It is God that justifieth.* Jesus is on our side. *Who shall separate us from the love of Christ?* No one, despite terrible hardship. Total victory will be ours,

For I am persuaded, that neither death, nor life, nor angels, nor principalities, nor powers, nor things present, nor things to come, Nor height, nor depth, nor any other creature, shall be able to separate us from the love of God, which is in Christ Jesus our Lord.

JEWS AND GENTILES

Paul was not blind to the irony that he, once a traditionally Jewish young man, was 9
spreading the word of my brother, another devout Jew, primarily among the
Gentiles. The failure of most Jews to believe that Jesus was the messiah pained
him to the point, he said, *I could wish that myself were accursed from Christ for
my brethren.*

It also raised the problem of God's promises to the children of Israel. Had he
gone back on his word? No, said Paul, arguing that God had never meant to lead
everyone to his kingdom, only a selected group. His favour wasn't earned, but
predestined; he chose among the sons of Abraham and Isaac, for example, before
they had even appeared: *the children being not yet born, neither having done any
good or evil, that the purpose of God according to election might stand, not of
works, but of him that calleth.*

Some might protest that this doctrine of the elect sounds a trifle unfair. Paul
replied by quoting God to Moses, *I will have mercy on whom I will have mercy,
and I will have compassion on whom I will have compassion.* God can even
choose, as with Pharaoh, to harden men's hearts, the better to punish them. With
Paul for an advocate, who needs critics?

He did no better with the next objection. How can God blame people when all
their actions are subject to his will? Not having much of an answer, Paul could only
abuse the questioners as impudent pups.

*O man, who art thou that repliest against God? Shall the thing formed say
to him that formed it, Why hast thou made me thus? Hath not the potter
power over the clay, of the same lump to make one vessel unto honour, and
another unto dishonour?*

Quite so: the potter can do what he likes with his pots. What he can't do is blame
them for being imperfect, or for being used as chamber-pots.

Coming back to the treatment of the Jews, Paul cited scripture to support his
claim that God had never intended to save more than a remnant; as Isaiah said, *a
short work will the Lord make upon the earth.* The Gentiles had made no effort
to be good, and yet were justified by faith. Despite considerable effort, the Jews
never achieved righteousness. *Wherefore? Because they sought it not by faith,
but as it were by the works of the law.* They tried too hard.

Brethren, Paul declared, *my heart's desire and prayer to God for Israel is, that* 10
they might be saved. He gave them credit for zeal, but regretted that it was
misdirected. Paul accused the Jews of going their own way, rather than God's –
unfairly, to my mind, given that their entire commitment was to obeying the divine
commandments. In his view, however, *Christ is the end of the law,* and they missed
what was essential: *if thou shalt confess with thy mouth the Lord Jesus, and shalt
believe in thine heart that God hath raised him from the dead, thou shalt be saved.*

Otherwise – e.g. because you had the misfortune to be born before my brother appeared – you'll have to take your chances.

Everyone, Jewish or Greek, is on an equal footing. Paul had the cheek to quote the prophet Joel's words that *whosoever shall call upon the name of the Lord shall be saved*, when the name he had in mind was Jesus, not Jehovah. The gospel had been spread far and wide; if the Jews didn't respond, they had no excuse. It seemed that they were at loggerheads with God, as scripture said they would be.

11　　*I say then, Hath God cast away his people? God forbid.* A few of us, Paul modestly observed, may be counted among the elect. And anyway there's a silver lining: *through their fall salvation is come unto the Gentiles*, who might otherwise have missed out.

Gentiles shouldn't feel superior, he cautioned. Israel was a tree,

And if some of the branches be broken off, and thou, being a wild olive tree, wert graffed in among them, and with them partakest of the root and fatness of the olive tree; Boast not against the branches.

You still depend on the sacred root. *Be not highminded, but fear: For if God spared not the natural branches, take heed lest he also spare not thee.*

In any event, the infidelity of the children of Israel is only temporary. When recruitment among the Gentiles has run its course, *all Israel shall be saved.* That 'all' sounds hopeful, but the indications are that Paul was thinking of the collective, rather than everyone in it. Once Gentiles were out, now they are in; the Jews are in the doghouse, but their day will come again.

God apparently enjoyed these overlapping affairs with different groups, where his favourites came and went in complementary cycles of estrangement and reconciliation. *God hath concluded them all in unbelief, that he might have mercy upon all.* Such relationships are too rough for my taste, but as Paul exclaimed (without taking it much to heart, I'd have to say), *how unsearchable are his judgments, and his ways past finding out! For who hath known the mind of the Lord?*

CHRISTIAN PROVERBS

12　　After this digression on the fate of the Jews, Paul offered some advice on how to behave.

I beseech you therefore, brethren, by the mercies of God, that ye present your bodies a living sacrifice, holy, acceptable unto God, which is your reasonable service.

Or unreasonable, depending on your point of view.

Speaking of bodies, just as the various parts have different functions, *we, being many, are one body in Christ, and every one members one of another.* We should each contribute according to our natural endowments. Prophets should prophesy, ministers administer, and teachers teach.

On the principle, I suppose, that moralists should moralise, Paul reeled off a long list of exhortations.

> *Be kindly affectioned one to another with brotherly love ... Rejoicing in hope; patient in tribulation ... given to hospitality. Bless them which persecute you: bless, and curse not. Rejoice with them that do rejoice, and weep with them that weep. Be of the same mind one toward another. Mind not high things, but condescend to men of low estate. Be not wise in your own conceits. Recompense to no man evil for evil. ... If it be possible, as much as lieth in you, live peaceably with all men.*

I've already expressed my views on appeasement. Paul justified his advice on the grounds that God would do the retaliating: *Vengeance is mine; I will repay, saith the Lord.* Make your enemy ashamed; *Be not overcome of evil, but overcome evil with good.* I just hope that my adversaries are all sensitive and misunderstood; perhaps Paul can take care of any violent mobs or deranged bigots.

His view of political rulers was just as optimistic as his method of dealing with evil.   13

> *Let every soul be subject unto the higher powers. For there is no power but of God: the powers that be are ordained of God. Whosoever therefore resisteth the power, resisteth the ordinance of God: and they that resist shall receive to themselves damnation.*

I knew he was a conservative, but this is ridiculous. He claimed that *rulers are not a terror to good works, but to the evil;* while we can certainly hope so, let's not get carried away. Paul claimed that governments act with divine authority; the sovereign *beareth not the sword in vain: for he is the minister of God, a revenger to execute wrath upon him that doeth evil.*

In consequence you should obey your rulers as a matter of conscience – and don't forget to pay your taxes. More generally,

> *Render therefore to all their dues: tribute to whom tribute is due; custom to whom custom; fear to whom fear; honour to whom honour. Owe no man any thing, but to love one another: for he that loveth another hath fulfilled the law.*

Try telling that to your tax inspector. Having reviewed the commandments, he reiterated that *love is the fulfilling of the law.*

Paul believed that the end was nigh (he might otherwise have rethought his advice). So, he urged,

> *now it is high time to awake out of sleep: for now is our salvation nearer than when we believed. The night is far spent, the day is at hand: let us therefore cast off the works of darkness, and let us put on the armour of light. Let us walk honestly, as in the day; not in rioting and drunkenness, not in chambering and wantonness, not in strife and envying. But put ye on the Lord Jesus Christ, and make not provision for the flesh, to fulfil the lusts thereof.*

You're not allowed to go out with a bang.

14   From there Paul turned, somewhat incongruously, to the finer points of Christian etiquette. Many followers observed the Jewish dietary laws (some going even further, becoming vegetarians), while others had no compunction about eating anything that moved. Paul appealed for tolerance, and the avoidance of *doubtful disputations. For one believeth that he may eat all things: another, who is weak, eateth herbs.* It's clear which side he was on.

Let every man be fully persuaded in his own mind. Whatever people eat, they thank God for it.

> *For none of us liveth to himself, and no man dieth to himself. For whether we live, we live unto the Lord; and whether we die, we die unto the Lord: whether we live therefore, or die, we are the Lord's.*

Why then should anyone pass judgment on another? On the contrary, we should avoid making life difficult for our brothers.

> *I know, and am persuaded by the Lord Jesus, that there is nothing unclean of itself: but to him that esteemeth any thing to be unclean, to him it is unclean.*

Quite a sympathetic point of view, I think: don't offend sensibilities gratuitously. *Let us therefore follow after the things which make for peace;* there are more

15   important things than food. Paul summarised his position by saying *We then that are strong ought to bear the infirmities of the weak, and not to please ourselves.* Noblesse oblige.

POSTSCRIPT

Patronising as ever, Paul offered his silken assurance that

I myself also am persuaded of you, my brethren, that ye also are full of goodness, filled with all knowledge, able also to admonish one another.

If he wanted to raise these issues, it was *because of the grace that is given to me of God, That I should be the minister of Jesus Christ to the Gentiles.* The demands of work had thus far prevented him from making the journey to Rome, but business now being slow in the eastern Mediterranean, he hoped to stop by on his way to Spain.

Before he did that, however, he needed to go back with the money raised by the Greek congregations as a *contribution for the poor saints which are at Jerusalem.* Despite his charity work, Paul didn't seem much taken with our part of the world; he asked the Romans to pray *That I may be delivered from them that do not believe in Judaea,* so that, duty done, *I may come unto you with joy by the will of God, and may with you be refreshed.* Thanks a lot, Paul; sorry that coming to see us in Jerusalem was such a hardship.

Paul tacked on a letter of introduction for a certain Phoebe, who served the   16
movement near Corinth. He then sent greetings to what, considering he had never been to Rome, was an astonishingly long list of people: over two dozen named individuals, together with some of their relatives. He began with Priscilla and Aquila, *Who have for my life laid down their own necks* (without losing their heads, fortunately), and likewise *the church that is in their house.* I didn't recognise most of the other names, though I'm tempted to suggest that he got a couple of them the wrong way around: *Salute Herodion my kinsman. Greet them that be of the household of Narcissus.*

Concluding his roll call, Paul suggested that they *Salute one another with an holy kiss.* Certain others, however, should be saluted with a kick:

mark them which cause divisions and offences contrary to the doctrine which ye have learned; and avoid them. For they that are such serve not our Lord Jesus Christ, but their own belly; and by good words and fair speeches deceive the hearts of the simple.

Surely not. Ah well, *the God of peace shall bruise Satan under your feet shortly.*

Paul passed on greetings from several of his companions, starting with Timothy. He closed by praising God and the existence of Jesus, *which was kept secret since the world began, But now is made manifest,* finally. He knows best; *To God only wise, be glory through Jesus Christ for ever. Amen.*

I Corinthians

1   A couple of years earlier Paul had written *unto the church of God which is at Corinth*. It seems to have been his second letter to them, not his first, but I'll come to that.

    Paul had been instrumental in founding the church, so it's natural that he had an interest in events there. The news, I'm afraid, was generally bad. They had split into factions – a common problem with new sects.

> *Now I beseech you, brethren, by the name of our Lord Jesus Christ, that ye all speak the same thing, and that there be no divisions among you.*

Some hope. People were claiming allegiance to Peter, or to Apollos (the Alexandrian scholar-turned-missionary), or to Paul himself. He wanted no part of it: *Is Christ divided? … were ye baptized in the name of Paul?* Fortunately he couldn't be held responsible. *I thank God that I baptized none of you, but Crispus and Gaius.* (Come on Paul, you were there for eighteen months.) Yes, all right, *And I baptized also the household of Stephanas: besides, I know not whether I baptized any other.* (Fine; no need to be defensive about it.)

    The way of Jesus calls for humility, not knowledge or power. Indeed, *hath not God made foolish the wisdom of this world?* As the so-called wise ignored him, *it pleased God by the foolishness of preaching to save them that believe. For the Jews require a sign, and the Greeks seek after wisdom: But we preach Christ crucified*, an executed messiah, which seems impossible to Jews and ridiculous to others.

    That's how God works, though. Take the congregation in Corinth: no offence, but

> *not many wise men after the flesh, not many mighty, not many noble, are called: But God hath chosen the foolish things of the world to confound the wise; and God hath chosen the weak things of the world to confound the things which are mighty; And base things of the world, and things which are despised, hath God chosen, yea, and things which are not, to bring to nought things that are.*

So be glad, you pathetic specimens of humanity.

2   Paul reminded them of how he had preached, not with polish and sophistication,

but *in weakness, and in fear, and in much trembling ... That your faith should not stand in the wisdom of men, but in the power of God.* (This might have been a backhanded slap at Apollos, who was known for his eloquence.)

There is, none the less, a kind of wisdom that belongs not to this world, but to divine mystery. For *as it is written, Eye hath not seen, nor ear heard, neither have entered into the heart of man, the things which God hath prepared for them that love him.* These gifts are spiritual, though Paul doesn't make it easy to understand just what's involved. Perhaps that's because, as he says, they can be spoken of *not in the words which man's wisdom teacheth, but which the Holy Ghost teacheth.* Then, too, for a man without the gift, matters of the Spirit *are foolishness unto him: neither can he know them, because they are spiritually discerned.* To such a man, I suppose, our new God-sent trappings would seem invisible.

Spiritual communication hadn't been possible with the Corinthians; they were   3 *babes in Christ. I have fed you with milk, and not with meat: for hitherto ye were not able to bear it, neither yet now are ye able.* Being preoccupied with sectarian quarrels, they obviously weren't ready for real food.

He and Apollos had the same aim. *I have planted, Apollos watered; but God gave the increase.* Among the gardeners, *every man shall receive his own reward according to his own labour* – an idea that sounds suspiciously like justification by works – *For we are labourers together with God: ye are God's husbandry.* That puts them in their place; the preacher gives God a hand, the congregation gets the manure.

To change the metaphor, *I have laid the foundation ... let every man take heed how he buildeth thereupon.* On the day of judgment we'll learn how well the building holds up.

> *Every man's work shall be made manifest: for the day shall declare it, because it shall be revealed by fire; and the fire shall try every man's work of what sort it is.*

In any case the foundation in Jesus should save his life, though it's then unclear what the rewards for structural merit might be.

What you don't want to do is vandalise the church.

> *Know ye not that ye are the temple of God, and that the Spirit of God dwelleth in you? If any man defile the temple of God, him shall God destroy; for the temple of God is holy, which temple ye are.*

(I don't think he had their bodies in mind here; he was referring to them collectively, not individually.)

As he had made plain, God wasn't impressed by worldly wisdom. People could   4 be no more than *stewards of the mysteries of God.* Paul, for his part, didn't give a fig what anyone said about him. He advised them to *judge nothing before the time, until the Lord come, who both will bring to light the hidden things of darkness, and will make manifest the counsels of the hearts.* Everyone deserving praise will get it (and I suppose everyone else will really get it).

To be a partisan of one preacher or another is simply presumptuous. With sarcastic humour – at least I believe that's what it was – Paul told the faithful that they had made their fortunes. Conversely,

> *I think that God hath set forth us the apostles last, as it were appointed to death: for we are made a spectacle unto the world, and to angels, and to men. We are fools for Christ's sake, but ye are wise in Christ; we are weak, but ye are strong; ye are honourable, but we are despised.*

He continued in the same vein, becoming quite carried away: *we are made as the filth of the world, and are the offscouring of all things.* No one could beat Paul at self-abuse.

This lecture, Paul explained, came simply from paternal devotion; if they had 10,000 Christian tutors he would still be their only father, *for in Christ Jesus I have begotten you through the gospel* – not a metaphor to dwell on. He was sending Timothy, one of his favourites, *who shall bring you into remembrance of my ways which be in Christ, as I teach every where in every church.* If some of them thought that he wouldn't be returning himself, they were in for a shock. The choice was theirs: *shall I come unto you with a rod, or in love, and in the spirit of meekness?*

SEX EDUCATION

5   *It is reported commonly that there is fornication among you, and such fornication as is not so much as named among the Gentiles, that one should have his father's wife.* To make matters worse, they hadn't even booted the fellow out of the movement. *For I verily,* Paul said, *as absent in body, but present in spirit, have judged already.* What they needed to do was clear:

> *with the power of our Lord Jesus Christ, To deliver such an one unto Satan for the destruction of the flesh, that the spirit may be saved in the day of the Lord Jesus.*

Love thy neighbour, unless he's loving his step-mother.

They were too pleased with themselves altogether. *Know ye not that a little leaven leaveneth the whole lump?* The yeast of sin should be thrown out, so that they could become as pure as bread for passover. That was only right,

> *For even Christ our passover is sacrificed for us: Therefore let us keep the feast, not with old leaven, neither with the leaven of malice and wickedness; but with the unleavened bread of sincerity and truth.*

To clarify his position, Paul mentioned that *I wrote unto you in an epistle* – an earlier one, apparently – *not to company with fornicators*. He hadn't intended that they should avoid all sinners in the everyday world; that would be impossible. It was other Christians he had mind; *if any man that is called a brother be a fornicator, or covetous, or an idolater, or a railer, or a drunkard, or an extortioner*, you shouldn't even sit down to eat with him. Let God judge the outsiders, but when it's one of your own, *put away from among yourselves that wicked person.*

Terrific; my brother stakes everything on forgiveness, and then Paul wants to excommunicate people. All I know is that if we toss out everyone tainted by sex, greed, swearing or drink we'll be out of business.

I think Paul had fond memories of life with the Pharisees, who were so respected   6 and well-behaved. Not liking to see dirty linen washed in public, he chastised believers for taking their disputes to court, rather than settling them privately.

Do ye not know that the saints shall judge the world? and if the world shall be judged by you, are ye unworthy to judge the smallest matters?

The work on judgment day is being delegated right down the line; first God was on the job, then Jesus, and now we have responsibility. Paul even asked *Know ye not that we shall judge angels?* No, and I imagine that it might come as a surprise to our friends in white.

Anyway, Paul was shocked that *brother goeth to law with brother, and that before the unbelievers.* Doing nothing would apparently be preferable: *why do ye not rather suffer yourselves to be defrauded?* The old boy seemed to think that everybody would be as concerned as we are to protect the reputation of the sect.

Wrong-doers will get what's coming to them.

Know ye not that the unrighteous shall not inherit the kingdom of God? Be not deceived: neither fornicators, nor idolaters, nor adulterers, nor effeminate, nor abusers of themselves with mankind, Nor thieves, nor covetous, nor drunkards, nor revilers, nor extortioners, shall inherit the kingdom of God.

So let's see: out of ten ways to end up in God's bad books, four originate below the belt, three concern property, and not one involves violence. That might just suit someone who's physically brave but sexually insecure. Having named these types of sinners, Paul notes *such were some of you: ... but ye are justified in the name of the Lord Jesus.*

There was a view – perhaps it was particularly common in Corinth, where people were relaxed about sex – that anything goes. We have the equipment, why not use it? Or as Paul forcefully put it,

Meats for the belly, and the belly for meats: but God shall destroy both it and them. Now the body is not for fornication, but for the Lord; and the Lord for the body. ... Know ye not that your bodies are the members of Christ? shall I then take the members of Christ, and make them the members of an harlot? God forbid.

Fornication is a sin against your own body. I wouldn't suggest you argue that there are no such sins:

What? know ye not that your body is the temple of the Holy Ghost ...? For ye are bought with a price: therefore glorify God in your body, and in your spirit, which are God's.

7   Given the depth of his fear of sexual immorality, you might suppose that Paul would be a strong advocate of marriage and the family. Not a bit of it. The Corinthians had apparently written to request his advice on these matters, and his answers were, well, different.

It is good for a man not to touch a woman. Nevertheless, to avoid fornication, let every man have his own wife, and let every woman have her own husband.

Not exactly a ringing endorsement of matrimony.

Husband and wife, Paul went on to say, each possessed the other's body and should not be denied conjugal rights. Although religious devotion might cause them to abstain for a time, it was best not to tempt Satan by doing so permanently.

Ideally, he declared, everybody would be as he was, i.e. unattached. Not everyone has the gift, however. His advice to the single or widowed was to stay that way, if they had the self-control. *But if they cannot contain, let them marry: for it is better to marry than to burn.* Probably.

Paul ruled out divorce, following Jesus (*I command, yet not I, but the Lord*, he said, raising the question of how the Lord might view his other statements). Neither should you separate just because your spouse is a heathen, *For the unbelieving husband is sanctified by the wife,* and vice versa, not to mention that a split would take the children away from God. If the infidel wants to leave, let him go, but don't forget that you could be the instrument of his salvation.

What I teach in all the churches, said Paul, is that you should take yourself the way God found you. *Is any man called being circumcised? let him not become uncircumcised. Is any called in uncircumcision? let him not be circumcised.* I won't argue about circumcision this time; hear instead what he has to say about slavery.

Let every man abide in the same calling wherein he was called. Art thou called being a servant? care not for it: but if thou mayest be made free, use it rather. For he that is called in the Lord, being a servant, is the Lord's freeman.

While no one is sure whether he meant that the slave should or shouldn't take an opportunity for emancipation, he didn't in either case seem overly concerned to protest that people aren't property. Support for the status quo has its limits.

I should say, in Paul's defence, that he thought the world was coming to an end, just as my brother did. This was not the time, in his view, to be making career moves. Marriage wasn't a sin, if that's the way you wanted to go, but you could save yourself a lot of trouble by avoiding it. For those already trapped, *this I say, brethren, the time is short,* and so let *they that have wives be as though they had none.* Eat, drink, and enjoy the bachelor life, for tomorrow we shall die? He must have had something else in mind, *for the fashion of this world passeth away.*

It's obvious that Paul's experience as a lone male was out of the ordinary. Care to guess the one thing a single chap has on his mind?

He that is unmarried careth for the things that belong to the Lord, how he may please the Lord: But he that is married careth for the things that are of the world, how he may please his wife. There is difference also between a wife and a virgin.

No kidding; a young woman (let's not limit ourselves) spends most of her time thinking about young men. If Paul imagines she's preoccupied with being *holy both in body and in spirit,* he met even fewer than I did.

To wrap things up, Paul considered couples living in chaste partnership;

if any man think that he behaveth himself uncomely toward his virgin, if she pass the flower of her age, and need so require, let him do what he will, he sinneth not: let them marry.

For a moment there I feared for her virtue. According to another interpretation, he was actually discussing what to do with a virgin daughter; to sum up, *he that giveth her in marriage doeth well; but he that giveth her not in marriage doeth better.* Paul never really got the hang of family values.

MANNERS AND MORALS

I suppose it was inevitable that Paul, having dealt with sex, would next tackle food. 8 The usual question was whether meat that had been offered to idols could be eaten. While the sophisticated had no qualms, their behaviour wasn't helping the more superstitious brethren.

Knowledge puffeth up, but charity edifieth. And if any man think that he knoweth any thing, he knoweth nothing yet as he ought to know.

The situation calls for a certain understanding. For all the gods there are supposed to be,

to us there is but one God, the Father, of whom are all things, and we in him; and (and?) *one Lord Jesus Christ, by whom are all things, and we by him.*

Not everyone, though, is rooted in this conviction. People who find it difficult to eat the products of heathen sacrifice with a clear conscience should not be coerced into doing so. It's all very well to eat with the idol-worshippers, but your example could be fatal to the weak-minded. Paul declared that he, for his part, would sooner abstain from meat than risk it.

9   Digressing for a moment, Paul pointed out that he declined to stand on his rights even in more important ways. As an apostle he might reasonably have expected certain benefits: to be wined and dined, or to travel with a wife, which was the practice of Peter and the other apostles, and *the brethren of the Lord.* (I'll have Paul to thank if my expense account is cut.) Should he and his friend Barnabas be the only ones required to work for a living? *Who goeth a warfare any time at his own charges? who planteth a vineyard, and eateth not of the fruit thereof?*

It wasn't just a matter of custom, either, *For it is written in the law of Moses, Thou shalt not muzzle the mouth of the ox that treadeth out the corn. Doth God take care for oxen?* In a startling – not to say unwarranted – departure from literalism, Paul insisted that the scripture really meant that the worker should receive some of the fruits of his labour.

These precedents notwithstanding, he had not claimed what would have been his due, *lest we should hinder the gospel of Christ.* The only gain he looked for was in new believers. Whatever helped to win converts, he had become: a Jew among Jews, an outsider among the rest. To come around to the original point, he was weak among the weak; indeed, *I am made all things to all men, that I might by all means save some.*

Corinth being the home of the Isthmian Games, it was only appropriate to throw in a sporty metaphor. *Know ye not that they which run in a race run all, but one receiveth the prize?* Only winning counts (so why bother, I'd say). To gain the winner's wreath you need a clear goal and discipline.

Now they do it to obtain a corruptible crown; but we an incorruptible. I therefore so run, not as uncertainly; so fight I, not as one that beateth the air: But I keep under my body, and bring it into subjection: lest that by any means, when I have preached to others, I myself should be a castaway.

These reflections brought Paul back to one of his main concerns, avoiding the 10
perils of immorality. Like their ancestors during the exodus, they were in danger
of taking too much for granted. Just to take an example, *let us not commit*
fornication, as some of them committed (with the women of Moab), *and fell in*
one day three and twenty thousand. (By my recollection it was 24,000, but who's
counting?)

We should thus be warned – we, *upon whom the ends of the world are come.*
Wherefore let him that thinketh he standeth take heed lest he fall. You can trust
God; he won't set a harder test than you can bear.

Paul returned, finally, to the issue of suspect meat: *flee from idolatry.* We
recognise the cup and the bread as sacred, letting us share in the body and blood
of Christ. Similarly Jews invest their sacrifices with sanctity. Does this imply that
food offered to an idol has been given special properties? Not at all, but *Ye cannot*
drink the cup of the Lord, and the cup of devils.

To forestall objections, *All things are lawful for me, but all things are not*
expedient. It's one thing to buy meat from the slaughterhouse, or to eat at the home
of an unbeliever, no questions asked; it's another if you're told *This is offered in*
sacrifice unto idols. Although *the earth is the Lord's, and the fulness thereof,*
you have to consider how others view these things.

Moving on from food at last, Paul demonstrated his uncanny knack for saying 11
the wrong thing.

I would have you know, that the head of every man is Christ; and the head
of the woman is the man; and the head of Christ is God.

In keeping with this hierarchy, it is shameful for a man to pray or to prophesy with
his head covered, while for a woman the opposite is true. She might as well shave
her head (the humiliation inflicted on a loose woman) as go without a veil.

For a man indeed ought not to cover his head, forasmuch as he is the image
and glory of God: but the woman is the glory of the man. For the man is
not of the woman; but the woman of the man. Neither was the man created
for the woman; but the woman for the man.

Paul then made an obscure comment about the need for a woman to have something
on her head *because of the angels.* Although some people believe he was referring
to wicked, excitable angels, I think his concern was probably for good angels who
would be shocked by impropriety.

Paul did, to be fair, go on to say that man and woman each depend on the other.
If woman originally came out of man, man now comes from woman, and everything comes from God. Sadly, the poor chap felt compelled to be stupid again:

Doth not even nature itself teach you, that, if a man have long hair, it is a shame unto him? But if a woman have long hair, it is a glory to her: for her hair is given her for a covering.

Nature itself, eh? I hope he never sees those pictures of my brother. As the final argument – the easy-going Corinthians must have been a trial to him – Paul resorted to the last ditch defence of the old guard. It just wasn't done for a woman to pray bareheaded: *we have no such custom, neither the churches of God.*

Paul had heard some unhappy reports of their communal meals; it seemed that *ye come together not for the better, but for the worse.* They didn't eat as a group, with the result that some would just be arriving, hungry, when others were already drunk. He reminded them of what they were commemorating, as expressed to him (Paul alleged) by Jesus himself:

That the Lord Jesus the same night in which he was betrayed took bread: And when he had given thanks, he brake it, and said, Take, eat: this is my body, which is broken for you: this do in remembrance of me. After the same manner also he took the cup, when he had supped, saying, This cup is the new testament in my blood: this do ye, as oft as ye drink it, in remembrance of me.

This ritual, bound up as it is with the death of Jesus, is not to be undertaken lightly. In fact, *whosoever shall eat this bread, and drink this cup of the Lord, unworthily, shall be guilty of the body and blood of the Lord. But let a man examine himself,* because if he shouldn't be there he brings *damnation to himself, not discerning the Lord's body. For this cause many are weak and sickly among you, and many sleep.* Uplifting the worthy, killing the unworthy: these sacred meals were big medicine.

SPIRITUAL GIFTS

12 *Now concerning spiritual gifts, brethren, I would not have you ignorant,* which is always a danger. *Now there are diversities of gifts, but the same Spirit.* We might be able to speak with wisdom or knowledge, to have faith, to heal, to work miracles, to prophesy, to sort out good spirits from bad, to speak in tongues, or to interpret such speech: each has its place. Members of the church depend on each other like parts of the same body, the body of Christ. *For by one Spirit are we all baptized into one body, whether we be Jews or Gentiles, whether we be bond or free; and have been all made to drink into one Spirit.*

That's not to say that there isn't a hierarchy.

God hath set some in the church, first apostles, secondarily prophets, thirdly teachers, after that miracles, then gifts of healings, helps, govern-ments, diversities of tongues.

Paul suggested that they *covet earnestly the best gifts*. That might seem unnecessary advice, human nature being what it is, but the Corinthians were apparently over-enthusiastic about speaking in tongues. I think he was trying to tell them, in a round-about sort of way, to give it a rest.

His advice – certainly the best known of any he ever gave, and probably an   13
extract from a standard sermon – was as follows (reading 'love' in place of 'charity' might make it clearer):

Though I speak with the tongues of men and of angels, and have not charity, I am become as sounding brass, or a tinkling cymbal. And though I have the gift of prophecy, and understand all mysteries, and all knowledge; and though I have all faith, so that I could remove mountains, and have not charity, I am nothing. And though I bestow all my goods to feed the poor, and though I give my body to be burned, and have not charity, it profiteth me nothing.

Charity suffereth long, and is kind; charity envieth not; charity vaunteth not itself, is not puffed up, Doth not behave itself unseemly, seeketh not her own, is not easily provoked, thinketh no evil; Rejoiceth not in iniquity, but rejoiceth in the truth; Beareth all things, believeth all things, hopeth all things, endureth all things.

Charity never faileth: but whether there be prophecies, they shall fail; whether there be tongues, they shall cease; whether there be knowledge, it shall vanish away. For we know in part, and we prophesy in part. But when that which is perfect is come, then that which is in part shall be done away.

When I was a child, I spake as a child, I understood as a child, I thought as a child: but when I became a man, I put away childish things. For now we see through a glass, darkly; but then face to face: now I know in part; but then shall I know even as also I am known.

And now abideth faith, hope, charity, these three; but the greatest of these is charity.

And so back to business. Paul had more to say about the ecstatic gabbling, or   14
speaking in tongues, of which the Corinthians were so fond. There was nothing wrong with it, but the benefit is personal; by contrast, prophesying is educational for the whole congregation. *I would that ye all spake with tongues, but rather that ye prophesied.*

The problem with glossolalia – and what better word could there be for speaking in tongues? – was that to listeners it was all gibberish. *For if the trumpet give an uncertain sound, who shall prepare himself to the battle?* Being possessed by the spirit was a fine thing, but they should endeavor to use their brains as well. Paul, as usual, wasn't bashful.

I thank my God, I speak with tongues more than ye all: Yet in the church

I had rather speak five words with my understanding, that by my voice I might teach others also, than ten thousand words in an unknown tongue.

He told them to grow up. Taking a passage from Isaiah out of context, he maintained that *tongues are for a sign, not to them that believe, but to them that believe not.* In apparent self-contradiction, however, he then observed that if unbelievers saw people speaking in tongues, *will they not say that ye are mad?* It was much better to prophesy. The visitor might then find *the secrets of his heart made manifest; and so falling down on his face, he will worship God, and report that God is in you of a truth.*

Worship was never so exciting where I came from. Even Paul felt that they needed limits. He advised letting just a couple of people indulge in glossolalia during a meeting, on condition that someone was on hand to interpret. They should likewise take turns when prophesying, *For God is not the author of confusion, but of peace.*

To tighten the screws even further, Paul had a rule for all Christian congregations.

Let your women keep silence in the churches: for it is not permitted unto them to speak; but they are commanded to be under obedience, as also saith the law. And if they will learn any thing, let them ask their husbands at home: for it is a shame for women to speak in the church.

Perhaps I shouldn't describe it as Paul's rule; according to him, *the things that I write unto you are the commandments of the Lord.* How could we not believe him?

The missionary's lot is not an easy one; the natives do any number of strange things, and before you know it a chap hardly feels comfortable in church. *Let all things be done decently and in order.*

LIFE AFTER DEATH

15   The heretical notion that bodies might not return to life was apparently being passed around in Corinth, and Paul felt obliged to remind them of their creed. Jesus *rose again on the third day according to the scriptures* (which ones I've never been able to discover), and was seen by Peter, then the gang of twelve, and then by 500 disciples at once.

After that, he was seen of James; then of all the apostles. And last of all he was seen of me also, as of one born out of due time. For I am the least of the apostles, that am not meet to be called an apostle, because I persecuted the church of God. But by the grace of God I am what I am.

Paul didn't leave me out, but I'm still going to ask by what right he counted himself in: if there's no difference between the resurrection and a vision months or years afterwards, he weakens his own case. When he confesses to being an 'abortion', you know that an immodesty is coming. God hadn't wasted his time, Paul said; no one else had accomplished as much. *I laboured more abundantly than they all: yet not I, but the grace of God which was with me.* Good of him to share the credit.

So, then, since we claim that Jesus rose, *how say some among you that there is no resurrection of the dead?* If that were true, we'd be liars and lost souls. *If in this life only we have hope in Christ, we are of all men most miserable.* The idea obviously upset Paul, anyway.

> *But now is Christ risen from the dead, and become the firstfruits of them that slept. For since by man came death, by man came also the resurrection of the dead. For as in Adam all die, even so in Christ shall all be made alive.*

He will come and reign over the world, *till he hath put all enemies under his feet. The last enemy that shall be destroyed is death.* Everything will be subordinate to God, including the Son, *that God may be all in all.*

There are people, Paul observed, who have themselves baptized on behalf of the dead. Why bother, unless there's another life in prospect? Or for that matter, why do we ourselves struggle through life?

> *If after the manner of men I have fought with beasts at Ephesus, what advantageth it me, if the dead rise not? let us eat and drink; for to morrow we die.*

(Ephesus doesn't even have an arena; perhaps Paul was fantasizing about the wild animals, but I like to think he was referring to his opponents.) As an aside, he quoted a Greek playwright to warn against keeping bad company: *evil communications corrupt good manners.*

Proceeding now to practicalities, *some men will say, How are the dead raised up? and with what body do they come?* Although Paul could agree neither that the original body was revived, nor that only the soul survived, he didn't have much patience: *Thou fool, that which thou sowest is not quickened, except it die.* He looked for bodily resurrection, but not of the old lived-in flesh. Like seeds in the ground, we would emerge in new form.

Things come in different shapes and sizes; indeed, *one star differeth from another star in glory.* What equipment you need depends on where you are. *So also is the resurrection of the dead. It is sown in corruption; it is raised in incorruption. It is sown in dishonour; it is raised in glory.* The end product Paul had in mind was neither natural body, nor spirit, but *spiritual body* – a daring attempt to play both ends of the field at once.

The natural body comes first, and then the spiritual. Likewise Adam gives way to Jesus;

The first man is of the earth, earthy: the second man is the Lord from heaven. ... And as we have borne the image of the earthy, we shall also bear the image of the heavenly.

Now *flesh and blood cannot inherit the kingdom of God,* so something will have to happen.

Behold, I shew you a mystery; We shall not all sleep, but we shall all be changed, In a moment, in the twinkling of an eye, at the last trump: for the trumpet shall sound, and the dead shall be raised incorruptible, and we shall be changed. For this corruptible must put on incorruption, and this mortal must put on immortality.

When that happens we can say with the prophets *Death is swallowed up in victory. O death, where is thy sting? O grave, where is thy victory?* He rather spoiled the effect, I fear, by adding *The sting of death is sin; and the strength of sin is the law.* On the contrary, sin is all too enjoyable, and the law exists because people do wrong, not vice versa. The attempt to associate the law with death doesn't help his credibility.

16   Before signing off, Paul reminded them to put money aside for his collection; he wanted the cash to be ready when he arrived. He planned to visit Corinth after a forthcoming tour of Macedonia, and invited himself to spend the winter with them. After that, *ye may bring me on my journey whithersoever I go.*

Should Timothy come calling, they were to be hospitable; Paul seemed to fear – why, I don't know – that they might be rude to him. As for Apollos, *his will was not at all to come at this time,* despite Paul's encouragement; I can only guess that he didn't want to abet their sectarian tendencies.

Watch ye, stand fast in the faith, quit you like men, be strong. Treat stalwarts such as the family of Stephanas with respect; *they have addicted themselves to the ministry of the saints.* The whole crowd sends greetings, particularly (surprise) Aquila and Priscilla. Give everyone a kiss.

After the dictated portion of the letter follows *The salutation of me Paul with mine own hand. If any man love not the Lord Jesus Christ, let him be Anathema.* More of a curse than a salute, really. But try this Aramaic rallying cry: *Maranatha* – Come, O Lord! From Paul, that's an order.

8

II Corinthians

This letter, from *Paul, an apostle of Jesus Christ by the will of God, and Timothy* **1**
our brother, is generally described as the second to the Corinthians. Its predecessor
was in fact the second, however, and this one seems to contain both the third and
the fourth, unfortunately in reverse order. Religious publishers never were much
good.

After the conventional blessings, the authors (or Paul using the royal we – I
wouldn't put it past him) declared that if *we be afflicted, it is for your consolation*
and salvation. I gathered that Paul had been going through a rough patch; how this
would help the Corinthians is hard to say. He acknowledged their prayers, and was
glad that there would be so many to give thanks when his recovery was complete.

Evidently he had made some change to an earlier itinerary; *I was minded to*
come unto you before, that ye might have a second benefit, but no such luck. The
cancellation wasn't made for some unworthy motive. With Jesus it's never *yea and*
nay, but simply yea. *For all the promises of God in him are yea.*

The point is, anyway, that Paul had been thinking only of them when he decided
to give Corinth a miss. He didn't want to risk a repeat of that painful experience **2**
(his previous visit, I assume). It would just make him depressed, and he had
confidence in you all, that my joy is the joy of you all. Naturally. It was *out of*
much affliction and anguish of heart I wrote unto you with many tears (the letter
tacked on to the end of this one); *not that ye should be grieved, but that ye might*
know the love which I have more abundantly unto you. It hurt him more than it
hurt them, in other words.

Word had reached Paul, however, that the person who made his last visit such
a misery had been punished. Wanting bygones to be bygones he urged forgiveness,
Lest Satan should get an advantage of us: for we are not ignorant of his devices.
Paul confessed that the conflict had made him very uneasy, and the belated news
from his envoy Titus had come as a great relief.

Now thanks be unto God, who uses us to spread the word like scent over those
heading for salvation, and over those heading elsewhere. *To the one we are the*
savour of death unto death; and to the other the savour of life unto life. One
man's meat is another man's poison. As Paul remarked, it's a tough job.

He had no need of letters of recommendation, Paul said; the very existence of **3**
the Corinthian congregation was a message from Christ. Not, he hastened to say,
that he had done it all himself:

our sufficiency is of God; Who also hath made us able ministers of the new testament; not of the letter, but of the spirit: for the letter killeth, but the spirit giveth life.

He was back on the idea that the law was *the ministration of death.* It belonged to the old covenant: splendid in its day, but no match for the glories of the new dispensation.

Seeing then that we have such hope, we use great plainness of speech (did he ever not?). Moses wore a veil to protect the people from the reflected splendour of God. Regrettably the children of Israel still can't see clearly, *for until this day remaineth the same vail untaken away in the reading of the old testament; which vail is done away in Christ.* They miss being transfigured *by the Spirit of the Lord.*

4   The believers renounce shameful old habits (not specified, sadly), avoid distorting God's word (the prophets don't count), and spread the faith. The good news is only hidden from people who are headed for perdition; *the god of this world hath blinded the minds of them which believe not, lest the light of the glorious gospel of Christ, who is the image of God, should shine unto them.* Not very sporting.

We have been given the revelation, *But we have this treasure in earthen vessels.* Our mortal weakness is redeemed by Jesus, and our troubles will be far outweighed by the glory to come. We look beyond what we can see; *for the things which are seen are temporal; but the things which are not seen are eternal.*

5   Paul likened the physical body to a tent. He wasn't comfortable, however, with the idea that death might leave our souls naked under the stars; he preferred to believe that a permanent dwelling would be provided.

For we know that if our earthly house of this tabernacle were dissolved, we have a building of God, an house not made with hands, eternal in the heavens.

He wasn't content simply to trade in the tent, however; he wanted the new house to be built over it, *that mortality might be swallowed up in life.* Having it all was an article of faith with Paul. On the one hand, he recognised that *whilst we are at home in the body, we are absent from the Lord: (For we walk by faith, not by sight:)*; on the other hand, he realised that the body is too much a part of who we are to contemplate giving it up completely.

Paul was going to have it both ways on another score: grace and judgment. My understanding was that while everybody sins, faith was all you needed for a free pardon. Nevertheless, it seems that

we must all appear before the judgment seat of Christ; that every one may receive the things done in his body, according to that he hath done, whether it be good or bad.

Perhaps the pardon comes after the punishment.

The role of holy madman was tempting – if *we be beside ourselves, it is to God* – but there was the church to consider; if *we be sober, it is for your cause*. I'm surprised that the whole congregation wasn't behaving strangely: *if any man be in Christ, he is a new creature: old things are passed away; behold, all things are become new.* Never quite new enough, though.

We should really make peace with God; after all, *he hath made him to be sin for us, who knew no sin; that we might be made the righteousness of God in him.* God always said that he was there when he chose to be: *behold, now is the accepted* 6 *time; behold, now is the day of salvation.*

The missionary's life was not an easy one, Paul said. While enduring the worst physical hardships he had to be patient and kind. He carried on *By honour and dishonour, by evil report and good report.* Still, there were compensations; he lived *As sorrowful, yet alway rejoicing; as poor, yet making many rich; as having nothing, and yet possessing all things.*

The following paragraph may be from Paul's very first letter to the Corinthians, in which (his later reference to it suggests) he admonished them against associating with immoral men. The law of Moses forbids working two different kinds of animals in harness; likewise,

> *Be ye not unequally yoked together with unbelievers: for what fellowship hath righteousness with unrighteousness? and what communion hath light with darkness?*

Separatism is so boring, though.

Paul suddenly remembered that he hadn't properly finished the story with which 7 he began this (final) letter. He had been overjoyed to hear from Titus that they had repented. Although his previous letter had been harsh, it had clearly served its purpose:

> *what carefulness it wrought in you, yea, what clearing of yourselves, yea, what indignation, yea, what fear, yea, what vehement desire, yea, what zeal, yea, what revenge!*

Yea, what a wild man. Not quite what my brother had in mind, I suspect.

Innovator in so much, Paul also devised the evangelical epilogue: the appeal for 8 funds. The beneficiaries would, by tradition, be churches overseas. The Macedonians had already contributed lavishly to Paul's favourite cause, and he knew the Corinthians wouldn't want to be left out. *I speak not by commandment,* he said – God forbid there should be any pressure – but to remind them of the sacrifice Jesus made on their behalf.

The scheme, though reminiscent of that communism we promoted in the early days, sounded more like a form of insurance: *now at this time your abundance may be a supply for their want, that their abundance also may be a supply for your want.* A sensible approach, if not quite in the spirit of charity. Perhaps my brother said 'scratch my back and verily I'll scratch yours someday', but it doesn't ring a bell.

Titus had volunteered to return, Paul said, just to ensure that the money was flowing nicely. A colleague of high repute would accompany him as a kind of auditor, *that no man should blame us in this abundance which is administered by us.* A third person would also be coming along.

9   Paul told them frankly why this advance party was being sent: he had boasted to the Macedonians about the zeal of the Corinthians, claiming that everything had been in place a year ago, and *if they of Macedonia come with me, and find you unprepared, we (that we say not, ye) should be ashamed.* To avoid embarrassment, therefore, it was important that he didn't have to start scrounging when he arrived. I'm not surprised people wanted the funds audited.

Remember that you reap as you sow. *God loveth a cheerful giver;* he'll look after you. Your offering will reflect well on him and on the grace he's given you. *Thanks be unto God for his unspeakable gift.*

A STERN LETTER

10   At this point the tone changes dramatically; the best guess is that what follows is from Paul's previous letter, the one that had such a salutary effect. Responding to charges that he was as feeble as his letters were bold, he declared his readiness, with divine help, to show them the rough side of his character. (People can be cruel: *his letters, say they, are weighty and powerful; but his bodily presence is weak, and his speech contemptible.* You can't blame him for feeling hurt.)

11   *Would to God ye could bear with me a little in my folly,* Paul said. He confessed to jealousy on my brother's behalf, *for I have espoused you to one husband, that I may present you as a chaste virgin to Christ.* It appeared, though, that they had been seduced, like Eve corrupted by the serpent. He wasn't thrilled to be ditched in favour of unnamed preachers he sarcastically described as *the very chiefest apostles. But though I be rude in speech, yet not in knowledge;* he had always told them the truth.

He had never charged them for preaching the gospel, and didn't intend to start. His opponents were impostors, *And no marvel; for Satan himself is transformed into an angel of light.* Their *end shall be according to their works.* (Deeds can't assure salvation, according to Paul, but even he wanted to believe that they could lead to perdition.)

Paul sounded increasingly bitter. Since they were determined to take him for a fool, he would claim the privileges of one; *ye suffer fools gladly, seeing ye yourselves are wise.* What did the others boast?

Are they Hebrews? so am I. Are they Israelites? so am I. Are they the seed of Abraham? so am I. Are they ministers of Christ? (I speak as a fool) I am more; in labours more abundant, in stripes above measure, in prisons more frequent, in deaths oft. Of the Jews five times received I forty stripes save one. Thrice was I beaten with rods, once was I stoned, thrice I suffered shipwreck, a night and a day I have been in the deep; In journeyings often, in perils of waters, in perils of robbers, in perils by mine own countrymen, in perils by the heathen, in perils in the city, in perils in the wilderness, in perils in the sea, in perils among false brethren, In weariness and painfulness, in watchings often, in hunger and thirst, in fastings often, in cold and nakedness. Beside those things that are without, that which cometh upon me daily, the care of all the churches.

A lot of that comes as news to me; he must have landed himself in even more trouble than anybody told us.

To cap his other credentials, there were the visions he had been granted. That privilege was balanced by physical infirmity: **12**

there was given to me a thorn in the flesh, the messenger of Satan to buffet me, lest I should be exalted above measure. For this thing I besought the Lord thrice, that it might depart from me. And he said unto me, My grace is sufficient for thee: for my strength is made perfect in weakness.

On those terms, Paul declared, pain is a pleasure.

He reproached them with the work he had done in Corinth, miracles included. Had they suffered by comparison with any other congregation – *except it be that I myself was not burdensome to you? forgive me this wrong.* He wanted their souls, not their money. He feared, however, that at his next visit there would be *many which have sinned already, and have not repented of the uncleanness and fornication and lasciviousness which they have committed.*

Paul warned them that he would be unsparing towards sinners when he returned. **13** After further pokes and prods, he closed with a blessing that helped to produce the idea of the trinity, the three-in-one God: *The grace of the Lord Jesus Christ, and the love of God, and the communion of the Holy Ghost, be with you all. Amen.*

Galatians

1 Paul, commissioned as apostle, he declared, by Jesus and God himself, wrote *unto the churches of Galatia*, in Asia Minor. Coming straight to the point, he told them that he was astonished to hear that they were turning away from his teachings towards another so-called gospel. *If any man preach any other gospel unto you than that ye have received, let him be accursed.* Freedom of expression can be taken too far.

He hadn't been giving them second-hand doctrine; his news came *by revelation of Jesus Christ*. God had chosen him from birth, and revealed Jesus to him in order that he should carry the word to the Gentiles. At that point *I went into Arabia, and returned again unto Damascus*; it wasn't until three years later, Paul claimed, that he travelled to Jerusalem to see the original disciples. Even then he only spent a fortnight with Peter, and *other of the apostles saw I none, save James the Lord's brother*. Protesting too much for comfort, he insisted that *before God, I lie not*. This was all by way of demonstrating that he was a real apostle, not dependent on any others, bearing a message straight from the divine mouth.

2 There is, of course, the difficulty of explaining his later trips to Jerusalem, when we had summoned him to examine his (lack of) requirements for conversion. He baldly asserts *I went up by revelation*. Quite so: our messenger revealed to Paul that he'd better appear on the double, or else. As a sign that he was his own man, he makes a point of saying that his friend Titus didn't have to be circumcised. His opponents wanted to *bring us into bondage* – they believed in obeying the law of Moses, in other words.

The solution had been to divide the world into two spheres of influence: Paul would take the Gentiles, and we would take the Jews. *And when James, Cephas* (i.e. Peter, the Rock), *and John, who seemed to be pillars* (do I detect sour grapes?), *perceived the grace that was given unto me* (do I detect self-congratulation?), *they gave to me and Barnabas the right hands of fellowship; that we should go unto the heathen, and they unto the circumcision.*

The deal – an especially bad one for us, as it turned out – was done, but in-fighting continued. There was an unfortunate squabble in Antioch, which had a mixed congregation of Jews and Gentiles. Paul blames me for the trouble with Peter, who had come to visit; *before that certain came from James, he did eat with the Gentiles: but when they were come, he withdrew and separated himself*. Even Barnabas decided to pay more attention to his diet. Paul was outraged:

when I saw that they walked not uprightly according to the truth of the gospel, I said unto Peter before them all, If thou, being a Jew, livest after the manner of Gentiles, and not as do the Jews, why compellest thou the Gentiles to live as do the Jews?

I think he was suffering from a lapse in logic. We would have preferred the Gentiles to live as my brother did, according to a liberally-interpreted law, but we had agreed not to force them to do anything. Likewise, however, they had an obligation to respect our ways. Peter had been lax, but I don't regret reminding him that he was still a Jew.

Paul claimed, in effect, that trying to keep the commandments is a waste of time. We'll never succeed in being good enough for God, so our only hope is that Jesus will save us – which he will, if we have faith. By focusing on the law *I make myself a transgressor*, turning my back on God's grace, *for if righteousness come by the law, then Christ is dead in vain.*

AVOIDING THE LAW

Some legally-minded missionaries had been contradicting his teachings, apparently. *O foolish Galatians, who hath bewitched you ...?* It wasn't obedience that inspired God to work his miracles. Inventive as ever in his use of scripture, Paul argued that from Abraham onwards faith had been the path to God. Moreover my brother's ignoble death, far from being an embarrassment, breaks the power of the law over us. *Christ hath redeemed us from the curse of the law, being made a curse for us: for it is written, Cursed is every one that hangeth on a tree.* A fine example of begging the question: we have faith that he wasn't really cursed, so the law can't really apply.

That's ingenious, but what followed is pure sophistry. Before the law was ever given to Moses, God sealed the covenant with Abraham. *Now to Abraham and his seed were the promises made. He saith not, And to seeds, as of many; but as of one, And to thy seed, which is Christ.* A lot of his offspring(s) are going to be disappointed. Thus, Paul reasoned, my brother's blessing has priority over the law, which was provided merely as a holding operation.

Wherefore the law was our schoolmaster to bring us unto Christ, that we might be justified by faith. But after that faith is come, we are no longer under a schoolmaster.

Not before time, our people having suffered the birch for some thirteen centuries.

While we see equality before the law, Paul saw equality in faith. *There is neither Jew nor Greek, there is neither bond nor free, there is neither male nor female: for ye are all one in Christ Jesus.* As such everyone could be heir to Abraham.

4 Now that God is ready to adopt you, *how turn ye again to the weak and beggarly elements, whereunto ye desire again to be in bondage?*

Paul acknowledged that it was flattering to have seducers; *it is good to be zealously affected always in a good thing.* He just didn't happen to believe that those men were a good thing. *My little children ... I desire to be present with you now.* Some mothers have trouble letting go.

To discourage their incipient lust for the law, Paul came up with another novel interpretation of the scriptures:

> *it is written, that Abraham had two sons, the one by a bondmaid, the other by a freewoman. But he who was of the bondwoman was born after the flesh; but he of the freewoman was by promise. Which things are an allegory.*

Hagar was like the covenant of Mount Sinai, bearing children into slavery. We can identify with Isaac, the freeborn heir. *Cast out the bondwoman and her son;* there should be no one around to dispute the inheritance.

5 While I can't agree that my brother's work freed people from the constraints of the law, I do at least understand the opinion. Paul went further, however, claiming that deliberate obedience (to what are, remember, divine commands) did more harm than good. Thus, *if ye be circumcised, Christ shall profit you nothing.* You oblige yourself to keep all the commandments, and then you've had it; *ye are fallen from grace.* The notion that you have to rely on grace to deserve it strikes me as wrong-headed. Grace should be bestowed on people who try in good faith to toe the line, not on those who take their salvation for granted.

Those of us who were making his flock confused, Paul said, would have to answer to God. For his part, he wouldn't stop at circumcision; he'd like to see us castrated: *I would they were even cut off which trouble you.* Good old Paul – always raising the level of the debate.

Having announced our freedom from the law, he had the problem of reconciling his puritanism with that liberty. His advice was simple.

> *Walk in the Spirit, and ye shall not fulfil the lust of the flesh. For the flesh lusteth against the Spirit, and the Spirit against the flesh: and these are contrary the one to the other: so that ye cannot do the things that ye would.*

What happens, though, if you don't succeed in repressing the bodily desires? Nothing, I would have hoped, with grace in operation, but perhaps salvation isn't so certain after all.

> *Now the works of the flesh are manifest, which are these; Adultery, fornication, uncleanness, lasciviousness, Idolatry, witchcraft, hatred, variance, emulations, wrath, strife, seditions, heresies, Envyings, murders,*

drunkenness, revellings, and such like: of the which I tell you before, as I have also told you in time past, that they which do such things shall not inherit the kingdom of God.

That's a blow, I must say; quarrels and envy alone would account for most of us. If we're good, though, *the fruit of the Spirit is love, joy, peace, longsuffering, gentleness, goodness, faith, Meekness, temperance.* According to Paul, *they that are Christ's have crucified the flesh,* and don't have a problem with passion and desire. Not if they're dead, anyway.

This may come as a surprise, but every now and again I find myself in wholehearted agreement with Paul. Sometimes I even agree with his self-contradictory remarks. *Bear ye one another's burdens,* he said; *if a man think himself to be something, when he is nothing, he deceiveth himself.* Comparisons with others don't help, *For every man shall bear his own burden.* 6

Perhaps we can't work out who should carry what, but the usual farming metaphor presents no problems (except for Paul; it doesn't sound like justification by faith to me):

Be not deceived; God is not mocked: for whatsoever a man soweth, that shall he also reap. For he that soweth to his flesh shall of the flesh reap corruption; but he that soweth to the Spirit shall of the Spirit reap life everlasting. And let us not be weary in well doing: for in due season we shall reap, if we faint not.

So, he said, let's go do good deeds for others, giving believers priority.

Taking over from his secretary, Paul wrote the last few lines himself, in big characters. *Ye see how large a letter I have written unto you with mine own hand.* He disparaged the motives of his opponents, saying that they *desire to have you circumcised, that they may glory in your flesh.* He himself was beyond reproach. *From henceforth let no man trouble me: for I bear in my body the marks of the Lord Jesus.* I hope he was being figurative, but with Paul you never know.

10

Ephesians

1   This is supposed to be a letter from Paul *to the saints which are at Ephesus*. Paul probably didn't write it, and if he did, it wasn't to Ephesus. Although he had lived there for years, the letter seems to address strangers. It might have been a circular, of course, a piece of ecclesiastical junk mail. I'll call the writer Paul, but to my mind, at any rate, the tract just doesn't read like his work.

Since before creation, he said, we were predestined to be pure and holy. God decided that in *the fulness of times he might gather together in one all things in Christ,* from both heaven and earth. This phrase 'in Christ', with my brother as a metaphorical wrapper, has been hugely popular – beaten to death, in fact.

Whatever message there was in the humble life and humiliating death of Jesus has now been transformed; God

> *set him at his own right hand in the heavenly places, Far above all principality, and power, and might, and dominion, and every name that is named, not only in this world, but also in that which is to come: And hath put all things under his feet.*

I rather had the impression (remember the temptation in the wilderness?) that he didn't want everyone at his feet, let alone under them.

2   We were followers of Satan, but Jesus changed that, *For by grace are ye saved through faith.* Jews and Gentiles have been brought together; he *came and preached peace to you which were afar off, and to them that were nigh.* All may now be part of God's house.

3   We're already aware, of course, that *Unto me, who am less than the least of all saints, is this grace given, that I should preach among the Gentiles the unsearchable riches of Christ.* God had kept his intentions hidden since the beginning of time, but now the cat was out of the bag: everyone would share in the new age.

Paul offered a prayer for the occasion:

> *I bow my knees unto the Father of our Lord Jesus Christ, Of whom the whole family in heaven and earth is named, That he would grant you, according to the riches of his glory, to be strengthened with might by his Spirit in the inner man.*

He wanted us to grasp the intangible, and to understand the incomprehensible: to comprehend divine love in its four (?) dimensions of *breadth, and length, and depth, and height; And to know the love of Christ, which passeth knowledge.* Nothing, however, is too much for God.

Now unto him that is able to do exceeding abundantly above all that we ask or think, according to the power that worketh in us, Unto him be glory in the church by Christ Jesus throughout all ages, world without end. Amen.

Paul had some general instructions for them. *I therefore, the prisoner of the*   4 *Lord, beseech you that ye walk worthy of the vocation wherewith ye are called.* They should be united in *One Lord, one faith, one baptism* (one wishes). Everybody has some talent, *according to the measure of the gift of Christ* – occasionally a meagre one, on the face of it.

After a confusing aside in which he misquotes scripture, and says that Jesus *descended first into the lower parts of the earth,* Paul returns to the vocational theme.

And he gave some, apostles; and some, prophets; and some, evangelists; and some, pastors and teachers; For the perfecting of the saints, for the work of the ministry, for the edifying of the body of Christ: Till we all come in the unity of the faith, and of the knowledge of the Son of God, unto a perfect man, unto the measure of the stature of the fulness of Christ: That we henceforth be no more children, tossed to and fro, and carried about with every wind of doctrine, by the sleight of men, and cunning craftiness, whereby they lie in wait to deceive.

Our society will be one body, with Christ as its head.

Unbelievers are nasty creatures. They are blind, and *being past feeling have given themselves over unto lasciviousness, to work all uncleanness with greediness.* The followers of Jesus, by contrast, put their lusts behind them to become new men; *we are members one of another.*

You can lose your temper, but don't harbour a grudge. *Be ye angry, and sin not: let not the sun go down upon your wrath: Neither give place to the devil.* Don't use profanity. Be nice.

The Paul I knew was never this syrupy. He can tell me to *walk in love,* but I   5 draw the line at hearing that my brother was *a sacrifice to God for a sweetsmelling savour.* There was nothing fragrant about it, believe me.

Some of the old fire (and brimstone) was still there, though.

But fornication, and all uncleanness, or covetousness, let it not be once named among you, as becometh saints; Neither filthiness, nor foolish talking, nor jesting, which are not convenient: but rather giving of thanks. For this ye know, that no whoremonger, nor unclean person, nor covetous man, who is an idolater, hath any inheritance in the kingdom of Christ and of God. Let no man deceive you with vain words: for because of these things cometh the wrath of God upon the children of disobedience.

That's more like it. And he was being discreet, *For it is a shame even to speak of those things which are done of them in secret.* Too bad, but it never hurts to leave some things to the imagination. *See then that ye walk circumspectly, not as fools, but as wise, Redeeming the time, because the days are evil.* If you need an intoxicant, try songs of praise:

And be not drunk with wine, wherein is excess; but be filled with the Spirit; Speaking to yourselves in psalms and hymns and spiritual songs, singing and making melody in your heart to the Lord.

Why be exclusive? Wine and song go together, I find. They go with something else, too, but I think he's covered that. If you succumb to marriage, Paul has a simple rule for you.

Wives, submit yourselves unto your own husbands, as unto the Lord. For the husband is the head of the wife, even as Christ is the head of the church: and he is the saviour of the body. Therefore as the church is subject unto Christ, so let the wives be to their own husbands in every thing.

Domestic slavery makes life so much easier. It's not a one-way street, of course. Just as Christ loved the church, *So ought men to love their wives as their own bodies. He that loveth his wife loveth himself.* How very gratifying. Since *no man ever yet hated his own flesh,* and a woman becomes part of it on marriage, she has nothing to worry about. Let him love her like an appendage, let *the wife see that she reverence her husband,* and everything is as it should be.

6 Paul didn't confine himself to sorting out the wives. Children must also be obedient, and to reciprocate, *ye fathers, provoke not your children to wrath.* Slaves are to do as they are told and to put their backs into it, as if under divine command:

Servants, be obedient to them that are your masters according to the flesh, with fear and trembling, in singleness of your heart, as unto Christ; Not with eyeservice, as menpleasers; but as the servants of Christ, doing the will of God from the heart.

I hate to see a slave who isn't cheerful in his work.

Finally, learn to wear the divine power.

Put on the whole armour of God, that ye may be able to stand against the wiles of the devil. For we wrestle not against flesh and blood, but against principalities, against powers, against the rulers of the darkness of this world, against spiritual wickedness in high places. Wherefore take unto you the whole armour of God, that ye may be able to withstand in the evil day, and having done all, to stand.

Stand therefore, having your loins girt about with truth, and having on the breastplate of righteousness; And your feet shod with the preparation of the gospel of peace; Above all, taking the shield of faith, wherewith ye shall be able to quench all the fiery darts of the wicked. And take the helmet of salvation, and the sword of the Spirit, which is the word of God.

Give me a chariot of fire and I'll be all set. With a request for prayers and a perfunctory reference to his messenger, Paul signed off.

11

Philippians

1 Paul wrote to the congregation at Philippi while imprisoned – probably in Rome, though I wouldn't swear to it. He expressed confidence that God, having set to work on them, would finish the job by judgment day. There were things he'd like to do before then; *For God is my record, how greatly I long after you all in the bowels of Jesus Christ.*

The possibility of death made Paul emotional, and who can blame him. Still, he expected to come out ahead whatever happened, *For to me to live is Christ, and to die is gain.* He was in two minds about it, *having a desire to depart, and to be with Christ; which is far better: Nevertheless to abide in the flesh is more needful for you.* Only thinking of others, as usual. They should face their opponents without fear, *which is to them an evident token of perdition, but to you of salvation.* Suffering for the faith was an honour.

2 He wanted them to be united. When it came to putting aside personal interest, there was no better example than Jesus.

> *Let this mind be in you, which was also in Christ Jesus: Who, being in the form of God, thought it not [worth] robbery to be equal with God: But made himself of no reputation, and took upon him the form of a servant, and was made in the likeness of men: And being found in fashion as a man, he humbled himself, and became obedient unto death, even the death of the cross.*
>
> *Wherefore God also hath highly exalted him, and given him a name which is above every name: That at the name of Jesus every knee should bow, of things in heaven, and things in earth, and things under the earth; And that every tongue should confess that Jesus Christ is Lord, to the glory of God the Father.*

I'm delighted for my brother, of course, but sacrifice seems to lose its punch when the person (or god-like being) winds up better off than before.

And so, Paul said, they should continue to be obedient. (The partisans of faith still want to give orders.) Even more worrying for those relying on God's grace, he told them to *work out your own salvation with fear and trembling. For it is God which worketh in you both to will and to do of his good pleasure.* That should help, at least, especially being *in the midst of a crooked and perverse nation, among whom ye shine as lights in the world.* Such a civilised place it was, too.

Paul was giving every appearance of closing the letter, mentioning that he hoped to send Timothy soon, and would return their emissary Epaphroditus forthwith, when he suddenly changed tack. *Beware of dogs, beware of evil workers,* beware 3 of the penis mutilators – the truly circumcised are those who *have no confidence in the flesh.* With his endearing immodesty, he said that if salvation were just a matter of form, there could be no better candidate than himself.

If any other man thinketh that he hath whereof he might trust in the flesh, I more: Circumcised on the eighth day, of the stock of Israel, of the tribe of Benjamin, an Hebrew of the Hebrews; as touching the law, a Pharisee; Concerning zeal, persecuting the church; touching the righteousness which is in the law, blameless. But what things were gain to me, those I counted loss for Christ.

He had renounced his advantages, *and do count them but dung, that I may win Christ.* It was not by obedience to the law, but through faith, that he would be made righteous. All he wanted – and I find this worrying – was to share in the sufferings of Jesus, *If by any means I might attain unto the resurrection of the dead.*

In fact, Paul admitted, he wasn't perfect yet. I'd see no reason to be, by his principles, but as usual he was having it both ways. Life was a race:

this one thing I do, forgetting those things which are behind, and reaching forth unto those things which are before, I press toward the mark for the prize of the high calling of God in Christ Jesus.

It's important to be well behaved, and again Paul suggested that they could use him as a standard. Among their number were *enemies of the cross of Christ: Whose end is destruction, whose God is their belly, and whose glory is in their shame, who mind earthly things.* (As most people do, I'd guess.) The rest of us, however, are citizens of heaven, and can look forward to having our bodies transformed by Jesus.

Rejoice in the Lord alway: and again I say, Rejoice. ... The Lord is at hand. 4
Don't be afraid; tell God what you want.

And the peace of God, which passeth all understanding, shall keep your hearts and minds through Christ Jesus. Finally, brethren, whatsoever things are honest, whatsoever things are just, whatsoever things are pure, whatsoever things are lovely, whatsoever things are of good report; if there be any virtue, and if there be any praise, think on these things.

Having extolled the power of positive thinking, Paul thought fit to thank them for their financial support. The money didn't really matter, of course; *I have learned, in whatsoever state I am, therewith to be content. ... I can do all things through Christ which strengtheneth me.* The contribution was so welcome *Not because I desire a gift: but I desire fruit that may abound to your account.* Altruistic to the last. Such offerings were sweet-smelling and much appreciated by God, who would in turn *supply all your need according to his riches in glory by Christ Jesus.* Everybody came out ahead.

With that, Paul passed on regards from the boys, and said farewell.

12

Colossians

Another of Paul's prison letters was sent to Colossae, a town well off the beaten track, about a hundred miles southeast of Ephesus. As far as I'm aware Paul never even saw the place, but he was always thankful to have new believers. Just what to believe is a problem for converts, and he gave them a helpful summary of the creed. (The angelic armies, classified by rank as thrones, etc., are officially recognised.) God 1

> *hath delivered us from the power of darkness, and hath translated us into the kingdom of his dear Son: In whom we have redemption through his blood, even the forgiveness of sins:*
>
> *Who is the image of the invisible God, the firstborn of every creature: For by him were all things created, that are in heaven, and that are in earth, visible and invisible, whether they be thrones, or dominions, or principalities, or powers: all things were created by him, and for him: And he is before all things, and by him all things consist.*

Not bad for a Jewish boy from the provinces.

The blood of Jesus has reconciled the universe to God. Before hearing the gospel they had been alienated from God because of their own wickedness; having been purified, they had only to keep the faith. The cosmic Christ, whose promises have been *preached to every creature which is under heaven* – that's a surprise – would take it from there.

Paul made one of his characteristically odd statements, claiming to *rejoice in my sufferings for you, and fill up that which is behind of the afflictions of Christ.* I don't think he meant to imply that my brother hadn't met his quota of suffering. He could have believed that pain brought the end of the world that much closer – or he might just have been over-enthusiastic.

For ages God had kept his secret from everyone, but now he, Paul, had been appointed to make the announcement. The secret was this: *Christ in you, the hope of glory*. Obviously God didn't waste words. I wonder why previous generations over thousands of years had to miss out.

The message, in fact, could be made even more succinct: Christ. Paul warned them against philosophical speculation that might lead anywhere else, *For in him dwelleth all the fulness of the Godhead bodily.* There was a danger of being misled 2 by angel worshippers, or by ascetics saying *Touch not; taste not; handle not.* They should be above all that.

3   Paul's orders, then, were to *Set your affection on things above, not on things on the earth.* That said, he went into detail about what to avoid (if it sounds familiar, most of it was copied in the letter to the Ephesians):

> *Mortify therefore your members which are upon the earth; fornication, uncleaness, inordinate affection, evil concupiscence, and covetousness, which is idolatry: For which things' sake the wrath of God cometh on the children of disobedience: In the which ye also walked some time, when ye lived in them. But now ye also put off all these; anger, wrath, malice, blasphemy, filthy communication out of your mouth.*
>
> *Lie not one to another, seeing that ye have put off the old man with his deeds; And have put on the new man, which is renewed in knowledge after the image of him that created him: Where there is neither Greek nor Jew, circumcision nor uncircumcision, Barbarian, Scythian, bond nor free: but Christ is all, and in all.*

Put on therefore, as the elect, God's chosen people, such virtues as compassion, gentleness, and patience. Be forgiving, and above all, be guided by love.

Applying these principles to domestic life, Paul came up with rules for wives and husbands, children and parents, slaves and masters.

> *Wives, submit yourselves unto your own husbands, as it is fit in the Lord. Husbands, love your wives, and be not bitter against them.*
>
> *Children, obey your parents in all things: for this is well pleasing unto the Lord. Fathers, provoke not your children to anger, lest they be discouraged.*
>
> *Servants, obey in all things your masters ... And whatsoever ye do, do it*
4   *heartily, as to the Lord ... Masters, give unto your servants that which is just.*

Let's just say that his theory looks better than the practice. Paul was a regular fountain of personal advice; in order to influence people, *Let your speech be alway with grace, seasoned with salt, that ye may know how ye ought to answer every man.*

It was time for greetings and goodbyes. Having named a few of his colleagues, Paul meant to say that they were the only Jews among his helpers, and that he appreciated their company. The way it came out, though, was wonderfully absurd: they were Jews, and *These only are my fellowworkers unto the kingdom of God, which have been a comfort to me.* Preachers can make your life miserable, all right.

Luke, the beloved physician, and Demas, greet you. Paul himself sent regards to the intriguingly-named Nympha(s) and everyone at her (his) house (the sex of this person is uncertain, curiously enough). At the bottom, he scribbled *The salutation by the hand of me Paul. Remember my bonds. Grace be with you. Amen.* He was an odd fellow, all right. (Remember my bank balance. Yours sincerely, James.)

13

I Thessalonians

1   A decade previously, Paul wrote what might be the earliest of all these letters to the fledgling congregation at Thessalonica. He credits Silvanus (otherwise known as Silas) and Timothy as joint authors.

We give thanks to God always for you all, making mention of you in our prayers; Remembering without ceasing your work of faith, and labour of love, and patience of hope in our Lord Jesus Christ.

They could count themselves among God's chosen. News of their conversion had spread far and wide, of how they turned away from idols and waited now for the appearance of *Jesus, which delivered us from the wrath to come.*

2   Reading between the lines, I gather Paul feared that they would take him for just another wandering preacher or teacher. He appealed to them in emotional fashion, denying any attempt to win fame or fortune.

But we were gentle among you, even as a nurse cherisheth her children: So being affectionately desirous of you, we were willing to have imparted unto you, not the gospel of God only, but also our own souls, because ye were dear to us. For ye remember, brethren, our labour and travail: for labouring night and day, because we would not be chargeable unto any of you, we preached unto you the gospel of God.

Paul didn't enjoy being defensive; he always seemed to be bursting to attack. If their new faith had led to hardship, they were in good company; the original group of followers in Judaea had had nothing but grief from

the Jews: Who both killed the Lord Jesus, and their own prophets, and have persecuted us; and they please not God, and are contrary to all men: Forbidding us to speak to the Gentiles that they might be saved, to fill up their sins alway: for the wrath is come upon them to the uttermost.

Charming. My brother dies trying to make us better Jews, and his self-appointed executor encourages a hate campaign.

At any rate, Paul still had some explaining to do, having left the congregation without guidance. He claimed that *we would have come unto you, even I Paul, once and again; but Satan hindered us.* It wasn't his fault. In the end he sent Timothy to find out what was happening, and had been pleased to hear *good tidings of your faith and charity, and that ye have good remembrance of us always.* For that he thanked God.

Although the reports were good, a few reminders never hurt. God wanted them to be holy, and therefore *ye should abstain from fornication,* respecting the body, not succumbing to lust like *the Gentiles which know not God.* Paul remarked, somewhat cryptically, that for a man to take advantage of a brother in this department would result in divine punishment. 4

Admitting that they needed no instruction in brotherly love, Paul urged them to go one better, suggesting that *ye study to be quiet, and to do your own business, and to work with your own hands.* Self-sufficiency can do wonders.

People were concerned, apparently, about the fate of fellow believers who died before the return of Jesus. Paul promised that they would be resurrected; indeed, they would be at the front of the queue.

> *For the Lord himself shall descend from heaven with a shout, with the voice of the archangel, and with the trump of God: and the dead in Christ shall rise first: Then we which are alive and remain shall be caught up together with them in the clouds, to meet the Lord in the air: and so shall we ever be with the Lord.*

We'll never have our feet on the ground again.

Just when this might happen was hard to say; *the day of the Lord so cometh as a thief in the night.* One moment people would be talking about peace, and *then sudden destruction cometh upon them ... they shall not escape.* The faithful were in a different category, though; *Ye are all the children of light, and the children of the day: we are not of the night, nor of darkness.* Not for them the drunken night-time stupor. *But let us, who are of the day, be sober, putting on the breastplate of faith and love; and for an helmet, the hope of salvation.* God doesn't have us marked down for perdition. 5

In closing, Paul asked them to be good to one another; *warn them that are unruly, comfort the feebleminded, support the weak, be patient toward all men.* (I wish we could be selective, but it goes against the policy of our founder.) *Pray without ceasing.* There was even a motto for sceptics: *Prove all things; hold fast that which is good.* As he said, he had something for everybody.

14

II Thessalonians

1   There's a follow-up letter to the congregation at Thessalonica. Paul had an explanation for the inexplicable: the suffering endured by God's people. Far from throwing doubt on divine justice, such hardship demonstrated it. The faithful were shown to be worthy, and trouble-makers to merit condemnation. Accounts would be balanced

> *when the Lord Jesus shall be revealed from heaven with his mighty angels, In flaming fire taking vengeance on them that know not God, and that obey not the gospel of our Lord Jesus Christ: Who shall be punished with everlasting destruction from the presence of the Lord.*

Most satisfying for those of us with enemies, though victims of disease, accident and disaster ('acts of God'?) might be less impressed.

2   On the matter of the apocalypse, Paul needed to clear up a few points. Some of them apparently believed that the day of the Lord had arrived – not so. First the leader of the opposition, a man of sin, doomed to perdition, would have to rebel against God. The power of lawlessness was already at work, in fact, but for the moment someone was holding it in check. When the restraining force was removed, *then shall that Wicked be revealed, whom the Lord shall consume with the spirit of his mouth, and shall destroy with the brightness of his coming.*

No one is quite sure what he meant. Paul made it clear that Satan, though responsible for the coming of the man of lawlessness, shouldn't be identified with him. The Roman emperor might fill a role as either the force of evil or restraint (or both?). Another popular suggestion is that Paul pictured himself as the restrainer, which wouldn't surprise me.

Steps will be taken to ensure that people destined for destruction have suitably mistaken ideas.

> *God shall send them strong delusion, that they should believe a lie: That they all might be damned who believed not the truth, but had pleasure in unrighteousness.*

He wouldn't want to risk condemning an innocent person.

3   Paul wrapped things up with the usual round of exhortations. Instead of appealing for unity, however, he ordered *that ye withdraw yourselves from every*

brother that walketh disorderly, and not after the tradition which he received of us. In particular, he heard that some of them were being lazy, which was completely contrary to the example he had set. When people believe that the end is at hand, I'm afraid they tend to lose interest in making a living. Paul insisted, however, that *if any would not work, neither should he eat.* That should take care of those who were *working not at all, but are busybodies.* Peace and grace.

15

I Timothy

I'm afraid we've almost seen the last of the real Paul. Although the next three letters – dealing largely with practical matters of church leadership, and hence known as the Pastoral Epistles – claim to be by the master, they look like forgeries to most people. I'd like to pin the blame on him, but it wouldn't be fair.

1   The first letter is addressed to Timothy, the young favourite. Paul wanted him to stamp out the teaching of *fables and endless genealogies,* which were no substitute for sound doctrine. Neither is the law a substitute for the gospel – in fact, the faithful might just as well ignore it:

> *we know that the law is good, if a man use it lawfully; Knowing this, that the law is not made for a righteous man, but for the lawless and disobedient, for the ungodly and for sinners, for unholy and profane, for murderers of fathers and murderers of mothers, for manslayers, For whoremongers, for them that defile themselves with mankind, for menstealers, for liars, for perjured persons.*

For believers, all you need is love.

Having mentioned his shameful past as a persecutor of the movement, Paul said *I obtained mercy, because I did it ignorantly in unbelief.* My impression was that ignorance and unbelief are no excuse, but I suppose timely repentance makes all the difference. He was confident that *Christ Jesus came into the world to save sinners; of whom I am chief.* That's authentic enough; he always had to be the best at everything.

Don't expect any favours, though. He told Timothy to battle on against error, lest he end up like *Hymenaeus and Alexander; whom I have delivered unto Satan, that they may learn not to blaspheme.* Some people have to be taught love the hard way.

2   After a rather windy exhortation to tranquillity, Paul turned to the place of women. They were to dress modestly, avoiding fancy hairstyles, fine jewellery and expensive clothes, arraying themselves instead with good deeds (not faith?). That was just for starters.

> *Let the woman learn in silence with all subjection. But I suffer not a woman to teach, nor to usurp authority over the man, but to be in silence. For Adam was first formed, then Eve. And Adam was not deceived, but the*

woman being deceived was in the transgression. Notwithstanding she shall be saved in childbearing, if they continue in faith and charity and holiness with sobriety.

Delighted to hear it.

Paul went on to consider the qualifications for leadership in the church; by the   3
sound of it, you can't take anything for granted.

If a man desire the office of a bishop, he desireth a good work. A bishop then must be blameless, the husband of one wife, vigilant, sober, of good behaviour, given to hospitality, apt to teach; Not given to wine, no striker, not greedy of filthy lucre; but patient, not a brawler, not covetous; One that ruleth well his own house, having his children in subjection with all gravity; (For if a man know not how to rule his own house, how shall he take care of the church of God?)

How odd that we ended up being led by a troop of childless bachelors.

A bishop shouldn't be a new convert, because of the temptations of pride, and there should be no risk of scandal from those outside the faith. For lower office the requirements are similar, and just as markedly negative. *Likewise must the deacons be grave, not doubletongued, not given to much wine, not greedy of filthy lucre.* Their wives (only one each) should be serious, not given to gossip.

Paul cited a prophecy: the time would come, the Spirit said, when *some shall*   4
depart from the faith, giving heed to seducing spirits, and doctrines of devils; Speaking lies in hypocrisy; having their conscience seared with a hot iron. These peddlers of diabolical doctrine wanted people to abstain from marriage and from certain foods. I had expected something more exotic; besides, Paul was notoriously cool on the idea of marriage, and had some sympathy for fussy eaters. Here, though, the rule was simply that *every creature of God is good* (to eat), *and nothing to be refused, if it be received with thanksgiving.*

That was the sort of advice, he told Timothy, that people ought to hear. *But refuse profane and old wives' fables, and exercise thyself rather unto godliness.* The advantages are felt now and in the life to come. *Let no man despise thy youth; but be thou an example.* Paul urged him to continue his religious education, making sure that people noticed the improvement. Everybody would come out ahead.

Widows are always in need of pastoral attention. Not every widow is a real widow, however; if she has offspring, *let them learn first to shew pity at home, and to requite their parents,* which takes a burden off the church. A real widow is alone, and prays day and night, *But she that liveth in pleasure is dead while she liveth.* Just as bad as a merry widow is someone who doesn't look after his relatives: *if any provide not for his own, and specially for those of his own house, he hath denied the faith, and is worse than an infidel.* So much for the priority of faith over works.

Only a widow past the age of 60 should receive church funds, and not even then unless she has been faithful to a single husband, is known for good works, has reared children, has given hospitality, has washed the feet of other church-goers, has helped the afflicted – in short has devoted herself to doing good.

> *But the younger widows refuse: for when they have begun to wax wanton against Christ, they will marry; Having damnation, because they have cast off their first faith. And withal they learn to be idle, wandering about from house to house; and not only idle, but tattlers also and busybodies, speaking things which they ought not. I will therefore that the younger women marry, bear children, guide the house, give none occasion to the adversary to speak reproachfully. For some are already turned aside after Satan.*

Not so much starving them back into marriage, as making a virtue of necessity.

If an elder works hard at leading, preaching and teaching, you can double his pension. An accusation against an elder should be supported by *two or three witnesses.* (More than one, in other words?) Public sentencing is to be recommended, *that others also may fear.* Paul further suggested – if I understood him correctly – that quick pardons aren't desirable; *keep thyself pure.*

Completely out of the blue, he said *Drink no longer water, but use a little wine for thy stomach's sake and thine often infirmities.* Now we're talking.

6 The instructions wouldn't be complete without a few words for slaves. *Let as many servants as are under the yoke count their masters worthy of all honour, that the name of God and his doctrine be not blasphemed.* Heaven forbid that any rudeness bring the gospel into disrepute. If the master is himself a believer, his slaves shouldn't try to take advantage; on the contrary, they should work even harder to serve. Hallelujah.

16

II Timothy

Passages in this letter sound like the real Paul, including the emotional opening. 1
Timothy was constantly in his prayers: *Greatly desiring to see thee, being mindful of thy tears, that I may be filled with joy.* Paul urged him to make the most of that *which is in thee by the putting on of my hands. For God hath not given us the spirit of fear; but of power, and of love, and of a sound mind.*

Paul admitted that preaching the gospel had landed him in hot water – he was apparently writing from prison in Rome. He still had faith, however. Perhaps sensing that time was short, he told Timothy to *Hold fast the form of sound words, which thou hast heard of me.* Paul complained that everyone in the province of Asia had deserted him (mentioning two of the culprits by name); happily a certain Onesiphorus had been a great comfort to him in Rome, *and in how many things he ministered unto me at Ephesus, thou knowest very well.*

In a rambling collection of exhortations and worthy sayings, Paul told Timothy 2
to continue his mission. He should *endure hardness, as a good soldier of Jesus Christ.* Changing metaphors, he was an athlete, a farmer, *a workman that needeth not to be ashamed, rightly dividing the word of truth.* There were heretics (Paul named a couple), whose *word will eat as doth a canker,* but God knows which people are on his side.

Flee also youthful lusts: but follow righteousness, faith, charity, peace, etc. Be firm but gentle with the misguided. *This know also, that in the last days* 3
perilous times shall come. By the sound of it, though, we won't be able to tell the difference.

For men shall be lovers of their own selves, covetous, boasters, proud, blasphemers, disobedient to parents, unthankful, unholy, Without natural affection, truce-breakers, false accusers, incontinent, fierce, despisers of those that are good, Traitors, heady, highminded, lovers of pleasure more than lovers of God; Having a form of godliness, but denying the power thereof.

Life as usual, in other words. Be on your guard if the catalogue reminds you of anyone; men *of this sort are they which creep into houses, and lead captive silly women laden with sins, led away with divers lusts, Ever learning, and never able to come to the knowledge of the truth.* That's it? Come the last days a few frolics are the worst we'll have to hold against the wicked?

For the faithful, life is much less fun. In fact *all that will live godly in Christ Jesus shall suffer persecution.* Nevertheless, Timothy was told, remember your lessons, not to mention the scriptures. I wouldn't have expected this from Paul: *All scripture is given by inspiration of God, and is profitable for doctrine, for reproof, for correction, for instruction in righteousness,* so that you're equipped to do good works. Obedience to scripture would have turned people into Jews, which was not at all Paul's intention.

4   He ordered Timothy to *Preach the word; be instant in season, out of season.* It would be his last wish, for *the time of my departure is at hand. I have fought a good fight, I have finished my course, I have kept the faith.* The valediction would have been more touching had he not gone on to say that there was *a crown of righteousness* coming to him.

Paul had a score to settle before dying. *Alexander the coppersmith did me much evil: the Lord reward him according to his works.* There were a few greetings to or from comrades, and that was it.

17

Titus

Titus was continuing the mission on Crete. Paul had asked that elders be appointed 1 in every town, and now he reviewed the necessary qualifications: *blameless, the husband of one wife,* and so on.

The congregation obviously hadn't impressed Paul favourably. For a start *there are many unruly and vain talkers and deceivers,* especially amongst the Jewish tendency. Their *mouths must be stopped,* as they are subverting entire households by *teaching things which they ought not, for filthy lucre's sake.* In his view, I gather, such faults were ethnic traits; one of their own countrymen had said *The Cretians are alway liars, evil beasts, slow bellies. This witness is true.*

You can't be soft with people like that. *Unto the pure all things are pure: but unto them that are defiled and unbelieving is nothing pure.* They claim to *know God; but in works they deny him, being abominable, and disobedient, and unto every good work reprobate.* Perhaps some preacher put too much emphasis on faith.

The old men should be *sober, grave,* etc., and similarly the old women should 2 be reverent, *not false accusers, not given to much wine.* If they could hold back from riotous living, the matrons might also teach their juniors *to be sober, to love their husbands, to love their children, To be discreet, chaste, keepers at home, good, obedient to their own husbands.* Obeying somebody else's husband can be a mistake.

Young men likewise exhort to be sober minded. Slaves should be told to comply with their masters' every wish, *that they may adorn the doctrine of God our Saviour in all things.* Adornment is a matter of taste, I suppose.

In general the idea was to deny *worldly lusts* in favour of righteous living, anticipating the reappearance of 'our great God and Saviour Jesus Christ'. (This label inspired a degree of discomfort among monotheists.) To conclude the duties 3 of obedience, people were to submit to the civil authorities.

We all know what it is to sin. We have been saved *by the washing of regeneration, and renewing of the Holy Ghost.* I don't think the real Paul would have described baptism that way; he saw salvation as a future, not a past, event. And although the writer refers to being *justified by his grace,* he also hopes *that they which have believed in God might be careful to maintain good works.*

No doubt we'll still be arguing when my brother returns. Who, though, is the heretic? It's not an idle question. *A man that is an heretick after the first and second admonition reject; Knowing that he that is such is subverted, and sinneth, being condemned of himself.* It might be lucky for Paul that he never met Jesus — or perhaps for Jesus, that he never met Paul.

18

Philemon

This is a peculiar letter. It's entirely personal, with no doctrinal or moral content. (Perhaps there's immoral content, but that's another matter.) Just because the man was on the road to sainthood doesn't mean that we have to treat every word he wrote as sacred. The poor fellow is lucky that no one copied his laundry lists.

At any rate, the letter is from *Paul, a prisoner of Jesus Christ, and Timothy our brother, unto Philemon our dearly beloved.* (I hesitate to guess why Timothy is included in a private message.) He went through the formalities, saying that he was *making mention of thee always in my prayers,* and generally buttering him up. Paul pointed out that it was within his rights to give orders, but that he would treat the matter as a personal request.

He finally came to the point; the business concerned one Onesimus, a slave. The man evidently belonged to Philemon; the usual inference is that he had run off to Rome, there becoming a convert. Paul felt duty bound to send him back to his master. He did so with some regret – not because of any qualms about slavery or the harsh punishment of runaways, but because he wanted to keep Onesimus for himself. Like a true gentleman, however, he deferred to the rightful owner: *without thy mind would I do nothing; that thy benefit should not be as it were of necessity, but willingly.*

Now that the slave was a brother in faith, Paul suggested, Philemon should *receive him as myself. If he hath wronged thee, or oweth thee ought, put that on mine account.* True to form, though, a gracious remark must be followed by a crass one. *I will repay it: albeit I do not say to thee how thou owest unto me even thine own self besides.* Good of him not to mention it.

Yea, brother, let me have joy of thee in the Lord: refresh my bowels in the Lord. You can get used to having a slave around. *Having confidence in thy obedience I wrote unto thee, knowing that thou wilt also do more than I say.* Perhaps he was referring to the welcome for Onesimus, but I suspect he was dropping a hint about generosity to preachers.

A few greetings, and that was that: the shortest letter of them all. I wish I knew what Philemon did with Onesimus.

Hebrews

I don't know who wrote this letter, who received it, or even whether it's a letter at all. As author, people have suggested Paul (always a favourite, though most unlikely here), Luke, Barnabas, Apollos, Priscilla – you name them, we've guessed it. The work seems to be aimed at Jewish, not Gentile, converts, with the intention of making them more enthusiastic about the faith. Whether it was written for a particular congregation, and if so where, is difficult to say: Rome is the most popular choice. Except for the ending I'd take it for a treatise rather than a letter;

1   it opens without a word of salutation:

> *God, who at sundry times and in divers manners spake in time past unto the fathers by the prophets, Hath in these last days spoken unto us by his Son, whom he hath appointed heir of all things, by whom also he made the worlds; Who being the brightness of his glory, and the express image of his person, and upholding all things by the word of his power, when he had by himself purged our sins, sat down on the right hand of the Majesty on high; Being made so much better than the angels, as he hath by inheritance obtained a more excellent name than they.*

Reading between the lines, I gather that some people must have taken my brother for an angel, or put him on that level. Needless to say he is much superior; God *maketh his angels spirits, and his ministers a flame of fire. But unto the Son he saith, Thy throne, O God, is for ever and ever.* The author is concerned throughout to show the fulfilment of prophecy, and doesn't mind playing fast and loose with scripture to make a point. That's common enough, but the effect is sometimes curious; would Jesus really have wanted God to say, for example, *Sit on my right hand, until I make thine enemies thy footstool?*

2   Mind you, the turn of phrase is often peculiar. Jesus was *crowned with glory and honour; that he by the grace of God should taste death for every man.* Some people might call it an honour, but the glory at least came later. God was right, *in bringing many sons unto glory, to make the captain of their salvation perfect through sufferings.* If Jesus fell short of perfection you'd think there might have been less sadistic means of improvement. The idea, though, is probably that he had to become human in order to be perfect for the job.

Whereas Paul (being afflicted by his conscience?) saw salvation primarily as release from sin, most people seem more interested in the escape from oblivion. Jesus was a man,

> *that through death he might destroy him that had the power of death, that is, the devil; And deliver them who through fear of death were all their lifetime subject to bondage.*

That's the emphasis we need; immortality is a bigger draw than reconciliation.

It should be no surprise that, being better than the angels, Jesus also outranks Moses. In the divine household one is a son, the other merely a servant. By implication, then, the law of Moses isn't the whole story. **3**

Nearly all of the Israelites who left Egypt failed to reach the promised land. Their persistent sinning and consequent punishment by God should be an example to us. *And to whom sware he that they should not enter into his rest, but to them that believed not?* I think it's a little unfair to label them all unbelievers, even if they did deserve to die in the desert.

What they missed – and what people continued to miss every time the opportunity arose – was a rest of the sort God enjoyed on the seventh day. *Let us labour therefore to enter into that rest,* if that makes sense. Slacking isn't recommended, **4**

> *For the word of God is quick, and powerful, and sharper than any twoedged sword, piercing even to the dividing asunder of soul and spirit, and of the joints and marrow, and is a discerner of the thoughts and intents of the heart.*

Vivisection should be unnecessary, though, because *all things are naked and opened unto the eyes of him with whom we have to do.*

JESUS THE HIGH PRIEST

Jesus is our high priest, which is not to say that he's stuffy and unsympathetic. Indeed, he *was in all points tempted like as we are, yet without sin.* Some people protest that he could never really have been tempted by temptation – wouldn't that be a sin, just like committing adultery in the heart? – but I can testify that he was as human as the next man.

It's well known, for example, how on the last night *he had offered up prayers and supplications with strong crying and tears unto him that was able to save him from death, and was heard* (not that God did anything). Despite being a son, *yet learned he obedience by the things which he suffered;* you always hate to see people learn things the hard way. Why would someone without sin need to learn to obey, anyway? **5**

Jesus was divinely appointed to fill the shoes of the great priest Melchizedek. The author of the letter realises that this is likely to go over the heads of his readers,

whom he abuses as dimwitted and infantile. What they need is milk; ***strong meat***
6   ***belongeth to them that are of full age.*** It was time to grow up, however; the basics
– repentance, faith, baptism, laying-on of hands, resurrection, eternal judgment –
should be taken for granted. ***And this will we do, if God permit.***

Evidently he did – no thunderbolt intervened, at least – and the letter continues
with a warning that anyone who lapses from the faith is lost forever.

> ***For it is impossible for those who were once enlightened ... If they shall***
> ***fall away, to renew them again unto repentance; seeing they crucify to***
> ***themselves the Son of God afresh, and put him to an open shame.***

Fruitful ground is blessed, ***But that which beareth thorns and briers is rejected,***
and is nigh unto cursing; whose end is to be burned. With transparent insincerity,
the writer quickly expressed confidence that his readers were destined for salvation.
He just wanted to rouse them from apathy.

God made his promises to Abraham, and ***because he could swear by no greater,***
he sware by himself. Thus we have his word, and his word on his word, ***That by***
two immutable things, in which it was impossible for God to lie, we might have
a strong consolation. I'd have felt more comfortable without all the fuss; with God,
as they say, nothing is impossible. What's important is the ***hope we have as an***
anchor of the soul.

7   After that digression, back to the high priesthood. The writer is determined to
see Melchizedek, king of Salem, who rated three lines in the scriptures, as the
forerunner of Jesus. For a start, his name could (with a little effort) be interpreted
as 'king of righteousness', and his title as 'king of peace'. Since the scriptures make
no reference to his birth or death, we can assume (I'm not making this up) that he
wasn't born and didn't die, but goes on forever. Moreover, Abraham gave him a
tenth of the spoils of battle, thus recognising his ascendancy over both Abraham
himself and his descendants (in particular the Levites). By my reading of the
passage it was Melchizedek who gave the tithe to Abraham, but at this point I'm
not going to fight over the ambiguity.

The upshot is that the Levites, who administered the law of Moses, must abdicate
the priesthood in favour of Jesus. He has been appointed by God – an appointment
sealed, moreover, with a divine oath. Members of the old order were constantly
dying and being replaced; with Jesus we don't have that problem. An ordinary high
priest had to atone daily (in fact it was annually) for his own sins, as well as those
of the people; Jesus made a once and for all sacrifice. He is the perfect priest.

8   It's only fitting that Jesus, being the ideal high priest, should operate from the
ideal sanctuary. The earthly tabernacle was only a copy, an ***example and shadow***
of heavenly things. Plato's doctrine was infiltrating our own; the Greeks were
going to run away with the movement.

Not only is Jesus a better priest, practising in a better place; ***he is the mediator***
of a better covenant, which was established upon better promises. (Some of God's

promises are apparently worth more than others.) The old covenant must have had its faults, because the prophet Jeremiah speaks of God inaugurating a new one. This new agreement would be written on the hearts of the people, and their sins would be forgiven. By implication, then, the *old is ready to vanish away.*

The tabernacle was very elaborate, but nothing that happened there could change   9
the inner nature of a worshipper. The ceremonies rested *only in meats and drinks, and divers washings, and carnal ordinances, imposed on them until the time of reformation.* (Every rebel argues that the old rituals are empty.) With Jesus everything is different, because the sacrifice was himself.

> *For if the blood of bulls and of goats, and the ashes of an heifer sprinkling the unclean, sanctifieth to the purifying of the flesh: How much more shall the blood of Christ, who through the eternal Spirit offered himself without spot to God, purge your conscience from dead works to serve the living God?*

I can't say it helps my conscience much, but the sacrifice was certainly imposing.

In the view of the letter's author, somebody had to die. Using an equivocation on the word 'testament' (meaning either 'covenant' or 'will'), he said that we have a new testament, and *where a testament is, there must also of necessity be the death of the testator.* I'm not sure how that applies to the first time, but Moses did sprinkle bull's blood over the people. Sacrifice is a necessity, and sacrifice means blood: *without shedding of blood is no remission.*

The ideal sanctuary requires an ideal sacrifice, and that's what Jesus provided. No repetition is necessary: *once in the end of the world hath he appeared to put away sin by the sacrifice of himself.* It only remains for him to *appear the second time,* bringing salvation.

The law offers only *a shadow of good things to come.* The continual round of   10
sacrifices obviously doesn't accomplish anything, as otherwise people wouldn't still be at it. Good news for animals: *it is not possible that the blood of bulls and of goats should take away sins.* Bad news for my brother: *we are sanctified through the offering of the body of Jesus Christ.* Having sacrificed himself, though, he can sit next to God *till his enemies be made his footstool. For by one offering he hath perfected for ever them that are sanctified.* I haven't noticed the faithful being perfect for five minutes, let alone forever; I hope this isn't a bad sign. In principle, nothing remains to be done.

FAITH AND FIRE

Jesus, then, has opened the gates to the inner sanctum. Skipping the meetings of the faithful, *as the manner of some is,* would be a mistake. We should rather give mutual support, especially *as ye see the day approaching.* Backsliders will be sorry,

*For if we sin wilfully after that we have received the knowledge of the truth,
there remaineth no more sacrifice for sins, But a certain fearful looking
for of judgment and fiery indignation, which shall devour the adversaries.*

After all, if breaching the law calls for stoning, of how much more terrible a
punishment *shall he be thought worthy, who hath trodden under foot the Son of
God.* With anyone who has sinned wilfully consigned to the fire, I don't imagine
Jesus will have much company in the hereafter. *It is a fearful thing to fall into the
hands of the living God.*

As before, the author claimed that only the other fellow needs to be concerned;
there wasn't long to wait, and *we are not of them who draw back unto perdition.*
Perish the thought.

11   *Now faith is the substance of things hoped for, the evidence of things not seen.*
Confident expectation, belief in a higher reality: I'm not sure Paul would have
agreed. His notion of faith had more to do with the heart than the head. Still, I think
he would have appreciated the rhetorical set piece that follows. His argument that
Abraham was driven by faith is here extended to all the greats.

*By faith Abel offered unto God a more excellent sacrifice than Cain ... By
faith Enoch was translated that he should not see death* (tradition has it that he
was taken straight to heaven). Good deeds don't impress God; *without faith it is
impossible to please him.* You have to believe that he exists, *and that he is a
rewarder of them that diligently seek him. By faith Noah, being warned of God
of things not seen as yet,* saved his household in the ark.

By faith Abraham left his home in search of the promised land; *he looked for
a city which hath foundations, whose builder and maker is God.* Sarah had a son
when she was an old woman, *because she judged him faithful who had promised,*
even if she did laugh out loud. They founded a nation, though it must be admitted
that not everything went according to plan.

*These all died in faith, not having received the promises, but having seen
them afar off, and were persuaded of them, and embraced them, and
confessed that they were strangers and pilgrims on the earth.*

They were really looking for a heavenly country, and that God was happy to
provide.

By faith Abraham offered up Isaac:

*By faith Isaac blessed Jacob and Esau ... By faith Jacob, when he was
dying, blessed both the sons of Joseph ... By faith Joseph, when he died,
made mention of the departing of the children of Israel ... By faith Moses,
when he was born, was hid three months of his parents, because they saw
he was a proper child.*

Wonderfully inspirational, but you can't help thinking that there was more to it than that. Sometimes the analysis hardly makes sense; if we're supposed to think about Moses running away after killing the Egyptian overseer, for example, it contradicts scripture to say that *By faith he forsook Egypt, not fearing the wrath of the king.* And given the recriminations from the people when the chariots were bearing down on them, he would have been surprised to hear that *By faith they passed through the Red sea as by dry land.*

To continue, *By faith the walls of Jericho fell down ... By faith the harlot Rahab perished not.* But enough:

> *time would fail me to tell of Gedeon, and of Barak, and of Samson, and of Jephthae; of David also, and Samuel, and of the prophets: Who through faith subdued kingdoms, wrought righteousness, obtained promises, stopped the mouths of lions, Quenched the violence of fire, escaped the edge of the sword.*

Not everyone was made successful by faith; some suffered terribly for it. *They were stoned, they were sawn asunder, were tempted, were slain with the sword.* These were people, poor and miserable, *Of whom the world was not worthy.* Yet despite their faith, they *received not the promise,* God having decided to wait for us to come along. Should I be happy about that?

We have a heavy responsibility – one calling for a sporting metaphor to do it justice. 12

> *Wherefore seeing we also are compassed about with so great a cloud of witnesses, let us lay aside every weight, and the sin which doth so easily beset us, and let us run with patience the race that is set before us, Looking unto Jesus the author and finisher of our faith; who for the joy that was set before him endured the cross, despising the shame, and is set down at the right hand of the throne of God.*

The thought of what Jesus suffered should help us bear our own burdens. Remember that *whom the Lord loveth he chasteneth ... God dealeth with you as with sons.* If he failed to apply discipline it would be a bad sign: *then are ye bastards, and not sons.* God has only our best interests in mind. *Now no chastening for the present seemeth to be joyous, but grievous: nevertheless afterward it yieldeth the peaceable fruit of righteousness.* I just wish God would explore the alternatives.

Keep people out of trouble, *Lest there be any fornicator, or profane person, as Esau, who for one morsel of meat sold his birthright.* Poor old Esau. Swindled by his younger brother, he's the one who ends up with a bad reputation.

Happily we're not waiting in terrified anticipation at Mount Sinai, where people were ordered that *if so much as a beast touch the mountain, it shall be stoned.*

We stand instead before Mount Zion and the celestial city, in the sight of angels and the citizens of heaven. We have come *to God the Judge of all, and to the spirits of just men made perfect, And to Jesus the mediator of the new covenant.* You'll want to be on your best behaviour; given the fate of those who ignored the prophets, there's obviously no escape for people who don't listen to God. He plans to shake up the world, *For our God is a consuming fire.*

13   There's not much more to say. *Let brotherly love continue. Be not forgetful to entertain strangers: for thereby some have entertained angels unawares.* Remember those in prison. Respect the marriage bed; God will judge those who don't. As for money and possessions, *be content with such things as ye have.* Besides, *The Lord is my helper, and I will not fear what man shall do unto me.* Follow the example of your religious leaders.

Our view (even if you wouldn't always know it) is of *Jesus Christ the same yesterday, and to day, and for ever. Be not carried about with divers and strange doctrines.* That said, we shouldn't be static, *For here have we no continuing city, but we seek one to come.* Praising God is worthwhile, and *to do good and to communicate forget not: for with such sacrifices God is well pleased.*

The anonymous author asks for our prayers, and reciprocates with one for us.

Now the God of peace, that brought again from the dead our Lord Jesus, that great shepherd of the sheep, through the blood of the everlasting covenant, Make you perfect in every good work to do his will, working in you that which is wellpleasing in his sight, through Jesus Christ; to whom be glory for ever and ever. Amen.

20

James

This letter is supposed to be from me. Although I'd go along with most of these exhortations, I'm afraid I don't remember writing them. Unless my memory is failing the epistle is a forgery (or as we say to be polite, a pseudonymous work), but I'll take credit (and blame) for it anyway.

I say something dubious right at the outset: *count it all joy when ye fall into divers temptations.* I wasn't really such a hedonist: for 'temptations', read 'trials', which makes me sound like a masochist instead. The idea was that *the trying of your faith worketh patience,* i.e. suffering breeds fortitude.

> *But let patience have her perfect work, that ye may be perfect and entire, wanting nothing. If any of you lack wisdom, let him ask of God, that giveth to all men liberally, and upbraideth not.*

God doesn't take people to task? What could I have been thinking?

The poor would be raised up, and the rich brought down. A rich man is like a flower, attractive only until the heat of the sun burns it into nothingness.

Going back to trying times, *Blessed is the man that endureth temptation: for when he is tried, he shall receive the crown of life.* So we hope, at any rate. *Let no man say when he is tempted, I am tempted of God,* because God doesn't tempt people. I'd have to admit that there are examples to the contrary, and at the very least God doesn't seem to stand in the way. Still, it's best to make the person accountable.

I don't believe in holding God to blame, but I wouldn't object if he accepted responsibility on occasion. Otherwise we just end up asserting that *Every good gift and every perfect gift is from above, and cometh down from the Father of lights, with whom is no variableness, neither shadow of turning.* That's fine, but we still have to account for a lot of unpleasant surprises.

Let's keep the focus on people, though; God wouldn't appreciate advice (especially not angry advice):

> *let every man be swift to hear, slow to speak, slow to wrath: For the wrath of man worketh not the righteousness of God. Wherefore lay apart all filthiness and superfluity of naughtiness, and receive with meekness the engrafted word, which is able to save your souls.*
>
> *But be ye doers of the word, and not hearers only, deceiving your own*

1

selves. For if any be a hearer of the word, and not a doer, he is like unto a man beholding his natural face in a glass: For he beholdeth himself, and goeth his way, and straightway forgetteth what manner of man he was.

That's the case with most people, I'd guess; they nod their heads approvingly at the gospel, and then go out and do whatever they would have done anyway.

If any man among you seem to be religious, and bridleth not his tongue, but deceiveth his own heart, this man's religion is vain. Pure religion and undefiled before God and the Father is this, To visit the fatherless and widows in their affliction, and to keep himself unspotted from the world.

2   Far from helping the poor, believers are inclined to discriminate against them, even in places of worship. If both a well-dressed and a ragged-looking man arrive, *And ye have respect to him that weareth the gay clothing, and say unto him, Sit thou here in a good place; and say to the poor, Stand thou there, or sit here under my footstool,* whose standards are you using? Not God's: he's chosen the poor to inherit the kingdom. A person *shall have judgment without mercy, that hath shewed no mercy.*

    This brings me to the heart of my argument. *What doth it profit, my brethren, though a man say he hath faith, and have not works? can faith save him?* Clearly not. *Thou believest that there is one God; thou doest well: the devils also believe.* This is a devastating point, if I do say so myself, though in fairness faith meant more than just belief to Paul; he imagined a kind of emotional surrender. I tackled the scriptural examples head-on. *Was not Abraham our father justified by works, when he had offered Isaac his son upon the altar?* Faith is only shown by deeds, and

Ye see then how that by works a man is justified, and not by faith only. Likewise also was not Rahab the harlot justified by works, when she had received the messengers, and had sent them out another way? For as the body without the spirit is dead, so faith without works is dead also.

People have gone to enormous trouble to paper over the gap separating my views from Paul's. I grant that we had different notions of some of the key terms, and even that he might have accepted my points (anybody sensible would), but that's not to say that there was no disagreement. The question of whether faith or works should take priority remains.

WORDS OF WISDOM

Not many people should become teachers; *we shall receive the greater condem-* 3
nation. One person can direct – or misdirect – an entire community, just as a small
rudder controls a large ship. *Behold, how great a matter a little fire kindleth! And
the tongue is a fire,* with the power to ignite the world.

Animals can be tamed, *But the tongue can no man tame; it is an unruly evil,
full of deadly poison.* You can hear praise and curses from the same mouth. That
shouldn't happen; *Doth a fountain send forth at the same place sweet water and
bitter?* I don't know what made me think that people should be so predictable; God
isn't.

As with faith, my view of wisdom is that the proof is in the practice. Modesty
is a good sign, while jealousy and selfishness suggest a different quality. *This
wisdom descendeth not from above, but is earthly, sensual, devilish.* True wisdom
is peaceful and even-handed.

From whence come wars and fightings among you? They come from trying 4
to satisfy all your desires, resorting to aggression when you fail. Wanting things is
dangerous. Don't you know *that the friendship of the world is enmity with God?
whosoever therefore will be a friend of the world is the enemy of God.* I must have
been drunk when I said that – or more likely hungover. I'm all for taking the long
view, but I don't see that God would have put us here unless we belonged.

Submit yourselves therefore to God. Resist the devil, and he will flee from you.
I was still in the grip of self-mortification, unfortunately. *Be afflicted, and mourn,
and weep: let your laughter be turned to mourning, and your joy to heaviness.*
Controlling your desires is admirable, but this is just perverse.

Don't speak evil of your neighbour. *There is one lawgiver, who is able to save
and to destroy;* we can leave judgment to him. On reflection I'm not sure that we
don't need earthly tribunals as well, but a little tolerance wouldn't hurt.

Our pretensions for the future are empty. *For what is your life? It is even a
vapour, that appeareth for a little time, and then vanisheth away.* Bear that in
mind when you're tempted to boast.

Go to now, ye rich men, weep and howl for your miseries that shall come upon 5
you. Unlike most people, I'm not going to ignore what my brother said about the
fate of the prosperous. Your money will turn into piles of rust, *and shall eat your
flesh as it were fire.* You have been fattening yourselves nicely for the *day of
slaughter.*

These happy thoughts give the rest of us something to look forward to.

*Be patient therefore, brethren, unto the coming of the Lord. Behold, the
husbandman waiteth for the precious fruit of the earth, and hath long
patience for it, until he receive the early and the latter rain. Be ye also
patient; stablish your hearts: for the coming of the Lord draweth nigh. ...
the judge standeth before the door.*

Think how well the prophets bore their sufferings. *Ye have heard of the patience, of Job* (he complained non-stop, if truth be told), and recall his ultimate reward. You can rely on God.

Jesus also told people (in another saying they prefer to forget) not to use oaths. As he said, *let your yea be yea; and your nay, nay; lest ye fall into condemnation.*

I'm not sure what got into me next; I must have thought that anything my brother could do, we could do just as well.

> *Is any sick among you? let him call for the elders of the church; and let them pray over him, anointing him with oil in the name of the Lord: And the prayer of faith shall save the sick, and the Lord shall raise him up; and if he have committed sins, they shall be forgiven him. Confess your faults one to another, and pray one for another, that ye may be healed. The effectual fervent prayer of a righteous man availeth much.*

To confess my own faults, I raised hopes too high. It would be dreadful for anyone to think that illness is caused by sin, or that prayers fail for lack of faith.

I closed by saying that if anyone returned a believer who had strayed back to the fold (something the last letter declared to be impossible, you might recall), he *shall save a soul from death, and shall hide a multitude of sins.* It's confusing, the way you can have eternal life one day, lose it the next, and then get it back again. Some people must pop up and down like fleas in a kennel.

I Peter

This letter, addressed to believers in Asia Minor, is supposed to come from the apostle Peter. Personally I'm inclined to be doubtful – apart from anything else, too much of it is lifted from Paul – but you never know.

Peter devotes a good deal of attention to bearing up under persecution, not generally a major concern in our day. It was worth suffering, he said, as would be shown at the return of Jesus,

> *Whom having not seen, ye love; in whom, though now ye see him not, yet believing, ye rejoice with joy unspeakable and full of glory: Receiving the end of your faith, even the salvation of your souls.*

What they needed was self-discipline: *be sober, and hope to the end for the grace that is to be brought unto you.* God is fair but firm; he is *the Father, who without respect of persons judgeth according to every man's work.* (I'm gratified to see the plug for good deeds.) We have been redeemed *with the precious blood of Christ, as of a lamb without blemish and without spot.*

Self-purification would lead them to love their fellow believers. They were born again, this time into an immortal family. As the prophet Isaiah said,

> *all flesh is as grass, and all the glory of man as the flower of grass. The grass withereth, and the flower thereof falleth away: But the word of the Lord endureth for ever.*

So, then, throw off all ill-will; *As newborn babes, desire the sincere milk of* *the word, that ye may grow thereby: If so be ye have tasted that the Lord is gracious.* We should make ourselves into a spiritual temple, with Jesus as its keystone. Unbelievers are destined to fall, *But ye are a chosen generation, a royal priesthood, an holy nation, a peculiar people.*

Peter had a few rules of behaviour for them. In the first place, they should *abstain from fleshly lusts, which war against the soul.* At the same time, he ordered, *Submit yourselves to every ordinance of man for the Lord's sake: whether it be to the king, as supreme, Or unto governors.* Being faithful, in fact, doesn't seem to allow much scope for unconventional behaviour. *Honour all men. Love the brotherhood. Fear God. Honour the king.*

For slaves the position is even worse. He told them to *be subject to your masters with all fear; not only to the good and gentle,* but to the unjust and cruel as well.

For what glory is it, if, when ye be buffeted for your faults, ye shall take it patiently? but if, when ye do well, and suffer for it, ye take it patiently, this is acceptable with God.

I'd rather he found it unacceptable, to be honest. Following in my brother's footsteps can go too far; the better the reason for his sacrifice, the less the need to imitate it. In Peter's view, however, *ye were as sheep going astray; but are now returned unto the Shepherd and Bishop of your souls.*

3   *Likewise, ye wives* – having dealt with the slaves – *be in subjection to your own husbands.* If your men haven't yet realised what the gospel has to offer, they're sure to be impressed when *they behold your chaste conversation coupled with fear.* Rather than worry about her hair, jewellery, or clothes, a woman should seek *the ornament of a meek and quiet spirit, which is in the sight of God of great price.* She should follow the example set by women in the good old days, who were *in subjection unto their own husbands: Even as Sara obeyed Abraham, calling him lord.*

Men have obligations too, of course. Husbands should be understanding, *giving honour unto the wife, as unto the weaker vessel.* Taking care of the little woman has the advantage, apart from anything else, *that your prayers be not hindered.*

In conclusion, then, aim for unity and be considerate, *Not rendering evil for evil, or railing for railing: but contrariwise blessing* No doubt people will walk all over you; still, *if ye suffer for righteousness' sake, happy are ye.* Ecstatic, even. *For it is better, if the will of God be so, that ye suffer for well doing, than for evil doing.* For my part I'd choose justice over injustice, even if it meant being bad first.

Peter mentions that Jesus, after his death, visited *the spirits in prison* – apparently the divine offspring who got up to no good just before the Flood. What we're supposed to make of this is a mystery. The sea on which Noah's family was saved, however, is like the baptism by which we are saved. (Both involve water, anyway.)

4   Going back to persecution, we should look on the bright side: *he that hath suffered in the flesh hath ceased from sin.* I'm sure that hardship builds character, but I'd hesitate to go quite that far. Although Peter claims that we've had our fill of sin – *lasciviousness, lusts, excess of wine, revellings, banquetings, and abominable idolatries* – I wouldn't bet on it.

Everyone will be judged, dead or alive: *for this cause was the gospel preached also to them that are dead.* The usual inference is that Jesus paid a visit to the underworld, perhaps during the day between his death and resurrection. I'm not sure why he bothered; it was too late for them to change anything they had done or believed. (One school of thought holds that he just went to tell them that they were sunk.) If salvation was still on offer, however, the dead had a considerable advantage over the living, who had to take everything on faith.

Supposedly we wouldn't have long to wait:

> *the end of all things is at hand: be ye therefore sober, and watch unto prayer. And above all things have fervent charity among yourselves: for charity shall cover the multitude of sins.*

Love cancels sin: there's some good news.

Beloved, think it not strange concerning the fiery trial which is to try you. Think of it as an opportunity to share my brother's pain. If anyone insults you for your faith, consider yourself privileged. We just happen to be first in line for judgment; however bad the verdict, we can always gloat:

> *the time is come that judgment must begin at the house of God: and if it first begin at us, what shall the end be of them that obey not the gospel of God? And if the righteous scarcely be saved, where shall the ungodly and the sinner appear?*

The remark about how hard it is to be saved doesn't sound very reassuring. That said, the entire event seems to have been postponed indefinitely.

Peter concluded by reminding the elders to look after the flock; *when the chief   5 Shepherd shall appear, ye shall receive a crown of glory that fadeth not away.* Other people have duties, too: *ye younger, submit yourselves unto the elder.* Humility, though, was just a start. *Be sober, be vigilant; because your adversary the devil, as a roaring lion, walketh about, seeking whom he may devour.*

Having passed on greetings from *The church that is at Babylon* – a code term for Rome – Peter signed off.

II Peter

1   I don't know who wrote this letter, but it wasn't Peter. For a start he wouldn't have called Jesus 'our God and Saviour', as much as he loved him. And did he really suppose that *ye might be partakers of the divine nature*? We'd be debasers of the divine currency, more like.

He advised supplementing faith with virtue, knowledge, and a host of other qualities. Some effort is required *to make your calling and election sure*, which makes salvation sound worryingly tentative.

He himself was not long for this world, Peter announced ostentatiously, *even as our Lord Jesus Christ hath shewed me*. There's a certain irony in hearing an impostor say that *we have not followed cunningly devised fables, when we made known unto you the power and coming of our Lord Jesus Christ, but were eyewitnesses of his majesty*. As an example, Peter cited the transfiguration (when Jesus was joined by Moses and Elijah on a mountain top).

With scripture *ye do well that ye take heed, as unto a light that shineth in a dark place, until the day dawn, and the day star arise in your hearts*. When Jesus comes back, I take it, the law and the prophets will be redundant.

2   In the mean time, however, *there shall be false teachers among you, who privily shall bring in damnable heresies ... And many shall follow their pernicious ways*. Needless to say, their fate won't be pretty. *For if God spared not the angels that sinned, but cast them down to hell*, and destroyed the whole world, except for Noah's family, and reduced Sodom and Gomorrah to ashes, saving only Lot (who had been *vexed with the filthy conversation of the wicked* – this of a man who later impregnated both of his daughters in a drunken stupor), then clearly God knows how to punish anyone who has it coming.

Alarmingly, the prime targets are those who indulge *the flesh in the lust of uncleanness, and despise government. Presumptuous are they, selfwilled, they are not afraid to speak evil of dignities*. That sounds like most of the people I know. The description, though, was expanded at some length; these false teachers are

> *brute beasts, made to be taken and destroyed ... they that count it pleasure to riot in the day time ... Having eyes full of adultery, and that cannot cease from sin ... to whom the mist of darkness is reserved for ever ... they allure through the lusts of the flesh, through much wantonness.*

I've had some bad teachers in my time, but never in quite that way. School could have been considerably more exciting.

Worldly backsliders will come to a worse end than unbelievers. It's better *not to have known the way of righteousness,* than to know and then turn back. I couldn't say why; perhaps it's something to do with setting a bad example. There's nothing permanent about grace, it seems. *But it is happened unto them according to the true proverb, The dog is turned to his own vomit again.*

Having consigned the wicked to judgment, we have to explain the embarrassing 3 fact that the world failed to end on schedule. Now

> *there shall come in the last days scoffers, walking after their own lusts, And saying, Where is the promise of his coming? for since the fathers fell asleep, all things continue as they were from the beginning of the creation.*

On the contrary: God destroyed the world once by water, and intends to repeat the trick with fire. *But, beloved, be not ignorant of this one thing, that one day is with the Lord as a thousand years, and a thousand years as one day.* You can understand that he might lose track of time.

As the apocalypse could come any day now, lack of devotion would be foolish. Shouldn't you be *Looking for and hasting unto the coming of the day of God, wherein the heavens being on fire shall be dissolved, and the elements shall melt with fervent heat?* Not if you have any sense, by the sound of it. My brother warned us about over-confidence in the face of judgment.

The idea of justification by faith seems (as I predicted) to have encouraged some people to be relaxed about morality. To be diplomatic, there are, in the letters of *our beloved brother Paul ... some things hard to be understood, which they that are unlearned and unstable wrest, as they do also the other scriptures, unto their own destruction.* Be warned.

I John

The next three letters are unsigned, but let's call their author 'John'. Although he wouldn't be any of the Johns my brother knew, the one whose name is on the gospel might just be the same man. The way he talks about Jesus certainly rings a bell: *That which was from the beginning ... the Word of life.* The images are similar, too: *God is light, and in him is no darkness at all.*

1

People can become carried away into thinking that Jesus wasn't really flesh and blood, or what's worse, that they themselves aren't subject to human constraints. *If we say that we have no sin, we deceive ourselves, and the truth is not in us.* We'll be forgiven, but only if we confess.

2   *And if any man sin, we have an advocate with the Father, Jesus Christ the righteous: And he is the propitiation for our sins: and not for ours only, but also for the sins of the whole world.* Unfortunately for a lot of people – especially the rich – John went on to assert that anyone who claims to know Jesus, *and keepeth not his commandments, is a liar.* The chief commandment (thank heavens somebody remembered) is love; *he that hateth his brother is in darkness.*

I have to say, though, that the exceptions seem bigger than the rule. *Love not the world, neither the things that are in the world. If any man love the world, the love of the Father is not in him.* What attracts us in the world doesn't come from God, and only God is permanent. (Do flower-lovers burn in hell?)

Little children, it is the last time. The proof is that the antichrist appears when the end has come, and *now are there many antichrists.* With a definition as loose as John's, any number of people could qualify: *He is antichrist, that denieth the Father and the Son. Whosoever denieth the Son, the same hath not the Father,* so don't bother trying to worship God in any other way.

3   We may be children, but at least we're God's children – or would be, if we were perfect. No one who lives in Jesus sins: *whosoever sinneth hath not seen him, neither known him.* Anyone who sins *is of the devil,* and Jesus came specifically to stamp out his work. That's it for us, I suppose. To repeat:

> *Whosoever is born of God doth not commit sin; for his seed remaineth in him: and he cannot sin, because he is born of God. In this the children of God are manifest, and the children of the devil: whosoever doeth not righteousness is not of God, neither he that loveth not his brother.*

As if that wasn't enough, John put a few more nails in the coffin.

He that loveth not his brother abideth in death. Whosoever hateth his brother is a murderer: and ye know that no murderer hath eternal life abiding in him.

Don't suppose that this hatred has to be active; simple neglect will do. Jesus gave up his life for us, and we ought to be ready to sacrifice ourselves for others. *But whoso hath this world's good, and seeth his brother have need, and shutteth up his bowels of compassion from him, how dwelleth the love of God in him?* Love is a matter of deeds, not words.

He that loveth not, knoweth not God; for God is love. He loved us enough to 4
have *sent his Son to be the propitiation for our sins. Beloved, if God so loved us, we ought also to love one another.* If you acknowledge that Jesus is the Son, God will merge with you. His love will give you no end of confidence on judgment day. *There is no fear in love; but perfect love casteth out fear.*

None the less, love is a demanding business. *If a man say, I love God, and hateth his brother, he is a liar: for he that loveth not his brother whom he hath seen, how can he love God whom he hath not seen?* John claimed that to love God is to obey him, and that his commandments are no burden. He should speak for himself.

John finished by trying to be reassuring. We can be confident in praying to God that

if we ask any thing according to his will, he heareth us: And if we know that he hear us, whatsoever we ask, we know that we have the petitions that we desired of him.

If this means that God always grants our requests, John can't have asked for much. If it just promises success when we ask for what God wants to do anyway, I can't get too excited. Perhaps God only takes action when somebody prays for it, but that would seem an odd way to run the world.

It's worth praying for the ordinary run of sinners, because God will give them life. *There is sin unto death,* however, and in such cases praying is a waste of time. I wouldn't like to guess which sin is which.

In conclusion, we know three things. *We know that whosoever is born of God sinneth not … we know that we are of God, and the whole world lieth in wickedness. And we know that the Son of God is come.* You can't say he didn't stick his neck out.

II John

The elder unto the elect lady and her children, whom I love in the truth: it sounds disconcertingly like a *billet-doux*, but the lady appears to have been a church. John was pleased to see followers upholding the truth; regrettably unorthodox ideas were starting to circulate.

Some people maintained that Christ was divine, and only appeared to be human; others held that the divine spirit descended on Jesus when he was baptised and left him at the crucifixion. In John's view Jesus Christ was and is both human and divine. He didn't have any time for rival theologians; *many deceivers are entered into the world, who confess not that Jesus Christ is come in the flesh. This is a deceiver and an antichrist.*

Anybody whose speculations are too advanced is ungodly, while an adherent of the conventional doctrine

hath both the Father and the Son. If there come any unto you, and bring not this doctrine, receive him not into your house, neither bid him God speed: For he that biddeth him God speed is partaker of his evil deeds.

This directly contradicts my brother's advice. If greeting people with different ideas makes you guilty of their sins, we're in even more trouble than I thought.

III John

This is a private letter to one Gaius; John didn't intend it to be edifying, and it isn't. Apart from praising the addressee for his kindness to some missionaries, he principally wanted to fume about a certain leader of the congregation.

I wrote unto the church: but Diotrephes, who loveth to have the preeminence among them, receiveth us not. Wherefore, if I come, I will remember his deeds which he doeth, prating against us with malicious words: and not content therewith, neither doth he himself receive the brethren, and forbiddeth them that would, and casteth them out of the church.

Having blackened the reputation of this cleric, John produced a single line of doctrine: *He that doeth good is of God: but he that doeth evil hath not seen God.* The first part sounds hopeful for deserving people outside the faith, but I think we're supposed to take correct belief for granted. In any case, the second part isn't very encouraging. Most of us do both good and bad; are we in or out?

I had many things to write, but I will not with ink and pen write unto thee. It was probably a wise decision.

26

Jude

This letter is credited to *Jude, the servant of Jesus Christ, and brother of James*. Much as I'd like to keep things in the family, I'm not convinced; my little brother wasn't the writing type. (Nor was my elder brother, come to that.) The tract is entertaining – most of the material was reused in the second letter attributed to Peter – if rather uncharitable.

Jude (as I'm happy to call the author) was in a hurry to warn the movement about certain infiltrators, *ungodly men, turning the grace of our God into lasciviousness*. Corruption can have unpleasant consequences. Remember how God, *having saved the people out of the land of Egypt, afterward destroyed them that believed not*. Remember how he keeps the fallen angels *in everlasting chains under darkness unto the judgment of the great day*. Remember how he dealt with Sodom and Gomorrah, where those *giving themselves over to fornication, and going after strange flesh, are set forth for an example, suffering the vengeance of eternal fire*.

You can imagine what's going to happen to teachers propagating false doctrine; *these filthy dreamers defile the flesh, despise dominion, and speak evil of dignities. Yet Michael the archangel* – a role model of mine, incidentally – *when contending with the devil* did not try to usurp God's authority. These people, by contrast, *speak evil of those things which they know not,* while being ruined by their animal instincts.

They are blemishes on the church, clouds without water, trees *without fruit, twice dead, plucked up by the roots; Raging waves of the sea, foaming out their own shame; wandering stars, to whom is reserved the blackness of darkness for ever.* You get the idea, anyway.

The irony is that, in condemning the unorthodox, Jude drew half his examples from folk tales rather than official scripture. He cited the apocryphal words of Enoch, for example, to show that God would convict *all that are ungodly among them of all their ungodly deeds which they have ungodly committed, and of all their hard speeches which ungodly sinners have spoken against him.* To forgive them would be ungodly.

Don't think that the apostles didn't see the problems coming; *they told you there should be mockers in the last time, who should walk after their own ungodly lusts.* The heretics are sectarian, claiming to separate out the spiritual when they themselves are nothing of the sort. The best defence is to keep the faith and say your prayers.

Almost as an afterthought, Jude suggested that we might just be able to save some of the doubters, *pulling them out of the fire*. Others may be too far gone; you can't help *hating even the garment spotted by the flesh*. (Uncleanliness is next to ungodliness.) *To the only wise God our Saviour, be glory and majesty, dominion and power, both now and ever. Amen.*

Revelation

1   After all those letters, it's time for something different. A certain John – yet another one, I'm afraid – came up with just what we needed. He had help, of course; God revealed to Jesus his plans for *things which must shortly come to pass,* and Jesus sent an angel to John with the news. The story isn't always easy to understand; perhaps it lost something in transmission from God to my brother to his messenger to the prophet to us. When it comes to the apocalypse, though, it's hard to mistake the drift.

   John was obsessed with the number seven; if you asked him how many fingers Jesus had, I wouldn't trust him to say 'ten'. Thus, *John to the seven churches which are in Asia: Grace be unto you, and peace, from him which is, and which was, and which is to come; and from the seven Spirits which are before his throne.* The spirit has multiplied, but there's only one Jesus. *Behold, he cometh with clouds, and every eye shall see him, and they also which pierced him: and all kindreds of the earth shall wail because of him. Even so, Amen.* Like an old man not quite following the conversation, God chipped in a few words. *I am the Alpha and Omega, the beginning and the ending, saith the Lord.*

   We'll be at the end before hearing the beginning, if we're not careful. John paused to explain how he came to know so much.

> *I John, who also am your brother, and companion in tribulation, and in the kingdom and patience of Jesus Christ, was in the isle that is called Patmos, for the word of God, and for the testimony of Jesus Christ. I was in the Spirit on the Lord's day, and heard behind me a great voice, as of a trumpet, Saying, I am Alpha and Omega, the first and the last: and, What thou seest, write in a book, and send it unto the seven churches which are in Asia.*

John turned to find the owner of this trumpet-like voice. *And being turned, I saw seven golden candlesticks.* More to the point there was a figure, fully robed,

> *girt about the paps with a golden girdle. His head and his hairs were white like wool, as white as snow; and his eyes were as a flame of fire; And his feet like unto fine brass, as if they burned in a furnace; and his voice as the sound of many waters. And he had in his right hand seven stars: and out of his mouth went a sharp twoedged sword: and his countenance was*

as the sun shineth in his strength. And when I saw him, I fell at his feet as dead.

Daniel had a similar vision, I recall, though the sword coming out of the mouth is a special touch. Amazingly, this fellow with the double-bladed tongue was supposed to be my brother. *Fear not,* he said, *I am he that liveth, and was dead; and, behold, I am alive for evermore, Amen; and have the keys of hell and of death.* This is reassuring?

He explained, incidentally, that the seven candlesticks represented the seven churches, and the seven stars the angels of those churches. It's hard to say whether these 'angels' were earthly leaders, heavenly representatives, or something else altogether.

Jesus dictated messages to the angels of each of the seven churches in the province of Asia, beginning with Ephesus. There the faithful had done good work in repressing the teachings of false apostles, and in upholding the cause. *Nevertheless I have somewhat against thee, because thou hast left thy first love.* They would do well to repent and to start loving again, or he would ensure that something unfortunate happened to the congregation. To their credit they rejected the doings of certain heretics, *which I also hate.* Fight the good fight; *To him that overcometh will I give to eat of the tree of life.*

The church at Smyrna was already suffering, Jesus acknowledged. *I know the blasphemy of them which say they are Jews, and are not, but are the synagogue of Satan.* There was nothing to fear, though. Granted, *the devil shall cast some of you into prison,* and there would be dreadful persecution for ten days, but *be thou faithful unto death, and I will give thee a crown of life.* Ah, the joys of martyrdom.

The town of Pergamum was distinguished as the place where Satan has his throne – that would be worth a detour to see. The church had kept the faith, but they were being undermined. *Repent; or else I will come unto thee quickly, and will fight against them with the sword of my mouth.* For that I'd make a special trip.

Jesus was getting into his stride. The church at Thyatira had much to recommend it, but it allowed *that woman Jezebel, which calleth herself a prophetess, to teach and to seduce my servants to commit fornication, and to eat things sacrificed unto idols.* He would throw her onto a bed of pain and inflict terrible suffering on her unrepentant lovers. *And I will kill her children with death* – usually the best method – *and all the churches shall know that … I will give unto every one of you according to your works.* (He'll give it to your children, too.) To the person who stands fast,

and keepeth my works unto the end, to him will I give power over the nations: And he shall rule them with a rod of iron; as the vessels of a potter shall they be broken to shivers.

It's such a relief to have righteous leaders.

3   The church at Sardis was criticised for lack of enthusiasm. Unless they pulled themselves together, Jesus said, *I will come on thee as a thief,* without warning. Here and there someone had remained uncontaminated, *and I will not blot out his name out of the book of life.*

At Philadelphia all would be well were it not for *them of the synagogue of Satan, which say they are Jews, and are not, but do lie; behold, I will make them to come and worship before thy feet, and to know that I have loved thee.* Very good of my brother, but it's so embarrassing to have people grovel at your feet. The faithful would be suitably labelled with God's name and the name of the new Jerusalem, *and I will write upon him my new name.* That should keep them from being mislaid.

Finally there was a warning for the half-hearted believers of Laodicea.

I know thy works, that thou art neither cold nor hot: I would thou wert cold or hot. So then because thou art lukewarm, and neither cold nor hot, I will spue thee out of my mouth.

It appears that they were comfortable and self-satisfied, not realising the danger of their condition. For their own good, Jesus would make them suffer. *Behold, I stand at the door, and knock*: it's a good idea to let him in.

That concluded my brother's messages. He didn't sound very mild-mannered; perhaps a few decades with God had toughened him up. *He that hath an ear, let him hear what the Spirit saith unto the churches.*

THE SEALED BOOK

4   No sooner had dictation ended than *a door was opened in heaven,* and a voice told John *I will shew thee things which must be hereafter.* Up he went, and what should there be but a throne. *And he that sat was to look upon like a jasper and a sardine stone: and there was a rainbow round about the throne, in sight like unto an emerald.* That's the first time I've heard God described as sardine-coloured.

And before the throne there was a sea of glass like unto crystal: and in the midst of the throne, and round about the throne, were four beasts full of eyes before and behind. And the first beast was like a lion, and the second beast like a calf, and the third beast had a face as a man, and the fourth beast was like a flying eagle. And the four beasts had each of them six wings about him; and they were full of eyes within: and they rest not day and night, saying, Holy, holy, holy, Lord God Almighty, which was, and is, and is to come.

According to Ezekiel the cherubim had four faces each and four wings, and all the eyes were mounted on wheels. God must have traded that throne in for a new model. (Isaiah had counted six wings as well, though, so perhaps God runs two thrones.)

In any event, the song of these four creatures is hardly sufficient; 24 elders prostrate themselves before the throne to praise its occupant, saying *thou hast created all things, and for thy pleasure they are and were created.* Or uncreated, presumably.

God held a scroll in his right hand, 5

a book written within and on the backside, sealed with seven seals. And I saw a strong angel proclaiming with a loud voice, Who is worthy to open the book, and to loose the seals thereof?

The answer appeared to be 'no one', and John was most upset. One of the elders told him to stop blubbing, because the Lion of Judah had qualified. When he looked, he saw not a lion but a lamb, albeit one *having seven horns and seven eyes.* God handed over the book, and

the four beasts and four and twenty elders fell down before the Lamb, having every one of them harps, and golden vials full of odours, which are the prayers of saints.

Seven-eyed creatures and incense seem to go together. Anyway, the choir sang *Thou art worthy to take the book, and to open the seals thereof: for thou wast slain, and hast redeemed us to God by thy blood.* Clearly the Lion/Lamb was none other than Jesus.

Next, John said, *I heard the voice of many angels round about the throne and the beasts and the elders: and the number of them was ten thousand times ten thousand, and thousands of thousands*: quite a few, in other words. Finally every creature from heaven, earth (on or under) and sea joined in with cries of *Blessing, and honour, and glory, and power.* I'm surprised anyone noticed when *the four beasts said, Amen.*

The excitement was only just beginning; John was about to see the four 6 horsemen of the apocalypse: war, revolution, famine and plague (or death). When the Lamb broke the first seal a white horse appeared, its rider carrying a bow, *and he went forth conquering, and to conquer.* With the second seal came a red horse whose rider was given the power to make men *kill one another: and there was given unto him a great sword.*

As the third seal was broken John saw *a black horse; and he that sat on him had a pair of balances in his hand.* Someone ordered the rider to drive up the price of flour and barley, leaving oil and wine unharmed. With the opening of the fourth *I looked, and behold a pale horse: and his name that sat on him was Death, and Hell followed with him.* They were given power over a quarter of the earth, to kill by violence, starvation, disease and wild animals.

The cracking of the fifth seal was accompanied by loud protests from martyred souls asking God *dost thou not judge and avenge our blood on them that dwell on the earth?* They were issued with white robes and told to settle down, pending the arrival of *their brethren, that should be killed as they were.*

So far, so routine; it was at the breaking of the sixth seal that the action really picked up. There was an enormous earthquake, the sun went black while the moon turned red, and the stars fell out of the sky to the earth.

> *And the kings of the earth, and the great men, and the rich men, and the chief captains, and the mighty men, and every bondman, and every free man, hid themselves in the dens and in the rocks of the mountains; And said to the mountains and rocks, Fall on us, and hide us from the face of him that sitteth on the throne, and from the wrath of the Lamb: For the great day of his wrath is come; and who shall be able to stand?*

Being buried by rocks is preferable to catching my brother on a bad day.

7   *And after these things,* John said, *I saw four angels standing on the four corners of the earth, holding the four winds of the earth,* so that nothing would be blown away. (I've always wanted to find the earth's corners.) A messenger from God ordered the four angels to *Hurt not the earth, neither the sea, nor the trees,* until seals had been placed on the foreheads of the chosen.

And I heard the number of them which were sealed: 144,000. The number seemed comfortably large at the time, but I'm beginning to have second thoughts. The end is constantly being put off, while the movement, not to mention the population, continues to grow; we're going to have a lot of irate customers when they discover how much we've overbooked. Each of the 12 tribes of Israel would contribute 12,000 qualifiers; for some reason the list of tribes omitted Dan while including both Manasseh and his father Joseph, which doesn't make sense.

At any rate, *a great multitude, which no man could number, of all nations, and kindreds, and people, and tongues, stood before the throne, and before the Lamb, clothed with white robes.* They all hailed the leaders at the top of their voices, *And all the angels stood round about the throne, and about the elders and the four beasts, and fell before the throne on their faces, and worshipped God.*

One of the elders asked John *What are these which are arrayed in white robes? and whence came they?* You tell me, he replied. Having established his superior knowledge, the old duffer said

> *These are they which came out of great tribulation, and have washed their robes, and made them white in the blood of the Lamb. ... They shall hunger no more, neither thirst any more; neither shall the sun light on them, nor any heat. ... God shall wipe away all tears from their eyes.*

You can have a hard life and a ghastly death, but God will make it all better.

And when he had opened the seventh seal, there was silence in heaven about 8
the space of half an hour. The suspense was killing me. What was in the book? Would the world finally come to an end? To my considerable frustration, nothing happened. The story just repeated itself in a slightly different form.

SEVEN TRUMPETS

I saw the seven angels which stood before God; and to them were given seven trumpets. Having offered incense, another angel threw some fire from the altar down to earth, producing thunder and lightning, an earthquake, and apocalyptic sound effects.

The first angel blew his trumpet, causing hail, fire and blood to fall from heaven. This cocktail scorched a third of the earth, and burnt all the green grass. At the second blast a burning mountain dropped into the sea, turning a third of it into blood, and destroying a third of all fish and ships. The next angel knocked a star into the rivers of the world; *the name of the star is called Wormwood,* and it poisoned a third of the fresh water.

When the trumpet of the fourth angel sounded, a third of the sun, of the moon, and of the stars, went dark. The unlikely result was that *the day shone not for a* 9
third part of it, and the night likewise. With the fifth trumpet call the abyss was opened, and out poured locusts in a column of smoke. They were ordered not to hurt the grass (wasn't it already destroyed?), *but only those men which have not the seal of God in their foreheads.* The people weren't to be killed, just tortured for five months.

The locusts were scorpion-like, and evidently unpleasant: *in those days shall men seek death, and shall not find it; and shall desire to die, and death shall flee from them.* No ordinary bugs, these locusts looked like battle horses, with human faces and lion's teeth, *and there were stings in their tails.* They even had a king named Destroyer.

It was a hard act to follow, but the sixth trumpeter didn't disgrace himself. Four angels were let loose from the river Euphrates to kill a third of humanity, which they did with the help of 200,000,000 mounted troops. The horses, if you can call them that, had *heads of lions; and out of their mouths issued fire and smoke and brimstone.* With snakes for tails, they could catch you coming or going.

The survivors of these God-sent horrors were strangely unwilling to give up their idols, *Neither repented they of their murders, nor of their sorceries, nor of their fornication, nor of their thefts.* Some people have no appreciation.

Before the last trumpet call another angel appeared, carrying a book and 10
shouting, and *seven thunders uttered their voices.* John was about to write down what they said when a heavenly command put it off the record. At that point the angel swore by God that there would be no further delay; it would all be over when the trumpet sounded. (Let me offer some advice: don't hold your breath.)

The divine courtiers were starting to give John a hard time; some statements he had to publicise, others he couldn't, and some words he had to eat. Under orders, he said, *I took the little book out of the angel's hand, and ate it up; and it was in my mouth sweet as honey: and as soon as I had eaten it, my belly was bitter.* I hope it was high in fibre.

11   Like a hallucination, the story is gradually becoming less coherent; fragments from the prophets are floating past. John was told to measure the temple, leaving the outer court to the Gentiles, who would trample Jerusalem underfoot over a period of 42 months. During this time two prophets would terrorise the infidels, but in the end the beast from the abyss would kill them. Their bodies would lie unburied for three and a half days, *And they that dwell upon the earth shall rejoice over them, and make merry, and shall send gifts one to another.*

Enough is enough, and God brought the prophets back to life, carrying them to heaven in a cloud. An earthquake decimated the city, so that *the remnant were affrighted, and gave glory to the God of heaven.* Their guts, his glory.

The seventh angel finally blew his trumpet, and voices in heaven were heard to cry *The kingdoms of this world are become the kingdoms of our Lord, and of his Christ; and he shall reign for ever and ever.* The ark of the covenant appeared in the heavenly temple as the sights and sounds of the apocalypse took an encore.

12   The world wasn't dead yet, however; *there appeared a great wonder in heaven; a woman clothed with the sun, and the moon under her feet, and upon her head a crown of twelve stars.* She was just about to give birth when, of all the luck, a seven-headed, ten-horned red dragon appeared. (Each head wore a crown; John doesn't mention where the spare horns were kept.) Oddly enough the dragon didn't eat her; waiting politely, it *stood before the woman which was ready to be delivered, for to devour her child as it was born.*

The infant was *a man child, who was to rule all nations with a rod of iron* – prime dragon bait, in other words. God snatched the babe away and *the woman fled into the wilderness,* leaving the monster's patience unrewarded.

And there was war in heaven: Michael and his angels fought against the dragon; and the dragon fought and his angels, And prevailed not ... the great dragon was cast out, that old serpent, called the Devil, and Satan, which deceiveth the whole world.

People assume that Michael used his sword on the old boy, but ordinary weapons wouldn't have nearly enough magic. A voice from heaven said that *they overcame him by the blood of the Lamb, and by the word of their testimony,* which seems more appropriate.

The dragon came down to earth with a bump, and went off in pursuit of the woman – no more playing pussycat. Although she was given the wings of an eagle, he tried to trap her in a flood of water: poor tactics to use with airborne prey, I'd have thought. The earth swallowed up the torrent. Furious, the dragon went to war against all her other children, those loyal to God and Jesus.

THE BEAST, THE SAVED AND THE DAMNED

John *saw a beast rise up out of the sea.* This one also had seven heads and ten   13
horns, but looked like a leopard. The dragon conferred its power on the beast, which
people worshipped, *saying, Who is like unto the beast? who is able to make war
with him?* The beast, it seems, was meant to represent the Roman Empire.

It was a foul-mouthed beast, full of blasphemy, and violent to boot. A two-
horned lamb with the voice of a dragon popped out of the earth to keep it company.
This creature made everyone worship the beast, just as the imperial priesthood
insisted on the divinity of emperors. It ordered the execution of those showing
insufficient reverence to the beast's image. Furthermore, everybody (excluding
rebels, presumably) would receive a mark on the right hand or the forehead, so *that
no man might buy or sell, save he that had the mark, or the name of the beast,
or the number of his name.*

There's a clue for the slow-witted. *Let him that hath understanding count the
number of the beast: for it is the number of a man; and his number is Six hundred
threescore and six.* Viewing letters as numbers you can turn any word into a total,
and the name of just about every unpopular character ever has been made to add
up to 666. The usual suggestion, though, is that Nero was the beast in question. He
was dead, as it happened, but more than a few people expected him to return.

John saw the Lamb standing on Mount Zion, accompanied by the 144,000   14
chosen ones bearing God's name on their foreheads.

> *And I heard a voice from heaven, as the voice of many waters, and as the
> voice of a great thunder: and I heard the voice of harpers harping with
> their harps: And they sung as it were a new song before the throne, and
> before the four beasts, and the elders: and no man could learn that song
> but the hundred and forty and four thousand, which were redeemed from
> the earth. These are they which were not defiled with women; for they are
> virgins.*

This was the worst news yet. It was bad enough that merely a select few would be
joining Jesus, and now I discover that only male virgins are eligible. (With some
things there's just no going back.) My harp and vocal abilities aren't up to much,
either.

A few angels flew overhead. The first shouted *Fear God ... for the hour of his
judgment is come.* The second announced that *Babylon is fallen, is fallen, that
great city,* because she made everyone drink the strong wine of her fornication
(Babylon being the code word for Rome). The third angel had a promise for anyone
receiving the mark of the beast:

> *he shall be tormented with fire and brimstone in the presence of the holy
> angels, and in the presence of the Lamb: And the smoke of their torment*

> *ascendeth up for ever and ever: and they have no rest day nor night, who worship the beast and his image.*

Entertainment in heaven won't be too highbrow, obviously.

Another celestial voice told John to take dictation: *Write, Blessed are the dead which die in the Lord from henceforth: Yea, saith the Spirit, that they may rest from their labours; and their works do follow them.* That's what Paul was hoping to avoid, I think.

It was time to harvest humanity; someone appeared with a sharp sickle and went to work on the earth. The grapes were gathered as well and thrown *into the great winepress of the wrath of God.* The blood poured from the press, flooding a couple of hundred miles to the level of a horse's bridle.

15   *And I saw as it were a sea of glass mingled with fire,* John said. People with harps stood around singing God's praises. Seven angels bearing seven plagues emerged from the heavenly tabernacle, and received *seven golden vials full of the*
16   *wrath of God,* which were to be poured out onto the earth.

The blood and guts are becoming monotonous, but I wouldn't want anyone to feel cheated. Angel number one poured out his bowl, and all the beast's followers were struck with nasty sores. Number two killed everything in the sea (so much for trying to save the whales), and number three turned all the rivers to blood (fish are infidels too).

Angel four burned men with the power of the sun; for some reason they only *blasphemed the name of God* instead of expressing high esteem, as required. There was a similar reaction to the next plague, when the empire was darkened and *they gnawed their tongues for pain.* Following that, at number six, the river Euphrates dried up.

Devils disguised as frogs hopped out of the mouths of the dragon, the beast, and the other creature (*the false prophet*), going off to rally the kings of the world to do battle with God. Jesus, meanwhile, gave his followers a reminder: *Behold, I come as a thief. Blessed is he that watcheth, and keepeth his garments, lest he walk naked, and they see his shame.* I hope he doesn't return at bathtime, but I'll risk it; you get a better class of convert if you don't sleep in your clothes. Besides, what with all the angels, trumpets, plagues and so forth, he shouldn't catch us off guard.

The demonic spirit having recruited the kings,

> *he gathered them together into a place called in the Hebrew tongue Armageddon. And the seventh angel poured out his vial into the air; and there came a great voice out of the temple of heaven, from the throne, saying, It is done.*

It was essentially a repeat performance. Various apocalyptic noises accompanied the greatest earthquake ever seen. The city was split in three. Every island and mountain disappeared. There were still survivors, however, because when hundred-pound hailstones started to fall, *men blasphemed God.* They clearly hadn't heard of loving your enemy.

THE WHORE OF BABYLON

As John was loitering, one of the angels approached and said   17

> *Come hither; I will shew unto thee the judgment of the great whore that sitteth upon many waters: With whom the kings of the earth have committed fornication, and the inhabitants of the earth have been made drunk with the wine of her fornication.*

Off in the wilds they found a woman sitting on a scarlet beast, another member of the seven-headed, ten-horned species. She was decked out in purple and scarlet and gold and jewels,

> *having a golden cup in her hand full of abominations and filthiness of her fornication: And upon her forehead was a name written, MYSTERY, BABY-LON THE GREAT, THE MOTHER OF HARLOTS AND ABOMINATIONS OF THE EARTH. And I saw the woman drunken with the blood of the saints, and with the blood of the martyrs of Jesus.*

The angel all but said that the Whore of Babylon was Rome. I gather that her steed was the empire, and its heads, the emperors. Although the symbolism fluctuates, it seems that the horns were other kings. *These shall make war with the Lamb, and the Lamb shall overcome them: for he is Lord of lords, and King of kings.*

He wouldn't have to deal with Babylon personally. The beast with its horns would come to *hate the whore, and shall make her desolate and naked, and shall eat her flesh, and burn her with fire. For God hath put in their hearts to fulfil his will.* Some jobs are best contracted out.

Another angel shouted *Babylon the great is fallen, is fallen, and is become the*   18 *habitation of devils, and the hold of every foul spirit, and a cage of every unclean and hateful bird.* I wonder why the birds kept such odd company; perhaps they were vultures.

That turning the cheek business was long gone, of course; God's people were invited to *Reward her even as she rewarded you, and double unto her double according to her works.* The high living will be brought to an end, *and she shall be utterly burned with fire: for strong is the Lord God who judgeth her.* Her ex-lovers will mourn, not to mention the merchants who supplied her with every luxury imaginable. Traders and seamen will be devastated by the loss (the effect on employment was going to be considerable). The faithful had a different response:

> *Rejoice over her, thou heaven, and ye holy apostles and prophets; for God hath avenged you on her. And a mighty angel took up a stone like a great millstone, and cast it into the sea, saying, Thus with violence shall that great city Babylon be thrown down, and shall be found no more at all.*

No music would be heard, no light would be seen, within her walls.

19   The celebration wasn't over. The population of heaven acclaimed God, *for he hath judged the great whore, which did corrupt the earth with her fornication, and hath avenged the blood of his servants.* It looked as though the party would go on indefinitely, with the guests shouting *Alleluia. And her smoke rose up for ever and ever.*

With the great whore burning, there could be no better time for a wedding. The moment for *the marriage of the Lamb is come, and his wife hath made herself ready.* She represented the faithful, of course, and the shining linen of her dress their righteous deeds. Just when I was enjoying the respite from mayhem, unfortunately, the bridegroom rushed out to fight.

And I saw heaven opened, John said, *and behold a white horse; and he that sat upon him was called Faithful and True.* (That sounds to me like something you'd call the horse, not the rider.) He had a name written on him *that no man knew, but he himself,* which is strange when it's stamped on his skin. Staring might be inadvisable, however; *he was clothed with a vesture dipped in blood: and his name is called the Word of God.* Just come as you are, everybody.

The armies of heaven tagged along, looking bright and shiny. To be honest, it didn't appear that their leader would need much help:

> *out of his mouth goeth a sharp sword, that with it he should smite the nations: and he shall rule them with a rod of iron: and he treadeth the winepress of the fierceness and wrath of Almighty God. And he hath on his vesture and on his thigh a name written, KING OF KINGS, AND LORD OF LORDS.*

An angel called on all the birds to come and enjoy a feast, *the supper of the great God, That ye may eat the flesh of kings, and the flesh of captains, and the flesh of mighty men, and the flesh of horses* – in short, horsemeat apart, *the flesh of all men, both free and bond, both small and great.* Poultry's revenge.

Meanwhile the rival armies had faced off, and the beast and the false prophet were taken prisoner. *These both were cast alive into a lake of fire burning with brimstone.* (After due process of law, I'm sure.) They were the only prisoners; our leader killed the rest of the opposing troops with his mouth sword, *and all the fowls were filled with their flesh.*

THE END OF THE END

In a mopping-up operation, an angel *laid hold on the dragon, that old serpent,*   20
which is the Devil, and Satan, and bound him a thousand years, And cast him
into the bottomless pit. He would be chained up there for a thousand years, *and*
after that he must be loosed a little season, presumably to provide heaven with
some excitement.

If it's any consolation to Satan, almost everyone else was in the same boat. True,

> *the souls of them that were beheaded for the witness of Jesus ... lived and*
> *reigned with Christ a thousand years. But the rest of the dead lived not*
> *again until the thousand years were finished.*

It's just as well for those who kept their heads, then, that Satan will be freed at the
end of the millennium. He'll summon the armies of the world (or *Gog and Magog,*
which make even less sense than when Ezekiel mentioned the names), only to see
them devoured by divine fire. (Hadn't they already been destroyed?) Satan will
join the beast and the false prophet in the burning lake, there to be tortured *day and*
night for ever and ever.

And I saw a great white throne, John said, *And I saw the dead, small and great,*
stand before God. He doesn't mention the living; I suppose by that stage we
shouldn't expect there to be any. Books were lying about, *and another book was*
opened, which is the book of life – just the thing for judging the dead.

> *And the sea gave up the dead which were in it; and death and hell delivered*
> *up the dead which were in them: and they were judged every man according*
> *to their works. And death and hell were cast into the lake of fire. This is*
> *the second death. And whosoever was not found written in the book of life*
> *was cast into the lake of fire.*

I'd hate to see any mistakes in that record.

The revelation did contain a dash of good news, by John's account.   21

> *I saw a new heaven and a new earth: for the first heaven and the first earth*
> *were passed away; and there was no more sea. And I John saw the holy*
> *city, new Jerusalem, coming down from God out of heaven, prepared as a*
> *bride adorned for her husband.*

Personally I rather liked the sea, but my own specifications for paradise don't carry
much weight. While I would have been happy enough to see the old heaven and
earth refurbished, after all the carnage I can understand why they had to be replaced.
The lucky residents will be better off:

God shall wipe away all tears from their eyes; and there shall be no more death, neither sorrow, nor crying, neither shall there be any more pain: for the former things are passed away. And he that sat upon the throne said, Behold, I make all things new. And he said unto me, Write: for these words are true and faithful.

Even at this point, I'm afraid, prospects seemed mixed. God said, on the one hand, *I will give unto him that is athirst of the fountain of the water of life freely.* On the other hand sinners of mundane stripe, whether cowards, sceptics, or the sexually impure, not to mention *all liars, shall have their part in the lake which burneth with fire and brimstone: which is the second death.* I wonder if there's room enough for everybody.

One of the angels of the seven plagues gave John a tour of the new Jerusalem, a cube 1,500 miles in length, width, and height. The city was solid gold, while the walls sparkled with jewels of every kind. There were twelve gates, each made from a single pearl, *and the street of the city was pure gold.* The sun and moon were unnecessary, as God's glory kept the place lit. In fact *the gates of it shall not be shut at all by day: for there shall be no night there.* Only people whose names are on the list will be allowed in. (I thought all the riff-raff had been dealt with, anyway.)

22   The angel, John said, *shewed me a pure river of water of life, clear as crystal, proceeding out of the throne of God and of the Lamb.* There was a tree of life on either side of the river. It's a useful tree; it produces a new crop of fruit every month, and *the leaves of the tree were for the healing of the nations.* God and Jesus would be on their thrones, served by the elect, who would have the divine name stamped on their foreheads. As mentioned, *there shall be no night there; and they need no candle.*

The end was expected any day; God was giving notice of *the things which must shortly be done.* John fell down to worship at the feet of the angel, who had to remind him that only God was a suitable object for that sort of thing. (It doesn't make me optimistic about John's chances on the big day.) He wasn't to hide this prophecy of the apocalypse,

> *for the time is at hand. He that is unjust, let him be unjust still: and he which is filthy, let him be filthy still: and he that is righteous, let him be righteous still: and he that is holy, let him be holy still.*

Jesus confirmed – incorrectly, as it turned out – that we wouldn't have long to wait.

> *And, behold, I come quickly; and my reward is with me, to give every man according as his work shall be. I am Alpha and Omega, the beginning and the end, the first and the last.*

The pure and unsullied will enter the heavenly city by the main gates; *without are dogs, and sorcerers, and whoremongers, and murderers, and idolaters, and whosoever loveth and maketh a lie. I Jesus have sent mine angel to testify unto you these things in the churches.* Too bad about man's best friend, but you've got to set the tone.

There's a final word of warning to preachers and commentators:

If any man shall add unto these things, God shall add unto him the plagues that are written in this book: And if any man shall take away from the words of the book of this prophecy, God shall take away his part out of the book of life.

My goose is cooked, but I'll be in good company.

John, I gathered, just wanted everything to be finished. When Jesus repeated *Surely I come quickly*, he replied: *Amen. Even so, come, Lord Jesus.* I won't try to guess why there's been such a delay, but it looks like good news to me.

Appendix

When Jesus or Paul referred to the scriptures, they were talking about the Jewish sacred writings. Not all of these are now regarded as authoritative; as well as the law, prophets, psalms, etc. – what Christians today call the Old Testament – Jesus and his contemporaries were greatly influenced by works later consigned to the Apocrypha. The standard collection of books making up the Hebrew Bible was not fixed until late in the first century.

Similarly, the canon of specifically Christian writings was fluid for many years. Some churches used documents that were ultimately excluded; others ignored works that were eventually recognised. In the year 367 the bishop of Alexandria produced the list of 27 books we know collectively as the New Testament, a selection that came to be accepted by the different regions of the church.

The fluidity is not difficult to understand. After Jesus died in about the year 30, stories and sayings circulated for decades among his followers. The gospels were created one or more generations after the crucifixion by author-editors using these written and oral traditions. Although Jesus would have preached in Aramaic, the gospels (like the other books in the New Testament) are in Greek, the lingua franca of the eastern Mediterranean.

Most scholars agree that Mark is the earliest of the four gospels, dated around the year 70, with Matthew, Luke and John following in roughly 80, 90 and 100. Matthew, Mark and Luke are called the 'synoptic' gospels, because they can be 'seen together', overlapping enough to be read in parallel columns. The consensus is that Matthew and Luke used Mark – and perhaps a collection of sayings labelled 'Q' – as a source, supplemented by their own contributions.

All four gospels are anonymous; tradition has supplied names, but the works themselves do not identify their authors. It is possible that Luke (as well as Acts, its sequel) was indeed written by Paul's medical companion of that name, but much less plausible that the scriptural Matthew, Mark or John produced those gospels. Likewise there is no real information on where the books were written. While certain suggestions are traditional – e.g. Mark in Rome, John in Ephesus – evidence is scant.

The genuine letters of Paul are the earliest Christian documents we possess. They were probably written during the period 50 to 62, in something like the following order: Thessalonians, Corinthians, Galatians, Romans, Colossians, Philemon, Philippians. (The authorship of Colossians and II Thessalonians is disputed, but on balance they may be assigned to Paul.) The pastoral epistles – I and II Timothy, and Titus – are pseudonymous, and very difficult to date: early in the second century may be the best guess. Ephesians is very likely not by Paul either, and seems to come from the late first century.

Although the unsigned letter Hebrews came to be attributed to Paul, few now hold to that view. I have therefore grouped it with the general epistles, a term usually applied to the seven explicitly non-Pauline letters. (Not being addressed to specific congregations – III John is an exception – the writings were called 'catholic', or general.) Dating is difficult, but Hebrews and James might be placed around the year 90, I Peter and the three letters of John in the first couple of decades of the second century, Jude slightly later, and II Peter about 150, making it the latest work in the New Testament.

Clearly the biblical James, Peter, John and Jude did not write the general epistles. The various Johns present a particular problem: there was the apostle, the evangelist, the letter-writer(s), and the recipient of Revelation. The three letters labelled John are probably by a single author. It seems possible, though no more, that the same hand produced the last gospel. John of Patmos, witness to the Revelation, is unlikely to have been that person. He would have been a contemporary, however; his book is usually assigned to approximately 95.

Thus about a century passed between the earliest and the latest compositions in the New Testament (by contrast the compilation of the Old spans close to a millennium). These dates are speculative, of course, and subject to much debate; studies of biblical authorship fill entire libraries. The above is provided merely to sketch the terrain.

Finally, a comment on the English Bible. The Authorised, or King James, Version was intended to supplant rival translations. It fulfilled this purpose more successfully than anyone might have thought possible: from shortly after its publication in 1611 to late in the nineteenth century, it was as little contested as scripture itself. Only Shakespeare has had a comparable effect on our language and literature. To most of us the King James Version *is* the Bible; modern translations simply offer a gloss.

There are two important objections to this version: scholars have made advances in the selection and understanding of the Greek sources, and people do not find it easy to read the English of four centuries ago. Neither difficulty is serious, I think, when the text is presented with commentary. A narrator can correct or explain as required. In any case, few problems of translation are crucial to general readers. The cultural importance of the King James Version triumphs over its faults – which is what could be said of the Bible itself.

Index